WASTING MORE POLICE TIME

Further adventures in la-la land

PC DAVID COPPERFIELD

and DAN COLLINS

MONDAY BOOKS

D0301088

© PC DAVID COPPERFIELD
and DAN COLLINS, 2012

The right of PC David Copperfield and Dan Collins
to be identified as the Authors of this work has been
asserted by them in accordance with the Copyright,
Designs and Patents Act 1988

All rights reserved. Apart from any use permitted
under UK copyright law no part of this publication
may be reproduced, stored in a retrieval system, or
transmitted, in any form or by any means, without
the prior written permission of the publisher, nor be
otherwise circulated in any form of binding or cover
other than that in which it is published and without
a similar condition being imposed on the subsequent
purchaser

A CIP catalogue record for this title is available
from the British Library

ISBN: 978-1-906308-19-3

Typeset by Andrew Searle
Printed and bound by
CPI Group (UK) Ltd, Croydon, CR0 4YY

www.mondaybooks.com
http://mondaybooks.wordpress.com/
info@mondaybooks.com

A note from the publisher

WHEN *WASTING POLICE TIME* was published, it was the first time that a serving police constable, with a detailed inside knowledge of the system, had risked his job to explain to the general public just what was going wrong in modern British policing.

As PC David Copperfield revealed, all was not well. Central *diktat* meant children were being arrested for playground fights, and Facebook name-calling could be treated like a serious offence; an ever-growing paperwork burden meant a simple arrest for vandalism or shoplifting could easily take an officer off the streets for an entire shift; serious criminals were being given joke sentences; response policing was being denuded by abstractions to various squads set up to manage the new, target-driven culture; in the midst of all this, the actual bobbies who come out when you dial 999, pulled in all directions, were often finding themselves unable to deliver a proper service to decent, law-abiding members of the public.

The obvious questions are: were the issues exposed in Copperfield's original book confined to one man and his opinion of his own force (he later revealed himself on the BBC's *Newsnight* programme as PC Stuart Davidson, a Staffordshire Police officer), and have things changed for the better since it was published?

The answer, in both cases, is a resounding 'No.'

First, Copperfield's message was later backed up by Inspector Gadget in his book, *Perverting the Course of Justice*, and by WPC E E Bloggs in her *Diary of an On-Call Girl* – the latter soon to be made into a TV series.

Now, in *Wasting MORE Police Time*, officers from all over England and Wales explain how things are now – if anything – even worse.

This book is based on a series of interviews with nearly 100 serving police officers, from PC to chief inspector, carried out over the last two years. In most cases, the officers have remained anonymous; in a small number of cases, they have either asked to be named or have given their stories on the understanding that they may be identified from the facts of a particular event. In many cases, some details have been altered or withheld so as to avoid officers, forces or members of the public being identified. Most interviewees are 'response' officers, though some were detectives and others worked in neighbourhood policing.

We are grateful to all our interviewees, but special thanks go to the following people: Adam, Ali and Sandi Gibb, Andy C, Andy S, APL, Bob, Brian, Buzz, Charlie Oscar, Caroline, Chez, CP, Delta Foxtrot 1, Dave S, Dave W, Eddie the Eagle, Foxtrot Oscar, Frank, Fliss, George, Gavin, Helen, Inspector Gadget, Jane, Jayne, John, Jon A, Jon L, Jack, Knighty, Lone Ranger, Met the Met, Mike, Minimum Cover, Response Monkey, Richard, Roy, Sgt NG (who always said he'd join the police), Shijuro, Sierra Mike, Totally un-PC, Uniform, Welshman, Winchester and Zulu Out.

The opinions expressed in this book are those of the interviewees.

A significant proportion of the author royalties from the book will be donated to the charity Care of Police Survivors (COPS).

Foreword

There was never a 'golden age' of law and order, when all officers were paragons of virtue, hardened criminals would grudgingly accept a 'fair cop', and youthful tearaways could be set on the straight-and-narrow with a clip round the ear from the local bobby: PC George Dixon (of Dock Green) was murdered on the street, after all. However, there's no doubt that the streets of the UK are more violent than they once were: ask any frontline police officer.

The reasons are complex and varied, and in many cases – family breakdown, poor education, the lack of opportunities for young people, weak sentencing – they are outwith the control of the police. But rank-and-file coppers are also sabotaged from within.

A year after *Wasting Police Time* was published, I left Staffordshire Constabulary and emigrated to Canada, where I now work as a police officer. The difference in working culture in 'the Job' in the two countries could not be greater.

My current force employs far fewer officers and spends much less money than a comparable UK force, and yet our results are far better.

I still face the same problems – drugs, sex offences, violent crime, domestic abuse, burglary and public order – as I did in the UK. I still tell people the time, and dish out parking tickets. But there are some important differences.

We're armed. We're (generally) fitter – British forces long ago abandoned any serious physical entry standards and there is no obligation on officers to stay in shape, whereas, in Canada, I can be fired for getting fat.

There is far less bureaucracy. When I worked in Britain, if I arrested a man over a fight in a pub, it could easily take six hours to deal with – even if he *admitted* the offence. Central custody can be 20 miles away or more. When you get there you have to wait to book him in, wait for his lawyer (and possibly his appropriate adult or interpreter), interview him on tape, fill in endless forms in longhand, usually duplicating the same information, fax it all to the CPS and wait some more while they tell you whether you can charge him. While I'm doing this, I'm not coming out to answer your 999 call.

In Canada, *I* decide whether to charge, after quickly running through the facts with my sergeant on the phone. I don't usually interview the guy – he can tell his story at court. I also decide whether to bail him. If I want to remand him, I'll have another short discussion and take him to jail, with a few pieces of paper and a copy of my brief report. We do all this while having regard for the proper rights of suspects: they get to talk to lawyers (over the phone, not in person), they get to make complaints, and it's all done on video. A Charter of Human Rights is written into Canadian law. Instead of six hours later, I'm back on the street a short while after the arrest.

I'm not alone on the street, either. The UK's Chief Inspector of Constabulary recently reported that, in some British forces, as few as six percent of warranted officers were available at any one time to deal with crime. The rest were either tied up with paperwork or were part of the huge cadre of cops who never leave the station. Over here, *everyone* is hands-on, almost all the time – even senior officers. My superintendent turns up to morning parade, takes a keen interest in crime on his patch and is a proper operational officer. In the UK, most superintendents have long ago abandoned any real policing in favour of managing statistics, holding meetings and 'developing strategies' to help them with the next bonus or promotion.

We're better equipped, too. My car carries a wireless laptop with a real-time crime map, detailing incidents, methods and likely suspects. I can check vehicles and people, access intelligence, update incidents, write reports and charge people without having to return to the station. I can see which calls are still waiting for police attention and how many minutes they've been waiting. (Unlike in Britain, I attend within minutes, not hours, and certainly not days.)

The final, crucial, difference in policing is that we are in no doubt who we serve – and it's not central government. We're financed by our local taxpayers, and we do what *they* want, not a police minister in an office a thousand miles away. There are no standing armies of crime auditors, policing pledge compliance teams or crime management units, either. It's just cops, policing.

The interviews in this book remind me of time spent in the van with my former colleagues, or waiting around to book-in prisoners. These officers sound like my old shift: fed-up, dispirited, doing their best despite all the ludicrous obstacles put in their way. British readers should educate themselves as to the true nature of modern policing; you have, the odd bad apple apart, some of the finest police officers in the world (which is why Canada, Australia and other countries have poached so many of them). I wonder if people will wake up to this before it's too late.

Of course, you could always listen to the Prime Minister and the Home Secretary, who are forever telling you that crime is down and that British streets are safer than ever. Meanwhile, they live behind fortified walls and travel everywhere with armed police guards. If they really believe their own spin, why don't they walk home alone through London late at night?

PC David Copperfield, 2012

Policing is all about people – strange, unpleasant, sad, lonely, depressed, violent and troubled people.

I'd sum it up like this: we deal with very nasty people, and try to keep a lid on them, stop them getting too close to the rest of the public. That's all I can really say. I've removed toddlers and babies from houses where there was excrement – cat, dog, human and lizard, they *love* their lizards – encrusted in the carpets, wiped on the walls, where the kids are crawling around in this eating their food, with maggots crawling on *them*. Where the stench stays on your nose and in your uniform for days afterwards.

I went to a house with a team on a pre-planned job to arrest a man who was handling stolen goods, the proceeds of burglaries in the nice part of town. We found him in bed with his 14-year-old granddaughter, with a 50-inch telly playing hardcore porn at the end of the bed. The telly had been stolen from the house of a doctor, and that was where it ended up.

I sat with an old lady of 90 who had been beaten so badly by a burglar that her own daughter, who was herself nearly 70, didn't recognise her at the hospital. Broken cheekbone, broken ribs, a broken arm, two black eyes, part of her scalp ripped out. We deal with the people who do things like that.

PC, 30, Northern force

As a PC, I arrested a man who was beating and raping his girlfriend and forcing her to eat his faeces. She did it because she was in mortal fear of him. Can you imagine that? He had himself been the victim of horrific abuse, in that he had been raped repeatedly by his own father from the age of five until he was big enough to fight back. It doesn't justify what he was doing to the girlfriend, but it does sort of explain it a bit. The idea that you can be treated like that as a child and then not turn out weird is unlikely.

Sergeant, 43, Midlands force

I think the public should be frightened by how crap things are. In my last role, it was my job to manage a team set up to monitor sex offenders on release from prison. Most of it was visiting them in their bail hostel or suchlike to ask them if they're hanging around schools, or attending partner agency meetings to talk about them. The whole thing is a joke – we don't 'monitor' them in any real sense. How could we? I had four officers under me, sharing one clapped-out Ford Mondeo. The Superintendent has a gold 5 Series BMW to drive to his meetings, of course. The bloody civilian *managers* have company BMWs, complete with blue lights and sirens … It would be illegal for them to ever switch the bloody things on! Anyway, these vile creatures are released, and it's my old team's job to go and visit them so the force can tick the box that says they're being monitored.

To give just one case, I dealt with a paedophile who was, in my opinion, probably working his way up to kidnapping and murdering a child. He had very serious images of child rape on his computer, and he was clearly a very dangerous man. It so happened that I had originally arrested this guy. He laughed in my face when I cautioned him. He was jailed for under three years and not much more than a year later he was given parole. A week or so later, I saw him hanging around Claire's Accessories on a parade of shops near where he was staying. He was trying to talk to the young girls going in and out, in breach of his parole conditions which included that he was not to approach children. I went over to him, arrested him and took him back to the nick, but the probation service felt that a warning was sufficient. He laughed at me again when I let him go. It was very frustrating.

Inspector, 44, Northern force

A lot of domestics we get called to are pants. They're both pissed, they might have slapped each other, who knows who did it first this time, it's really a case of who gets to the phone first. You'll probably nick the male just to get him away from the address for the night, but the female – if she doesn't switch sides and leap on you to stop you taking him away there and then – will never make a statement the next day, so it all goes nowhere. I know it sounds cynical, but it's the truth. A lot of the people we deal with are pissheads and they get bored and they enjoy knocking lumps out of each other.

However, there *are* serious domestics. For instance, my colleague and I attended reports of a female screaming in a house. We could hear the racket almost before we got out of the car. We couldn't get any response from knocking, so we decided to put the door in. Ideally, we would all carry an Enforcer [*a heavy metal tool used to effect entry*] but our health and safety policy was recently updated so as to disallow it from being carried in standard patrol vehicles, in case we crash and this thing damages us as it flies out of the boot. Plus it weighs a tonne and that adds to the petrol bill. Anyway, we put the window in and reached in to click the Yale. Inside was a woman, about 50, 5ft 2in tall, cowering on the floor with a 16-stone bloke standing over her with a belt, buckle end down. He was roaring and spitting, she was screaming and begging to be left alone. He threatened us with the belt, but my colleague, who is TASER-trained, quickly won that one. TASER is a Godsend, by the way. [*TASER – Thomas A Swift's Electric Rifle – is a (usually) pistol-style electronic weapon designed to incapacitate but not permanently injure assailants.*]

He was arrested, and we got the woman to a place of safety. Although she was too scared to make a statement, there are provisions for us to proceed without the victim making a statement and in this case he was bang to rights and was charged.

I spent quite a bit of time getting to know that lady over the next few months, and the story she told was horrific. She had been threatened and bullied and beaten all her marriage, but she had never contacted us and I guess the neighbours hadn't previously got involved. On this occasion, she had been unable to explain one of the numbers on their itemised phone bill, and he'd gone berserk. Like a lot of womanisers, he was madly jealous himself. She showed us marks on her back where he had burned her with the iron on other occasions. One of his favourite tactics was to sodomise her while pushing her head down the toilet. She had never told anyone about any of this, just suffered in silence. As a woman, I almost cried listening to her. She never went back to him, and he was convicted and given a jail term, and on the day he went down I met her for a coffee and she looked 20 years younger. I thought, *That is why I joined the police.*

PC, 30, Northern force

We arrested a mid-level drug dealer and all-round unpleasant character who kept his customers and slingers honest by injecting urine into their buttocks if they didn't pay their debts, or got creative with his gear. He thought this was highly amusing. It was like a perk of the job. I don't know whether he was a sadist, clinically-speaking, but he certainly had no compunction whatsoever about causing pain to others if it got him what he wanted.

A regular earner for him was to rob other drug dealers or general crims. A lot of them are into this now. The old cash-in-transit Securicor robberies of yesteryear, they are less common because the vans are better, the comms are better, the money cartridges all have DNA dye in them. There are ways around the dye, which I won't go into, but it makes it a bit harder for them. You can buy trackers from spy shops or online which will track vehicles, so they follow their targets until the point when they know they've got a decent stash of either drugs or money on board, and then they have them. They are certainly not averse to torturing people to get the intel they need. 'Where's Dave gonna be with his gear?' Meanwhile, the guy's tied to a chair with his feet in a bucket of petrol, or they're threatening to snip his fingers off with bolt-cutters.

We took this particular chap off the streets and he went away for a decent bit, but there is, unfortunately, an endless supply of amoral scum champing at the bit to step up a level. In one sense, people like this are no threat to honest people, but every now and then the law-abiding public get involved through no fault of their own. We had a guy turned over who ran a chain of takeaways. If you run kebab shops, most of your take is in cash. It's not hard to siphon off 20 percent of your monthly take and keep it. The downside of this is that people are after you. One lot is the Inland Revenue, but there's also criminals. They know you've a load of wedge stashed away, they know you're unlikely to come running to us, you're not a hard case, you're just dodging a bit of tax. It's easy money. So what this particular crew did was they hard-stopped the takeaway owner in his car – 9am, broad daylight, in a residential street – dragged him out, bundled him into their car and away they went. The only problem was, a woman saw it happen, wrote down a few details as an *aide memoire* and called us. The result is that she is a witness, she's under grave threat from some very nasty people, she's had to move home, move the kids from school, her life is changed beyond all recognition.

DC, 40, Southern force

People are strange, no doubt about it. Out and about one night, call to a guy bleeding in the street, we pitch up and there is claret everywhere, the guy is bleeding from the head from multiple stab wounds, but he's still conscious and breathing. *What happened, fella?* 'I was robbed coming out of the bookies round the corner.'

Ambulance are on scene and dealing, so me and a mate leave him with colleagues and go looking for the blood trail. Nothing to be found, but we'll get the CCTV so not really bothered, we head back to set up crime scenes and whatnot. As our vic is being loaded into the ambulance, his wife, who has been beside her husband's side the whole time, suddenly says, 'All right, I confess, he was ignoring me so I stabbed him in the head whilst he was asleep.'

Me and three other officers, one of which was an area car driver, just stood, gobsmacked. Then she asked if she could go to the hospital with her husband. Oh, how we laughed. We got a QSR [*quality service report – a kind of commendation*] out of that one.

PC, 35, Southern force

The people we deal with, you don't know what they're like. No commentator or reporter or politician really knows. Only the police know, and only frontline police. Maybe, I suppose, the paramedics, the nurses and the screws [*prison officers*] have an idea. But no-one else. The media and the politicians, the bleeding hearts, they think these people are all hard done-by, struggling valiantly against the system, but the vast majority of them are taking the absolute piss. I could give thousands of examples.

They're short of cash for the kids' clothes, but there's money for fags, booze, drugs, big tellies, iPhones, PlayStations, the heating's on full-bore all year round... I arrested a woman on a Tuesday night who'd abandoned her two children, aged three and five, in her flat while she went out on the razz. The kids were crying, we had an anonymous call, we found them malnourished, filthy, covered in fleas and lice, all scabby. The flat stank to high heaven and was full of dirty nappies and soiled clothes. The kids were taken into care on the spot and the woman was nicked when she came back to the flat at 7am the next morning, off her face on vodka and cocaine. She kicked off like a harpy when she found the kids had been taken away.

It was handed over to the Child Protection Unit, who are quite proactive in our force, and that was pretty much the end of it for me. But I heard later that obviously her solicitor tried to claim that she was a victim of the system, a struggling single mum, no cash. But if that's the case, how can she afford to get blinding pissed? How can she afford coke and fags and a taxi back? Her hair was styled and properly coloured – that costs at least £60, I can't afford it myself! Coming in at 7am on a Wednesday, you're not looking for work, are you?

The annoying thing is, we spend all our lives running round after people like this. I'm forever attending council houses where they've got a bigger telly than me, a bigger car than me, several kids – when me and my husband have decided we can't afford them yet – where you need breathing apparatus to survive the fag smoke and you're tripping over the empties and pizza boxes, and where they all think they know better than I do how to do my job, despite the fact they've never had a job themselves. We're told these people are 'vulnerable'. My arse. We're round their places all the time. Last week we're going round to sort out their domestic troubles or investigate their stolen Giro-stroke-attempt fraud, this week we're arresting them for whatever it is. Meanwhile, we can't offer a decent service to ordinary people, and they are rightly mithered by that.

PC, 30, Northern force

There's good and bad things in the Job. Personally, I find some of the worst areas to work are the middle class places, where the people look down on you as though you're a servant or something. We got a call from a posh part of our city about a man acting suspiciously one evening. OK, fair enough, we're always going to sus calls. I stick the blob [*blue light*] on and several of us race over there. I get there first. There's this young black guy sitting on a wall minding his own business, smoking a fag. It's immediately clear he's doing nothing – as the car pulled up, he didn't even realise we'd come for him.

I said, 'I'm sorry, mate, but do you mind me asking what you're doing? Only we've had a call about someone acting suspiciously?'

He said, 'Yeah, I'm waiting for my mum.'

And basically, what it was, he hadn't got a job and his mum worked as a cleaner or something in this building nearby, so every night he would walk over to walk his mum back home. I immediately cancelled the job and apologised to him for bothering him. The only reason they had called us was because he was black. It's terrible, really. He's coming over every night to walk his mum back home to make sure she's safe… *I've* never done that for *my* mum. Who's the better person here, me or him?

Sergeant, 43, Midlands force

I was working a night shift, teamed up with a rather naïve Geordie officer. We were asked to attend at a report of an assault which had taken place inside one of our local brothels, such-and-such a 'Health Studio'.

When we arrived we were led inside by the very friendly if somewhat haggard mistress to find a sheepish-looking young man in his 20s whose amorous intentions had apparently been squashed – along with his nose, which was splattered, along with a fair amount of claret, across his face.

I asked him what had happened and he told me he had been beaten up outside and had run inside the 'health studio' to escape, not actually knowing what the place was. I found this version of events a bit lacking, as the entrance to the studio is down a dark alley around the back, and is not well-advertised. I spent some time trying to convince him I was more interested in him being assaulted than what he was doing in a brothel.

Meanwhile, my colleague had struck up a rapport with the mistress, and while I was trying to give the victim a dose of sympathy I could see my colleague looking around and questioning her.

'So, do you have a gym in here, then?'

'Er… No, we're not that sort of health studio.'

'Swimming pool?'

'No, we haven't got a pool… We do massages, and stuff.'

'You're open late, for a physio…'

My colleague's eyes then drifted to a bumper box of 100 Durex, and, after turning a fetching shade of crimson, he said, 'Oh.'

At which point, the mistress, me and indeed the victim threw back our heads and laughed like musketeers, while he wandered outside muttering.

PC, 24, Northern force

I arrested and interviewed a chap who was forging pound coins. The guy worked as a toolmaker, so he had the skills and equipment to make very good copies – they wouldn't pass inspection, but his plan was to use them in vending machines. He'd bought some metal sheet of the precise thickness of a £1 coin – I forget the metal exactly, but it needed to be almost the exact weight also, and wasn't cheap. He'd only pressed a few in his shed before the offence had come to light.

So, I sat in the interview listening to my mate interview him, with his solicitor there, and he's admitting to all this. And he tells us how much the metal cost, and it starts nagging at me, so I do a few quick sums on a bit of paper and then I pass it to my mate. Who starts giggling.

'What's funny?' says the crim.

I said, 'It's just that the cost of the metal you bought is greater than the amount of pound coins you could have made with it. It was costing you money to make them.'

The solicitor twigged and began laughing, most unprofessionally, while his client sat there, saying, 'What? What?', over and over.

DC, 40, Southern force

There was a report of a woman threatening to kill herself at a hostel in the town centre. I was only just out of probation. I went with a colleague who I didn't know very well and, from what I did know, didn't particularly like. Been in years, a real 'the Job's fucked' type. Not very friendly, always moaning, always running down recent joiners, always away from work as close to bang on time as possible. And extremely cynical. All the way there he was, 'This is a load of bollocks. This is a waste of time. What about doing some real police work? Blah blah.'

Anyway, we gets there and the manager of the hostel is outside and she says, '[*Name*] is in her room, the door's locked, it's on the top floor and she's threatening to jump.'

The room looks onto an inner courtyard, so I go up the stairs, my colleague goes through to the courtyard, shaking his head and chuntering to himself. Get to the top floor, the manager shows me her room.

I say, 'Can you unlock the door please?'

Manager says, 'Oh no, we can't do that, it's her room, it would be an invasion of her privacy.'

We get this nonsense all the time. I say, 'But *you* called us... How am I supposed to stop her jumping if I can't even *see* her?'

Basically, it turns out that's *my* problem. I start shouting through the door, '[*Name*], come on, let me in, we can talk about this... This is silly, you don't want to hurt yourself.'

She's shouting at me to go away. I can hear my colleague shouting stuff at her, too, and she's basically telling him to fuck off as well. This goes on for a few minutes. I say to the manager, how serious does she think this girl is? She doesn't know. She's not long out of prison, but she seems very depressed, is all she can say. The girl has markers [*warning notes on the police computer*] for drugs, depression, alcohol, violence and a previous semi-serious suicide attempt with pills where she ended up in hospital. We get *so* many people threatening to kill themselves that even if you've not been in long you do become blasé if you're not careful, but maybe she's serious? I dunno. I carry on talking to the girl, but now she's not replying. I start thinking about trying again to convince the manager to unlock the door, then whether I can put the door in, when there's this shout from down below from my colleague. Then about 15 seconds later, he comes charging up the stairs, runs straight past me and the manager, shoulders the door straight in, falls through into the girl's room and is up again in about a second-and-a-half, and dives for her. He grabs her round the neck, and sort of by the scruff of her top, just as she slides from the windowsill where she was sitting.

She was dangling fully out of the window, gurgling and spitting as he was holding her by the chin and under one armpit, and he was himself leaning half way out of the window. Looking back, he could easily have over-balanced and gone with her. I got across the room as quick as I could, grabbed him round the waist with my right arm and got my left hand wrapped round her left arm, and, gradually, we managed to stabilise both her and my colleague and pull her back in. We all then collapsed onto the floor. The girl started crying, and my colleague just sort of cuddled her and stroked her head for a while. Going, 'There, there, love, you're OK now.' Turned out he wasn't such a cynic after all.

She was detained under the Mental Health Act. I'd love to say there's some sort of happy ending, where we saved her life and she went on to make something of herself, but last I heard she was in prison for handling stolen goods, various assaults and kiting [*cheque fraud*].

PC, 28, Southern force

Police officers are regularly called upon to deal with death.

Very early in my service, I was sent to a house where the occupant hadn't been seen for a few days. I spoke to the neighbour who'd called us. She said he was a single bloke in his mid-20s, kept himself to himself but always asked her to keep his key for him if he went away so she could feed his cat. She thought he might have gone away and she was more worried about the cat. I mooched around for a bit but couldn't see anything through the nets and there wasn't a letterbox you could look through, so I was a bit stumped.

I thought about kicking the door in, then thought I'd try the handle first – not sure why I hadn't done that already, actually – and it was unlocked. As soon as I entered I knew. His cat shot out of there at a rate of knots. It was the height of summer, the smell was terrible and the place was full of flies. The guy was sitting on his sofa with a needle in his arm and the telly on, muted. I remember there was a big Clash *London Calling* poster on the wall. He's got home from scoring, turned the TV on, sat down, stuck the needle in and just died. The thing I remember most was that the sofa was crawling with maggots and heavily stained, from where he had voided himself and then sort of melted as he decomposed. The oddest thing about this for me at the time, I now understand why, is that the control room skipper [*sergeant*]

17

wouldn't take my word for it that he was dead. I had to wait for a doctor to come and certify life extinct. I was like, 'I'm pretty fucking sure life's extinct, sarge… He's got maggots in his eyeballs.'

I wasn't bothered about it, other than it was a sad way for anyone to go, especially at that age, though these are the risks you take if you're on the brown, of course. That and the fact that I couldn't get the smell out of my clothes for ages.

Sergeant, 43, Welsh force

I've been to a lot of dead bodies. They never really bothered me – young, old they're still dead. In my area, a lot of them are ODs, suicides or just old people. Went to one, though. Her workmates called us on a Monday morning at 0930. She hadn't shown up for work. This lady, it seems, was as regular as clockwork and well-liked in her office, so her mates decided to pop round. They were outside her front door.

I went in, and there she was on the floor of her bathroom, bottom stuck up in the air, face first on the floor, having come off the toilet – note to self: don't strain.

We did the usual, I went outside to inform her friends, then went back inside to finish off the bits I needed to do. What struck me, and still does, is from what I could tell she was a nice, ordinary, well-liked woman who just went home one night, made her microwave dinner and her cup of tea, popped on her favourite TV show, went to the toilet and died, at the age of 42. And because of the position she was in, my mates made the usual joke about bike racks, and I wanted to deck them. I went home and sunk into a bottle of whisky. You never know which one is going to get you, and it's illogical that that was the one, but it did and it still does. The sadness of that lonely death.

PC, 35, Southern force

I went to a cot death. The little boy who had died had been born the day before my own son, and after that I spent more money than any sane man should on baby monitoring equipment, listening devices, mattress sensors. I would wake up in the middle of the night and go in to check my son was still breathing. Having seen what the parents had gone through, I was seized with an almost supernatural dread of it happening to us. Whenever I hear people bitching about us because we give out too many tickets or murder people at riots, I always think, 'You only see about two percent of what we do, you have absolutely no fucking idea. Or if you *do* have an idea then you're a moron. I wonder how you'd cope with a cold house and a dead one-year-old?'

PC, 36, Midlands force

I thought I was lucky, in that I'd never been badly affected by any of the things I have seen in my 20-plus years of service. I thought I had this sort of ability to zone it out. Suicides, road traffic collisions, accidents in the workplace, sudden deaths, like most police officers I've had my share of all of them.

Some years ago, I went to a house fire where a toddler was burned alive, and we physically had to hold the father back from going into the burning house to save his child. Same thing – no real effect on me. I don't mean I didn't care, just that I was able to think, *This is a job of work and I'm really just at the office*. I felt very sorry for the father, as I've always felt for the relatives of people who have died before their time, but it didn't play on my mind.

Or so I thought. A long time after that house fire, I found myself driving down the street where it had happened on the way to some bullshit call, and for some reason I looked at the house. I must have driven down there many times before in the intervening years but, for some reason, this time it caught my eye. It had obviously been repaired and renovated and sold on, and there was a little girl of about six or seven playing on a swing in the front garden. And, I don't know why, I just crumpled. I actually had to pull the car over to the side of the road and I got my notebook out and a pen and I buried my head down, like I was writing, but really it was so no-one could see me having a good little weep to myself.

I sat there for probably five minutes, just down the road from the house, and then I wiped my eyes and blew my nose and sorted myself out and then I was off. Never happened before or since, but I have lost that hard shell I thought I had. Intellectually, I know that whatever happens to a person, life moves on for the rest of us. Emotionally, however, I find it much harder now. I haven't told anyone about it before this, actually.

Sergeant, 44, Eastern force

Fires to me are the worst. We like to have a laugh at Trumpton [*the fire brigade*], the world's best-paid landscape gardeners, but I couldn't do their job. There's something about the smell of a burned body, be it from a car or a house or whatever. I know it's a cliché, but the first time I smelled it was in the summer, and it was a hot summer with lots of people having barbecues. Spare ribs… The smell of accelerant and burning flesh… I spent most of July and August retching.

PC, 30, Southern force

If anyone dies unexpectedly, we need to attend to establish whether it's a suspicious death or not. Quite often, we have also been the ones to break the news to the parents, or children, or husband or wife that they are never going to see their loved one again. For me it is the worst part of the Job by a long way, and I would be lying if I said I didn't dread having to do a death knock after all these years.

It makes me sick when I hear people running down the police service as just a bunch of thugs, as fitting people up, as being racist and this that and the other. They have no idea what we do. The bloke in riot gear who you called a 'scumbag' because he was supposedly 'kettling' you to stop you rampaging round the streets, yesterday he was telling a mum that her 10-year-old son had just been squashed under a bus. The Stephen Lawrence report comes out and says we're all racists… A couple of weeks ago I spent half an hour hugging a black lady who was sobbing in my arms because I'd just had to tell her that her son had been killed in an accident at work. *She* didn't think I was a racist.

PC, 42, Southern force

I've been to a couple of blokes who've shot themselves. One guy whose haulage business was in trouble, he planned it to the nth degree. Sent his wife and kids away to the seaside for the weekend, and did it in his garage with the doors open. He'd worked it out so that he was sitting on a chair in the middle of the garage, he'd got the shotgun under his chin and… The garage opened out onto the drive, which was quite long but gave out onto the pavement. I think he wanted to make sure someone other than his wife and kids found him. Which I suppose is good of him, in a way, but *someone* had to find him.

He must have stayed up all night drinking because he had a lot of alcohol in his bloodstream, and he did it at about 5am on the Saturday. You'd think in a quiet residential street, someone would hear a gunshot, but no-one did. One of the neighbours thought it was a crow scarer or a car backfiring. It was the postman who actually found him. As luck would have it, he was a former soldier who had served in the first Gulf War and had seen a few dead bodies, so he wasn't as fazed by it as the Avon lady might have been. The guy had used both barrels under his chin and the whole top and back of his head was missing, and his face was attached to the front of his neck like a rubber mask. One of the most bizarre things I've ever seen, and sometimes I still see it in my mind's eye now.

I watched the undertakers load him up and I wondered how and why a bloke in his 40s, basically my age, with two young kids, a lovely wife, a nice house and everything to live for… How does he do something like this? It turned out later that the business was on the brink. He was living above his means, he thought he'd lose his BMW and the house and that his wife wouldn't have stayed with him. She said, 'I'd have stayed with him if we lived on a park bench.'

The lesson I took from that, which I have always tried to pass on to people, when they're threatening to do this and that to themselves, is there's *always* a way out. You might have to trade down to a smaller house and car, but to do that to your kids… Unthinkable. The irony was that at the inquest his wife said that on the Monday a letter had arrived asking him to tender for some work, which he might well have won and which would have lifted him out of the hole he was in.

PC, 43, Northern force

I've seen lots of terrible things. In Northern Ireland, when I was in the Army, I saw a guy who had been machine-gunned in the face, so that there was nothing left of his head but a stump. In the police, I've seen a family minced in a car. But for some reason, none of it really bothered me. I can remember it, in the way that you would remember anything significant – I can't remember the last time I stopped a vehicle, because I do that all the time, but you do remember unpleasant things. I just don't dwell on them, and it doesn't affect me like it does some people.

The one and only time I've been affected on the job, I had been working a day shift and we were short-handed and they asked me to stay on. I ended up working 16 hours solid. Towards the end of the second shift, I was basically shattered. I didn't have my radio ears on, and a call came through, 'Go to such-and-such an address and...' And I sort of half-caught it, it was something like, someone has fallen down the stairs or something. So, OK, didn't think much of it, off we go to the address.

When we got there, it was actually a toddler who had been killed by his father. He had been beaten by the man, and had died from a ruptured stomach. That is one of the most painful deaths possible – I know, again from my time in the Army, that a stomach wound is terrible, the worst place to get shot. And the thing that got me was, when I saw the little boy's body he was lying in exactly the same position as my own baby son had been when he had died a few years earlier. I came out of the hospital later, and I remember I just stood there and beat the crap out of a road sign. When I got home after work, I just burst into tears. And later on that evening, I went out for dinner with my wife, and I started crying in the restaurant. She was like, 'What's the matter?' It was just the way the poor little lad had been lying, it reminded me of my own son.

PC, 30, Southern force

I absolutely love my job, but I do hate dealing with death. I know it's just part of it, but especially if it involves kids, probably because I have children of my own, that destroys me.

The worst day of my policing career has also been one of the worst days of my life to date. I attended an incident outside a school at going-home time where a young lad had been knocked down by a boy racer, who had then made off from the scene. There was a crowd of people gathered around the lad, who was unconscious and bleeding heavily from the head. He was nine or so years old, I won't be specific. It looked very bad. As the first member of the emergency services on scene, people looked to me. What could *I* do? Response officers do get *some* first aid training, but it's at about St John Ambulance level, if that. We carry a few items in the car, but realistically I could only get the control room to hurry up the ambo as much as possible and try to staunch the bleeding. I don't want to make this a political point, but with the mania for centralisation over the last decade or so, which has affected the police just as much, they had closed the local ambulance station. The idea is that they would have their vehicles plotted up and waiting up in various locations, but if they are all in use or whatever then they have to send from some distance away. To be fair, as it turned out, it could have been parked up across the road, and I'm not sure that it would have made much difference.

Anyway, I knelt there actually in this boy's blood, talking to him, trying to get some sort of response, and I sort of became aware of a little girl looking at me, and crying. It was his sister, who was six or so years old. Basically, she watched her big brother die in the road, and there was nothing I could do about it.

Eventually, the paramedics arrived, pronounced life extinct and that was that. I couldn't do the death message because I had the lad's blood all over me, which was a 'be grateful for small mercies' moment, though I felt very guilty feeling that. My guv'nor [*inspector*] sent me home to clean myself up and I stood at my kitchen sink, trying to scrub this brown, coagulated blood from under my fingernails, and I just started sobbing. Luckily, my own kids were still at school, and my wife was at work. I try to keep this sort of thing from them. It can wreck your home life. Most of the people on my shift have broken marriages.

I couldn't get the image of that little girl looking at me and crying out of my head for a long, long time. For quite a while after that, I dreaded calls to incidents near schools and I would avoid driving past that particular spot if I could.

Again, not to make this a political issue, but what really pisses me off is we spend very little time learning how to deal more effectively with serious injury, and next to no money on equipment, yet we spend days and days in courses learning not to be rude about travellers and gays. Which, I'm like, 'Fair enough, I understand that's important, but which should we spend three *days* on and which should we spend three *hours* on? Which is our priority?' I could not have saved that little boy, I don't even think HEMS [*Helicopter Emergency Medical Service*] could have if they'd been across the road when it happened, but that's not the point.

The other thing… Speeding drivers. *Slow down*. It's not hard. Lift your right foot half an inch, for fuck's sake.

PC, 36, Southern force

The worst death I have ever attended was that of a seven-month-old baby girl whose mum had found her blue in the cot in the morning. Obviously, we have to attend to make sure the woman hasn't killed the child, but in this case there was absolutely no suspicion of this, the doctor on scene was very happy that it was just a tragic cot death. A nice couple, nice house, nice people, no previous history, just a terrible tragedy.

The father was out at work, he was a dry-stone-waller, and he was out of mobile range up in the middle of nowhere, so we sent someone over to roughly where he was, looking for him, while myself and a WPC sat with the mum until he arrived. We asked the undertakers to wait outside, and this poor woman just collapsed, sobbing, into my arms. I mean, her whole body was heaving with it, she was utterly incoherent with grief. I didn't know a human being could be so – bereft, is the only word that comes close. She howled like a wounded animal. We sat with her for two hours until they found the father, who was just as inconsolable; as we were leaving, he managed to tell me that they'd been trying for a child for eight years.

I went from there to a report of a shoplifter stealing bacon from Morrison's. When I got there, the bloke had been detained by the store security guards but he wouldn't come quietly, would he, so I spent a few minutes wrestling him to the ground to get the cuffs on him, while he spat at me and tried to gouge my eyes out, and his mate shouted at me that I was pig scum from across the car park. I remember my top was still wet where the woman had cried on my shoulder.

That bloke had four children by four different women. He'd never worked, they'd never worked, and it crossed my mind that the other poor guy is going to be out in the wet and the cold all winter to earn the money to pay the tax to keep thieving scum like this in their beer and fags. And I'm ashamed to say that it also crossed my mind that I would like to take our shoplifter friend up on the moors, have him dig his own grave and then put him in it. That feeling eventually went away, but the lingering sense of, how can life be *so* cruel and *so* unfair, has never left me.

Sergeant, 40, Northern force

There was a woman on top of a multi-storey car park opposite the old cinema threatening to throw herself off. Most people accept the road's closed, there must be a sensible reason, but there's always someone who insists on trying to get through – usually either a scrote with an exaggerated sense of his own importance, or, at the other end of the scale, a bloke in an expensive suit who just won't accept that you can possibly 'bar the public highway' to him. And sure enough, one of the latter type appeared. He started complaining that he was late for a business meeting and did all that, 'I want your name and number!' stuff. So I gave him those and said, 'Nothing's changed, except now you know my name and number… You still can't go down there.'

He wouldn't have it, he kept moaning and muttering. Eventually, he said, 'Can't you just tell her to jump and get it over with?'

I said, 'You've never seen someone jump from six storeys up, have you?'

He goes, 'No.'

I said, 'I have. I've seen their arms and legs come off when they hit things on the way down, I've seen their brains splattered in a 15 foot arc on the pavement, I've seen them lying there blinking after impact, with their brain still working but nothing else, and you can see they're slowly realising that they've actually done it this time, and, whether they really want to or not now, they are going to die in that ambulance before they get to hospital. So please don't say things like that.'

PC, 30, Midlands force

We had a guy hang himself by means of a thin nylon rope which he had tied round a branch high up on a tall tree. Must have taken him some time to climb up there. It wasn't a cry for help, put it that way. He put the noose around his neck and jumped off, and the length of the drop pulled his head off. Imagine seeing that on early turn on an empty stomach. That afternoon I'd been booked in to give a talk about policing to the sixth formers at the college and one of them put his hand up and said, 'What have you done today, then?'

I looked at them and thought, 'Shall I tell them?' But I thought, *One of them might have known the guy and, anyway, it would be just for shock value.* So I said, 'I attended a sudden death, and then I patrolled.'

Probably not the most exciting talk they ever had.

Sergeant, 36, Welsh force

Death knocks are the worst part of the Job for me. That said, I had one where a bloke was killed in a car crash and I had to break the news to the widow. I hadn't been to the scene and was just sent round there. She opened the door and said, 'Yes, can I help?'

I said, 'I wonder if I can just come in for a moment, I've got some bad news.'

She said, 'No, tell me now.'

I told her, and she said, 'Good. I hate the bastard.'

She started going on about the insurance payout she was in line for, and it was so odd I actually radioed the officers at the scene and asked if there was any sign of interference with the vehicle, but he'd been hit by a lorry which had crossed the white line. Couldn't pin that on her!

PC, 36, Midlands force

I was less than a fortnight on the Job, it was about 4pm, we got a call to a little old lady, a widow who hadn't been seen for a couple of days. She lived in the middle of a row of terraces round the back of the Spar shop, so once we couldn't get any response from the front door we nipped round to the Spar car park, counted along to her house, then over the wall into her back garden. I looked in through the window. It was dusty, it's a busy road beyond the Spar, lots of traffic, and she had nets up, but I wiped the dirt a bit and there was a gap in the nets. I could see her sitting in her chair, watching the telly. I knocked on the back door, no reply. Knocked again. No reply. Then I knocked on the window and shouted 'Hello! Police!'

It was the first time I'd shouted 'Police!' to anyone, and it felt really weird. I thought, 'She's going to have a heart attack when she turns round and sees me here through the window.'

Of course, she didn't turn round. I don't know whether I was just not sparking, or I didn't want to think about it, but I think I said, 'She must be deaf, we'll have to knock a bit louder.'

The guy I was with, who's sadly since passed away himself, he was an old sweat, he said, 'I don't think she's deaf. Change a consonant.'

I couldn't work out what a consonant was for a moment, so that threw me, but then I twigged and my stomach started lurching. He was trying the windows and looking at the back of the house, and he said to me, 'We're going to have to break the door down.'

That's another thing I remember. Most of us, again, have never broken into a house... How do you do it? You don't get taught at police school, at least, I didn't. I said, 'How?'

He said, 'Break the glass in the door with your truncheon.'

It was one of those half-glass doors, with an orange nylon curtain, about 30 years old, on the inside. I started tapping it gingerly. By this time, my colleague didn't know whether to laugh or cry. I remember it felt very odd. Took me three or four goes, I think psychologically I didn't really want to go into the house. But I broke the glass. Reached in to see if there was a key in the lock. No key. Looked at my colleague, he said, 'Climb in, then.'

I pushed all the glass out, got my leg up and over the door, got myself inside. I remember the crunch of the glass on the floor under my boots. And immediately it was obvious something was not right because of the smell. It's a smell I now recognise as that of a healthily decomposing body of about four days' vintage. Hard to describe. Leave a raw chicken out on the side in your kitchen in July, it's a bit like that.

I walked into the living room, virtually gagging, and the little old lady was sitting in her chair, just staring at *Countdown* or whatever was on. On the mantelpiece, pictures of her grandchildren in their school uniforms and one of the old lady on holiday with what was obviously her late husband in Spain or somewhere. The chap I was with, he was a pretty sensitive bloke. He just said, 'She's gone to be with the old man now, that's all.'

It was actually very affecting. Maybe because she looked a bit like my granny. I don't know. In parts of the world, you might unfortunately expect to see dead bodies occasionally; Western society is very good at sweeping all that away, so that only a few of us actually have to see it and deal with it.

PC, 34, Midlands force

I get really quite fed up with people moaning at me for stopping them for speeding or giving them a ticket for driving while on their phones. I've been called a wanker, I've been asked many times why I'm not out catching burglars and rapists instead of hassling innocent motorists. Mostly, beyond warning them they'll be arrested if they carry on swearing, you try not to get involved. There's a satisfaction in remaining professional and letting them rant on. But one time I caught a guy doing 48mph in a 30mph zone, and as I was writing his ticket he just would not shut up about how we were just revenue-gatherers, the public hate us because we don't catch criminals. I was like, 'Yeah, yeah, whatever, mate,' but eventually I'd had enough. I turned to him and said, 'Six months ago, someone doing *exactly* your speed came through here, and half a mile up there he ran over a nine-year-old boy, squashed his skull and trailed his brains up the road for 20 metres. Now, if it weren't for people like you driving like this maybe I *could* be out catching burglars, but the trouble is we keep getting little kids killed, don't we?'

He apologised, got in his car and drove away, slowly. I'd like people to understand that it's not some sort of personal vendetta, as in us-versus-them, it's done for a reason. If people had more of an idea I think they would be more onside with us.

PC, 36, Southern force

I was working response duties teamed up with a colleague when we heard one of our traffic colleagues pursuing a vehicle which had sped off when he tried to stop it. We soon heard that the vehicle had crashed and turned over and rushed to the scene to help. There were three people in the car – two lads in their early 20s and a girl aged 18. The car had gone through a crossroads at around 90mph, hit a pothole and then the kerb and turned upside down. It had then skidded down the road on its roof, the roof having collapsed.

We tried our best at first aid, but they were well and truly trapped by seatbelts and twisted metal. They were all unconscious, and it was pretty clear some of them wouldn't be walking away. Ambulances and fire crews were on the scene very quickly, and after a quick examination they cut one of the young men out and loaded him into an ambulance to convey him to hospital.

One of the other paramedics then came over to me with the fire watch commander and said, 'The other two are dead, I'm afraid.'

The fire-fighter said, 'We'll get the girl out of the back next… Can you give us a hand?'

So I stood there with a colleague, holding up a big sheet to protect the car from view, with both of us feeling the way cops always do at a serious RTC [*road traffic collision*], like a spare part. She had long, blonde hair, she was hanging upside down from her seatbelt, and I still remember seeing her hair draped onto the road and watching the red slowly soaking down her hair and pooling on the tarmac. I looked up and I noticed a man stood in an upstairs window with a boy of about 10, watching us pull a dead body from the car. The watch commander tried to wave him away, but they stayed and watched.

After the girl had been removed I walked around the other side of the car and saw a fleshy shape poking out from under the door pillar. I stared at it for about 10 seconds, trying to work out what it was, before noticing the eyes. It was a face, but the head had been squashed almost flat. I have no idea what part of the car did it, or how. I can only hope it was quick. In the end, it was decided to leave this second lad in the car and have it recovered so he could be removed out of public view.

My colleague and I went back to our van, tasked with keeping an eye on the scene. I used to keep an iPod and a small speaker in the van on nights. It was set to shuffle. When we turned it on, Snow Patrol's *Chasing Cars* came on! We talked about the dead blonde girl, and how easy it would be for one of us to kill the other with a single mistake while driving fast. Now, when I catch myself on a response drive, pushing the car hard, I think about the blood soaking down that blonde hair, and I ease off.

It was probably one of the most surreal experiences of my life. The other lad survived. I later learnt that he and his mate had met the girl in town that night. The blonde girl had accepted a lift, her mate had gone home in a taxi.

PC, 24, Northern force

I'd just got in from spending the entire morning on a fruitless wild goose chase looking for a missing lad – lest you think I sound heartless, this was a kid who was *always* going 'missing' from care, by the simple expedient of walking out the door. No-one, sadly, can stop them – some of these 'MISPERs' [*missing persons*] are missing four or five times a week, mostly getting off their faces. Anyway, I'd no sooner sat down in the report room and got my snap out than the Sergeant pops his head in and says, 'Can you nip down to *x* junction for me, there's been a smash.'

This particular junction is out in the cuds about 15 minutes from town, so 20 minutes from the nick. It's the crossroads of a very straight old Roman road and a quick, straight stretch of country lane, which would have been fine but for the fact that the Roman road kinks slightly on either side of the lane, and approaching it, from the south particularly, an awful lot of drivers just didn't see the junction. Every year or so, someone would sail across it straight into the side of a vehicle travelling the other way. Luckily, there are wide verges and dry ditches on all sides as you go through the junction, so usually what happened was both vehicles would end up in the ditches and often people were shaken up but not too badly hurt. Lately they've put in place radar-triggered warning signs which light up, and big 'give way' signs with yellow-and-black checkered borders, so it's not so common.

Anyway, I knew where it was so I put my snap back in the fridge, got the keys to one of the pandas and stuck the blue bellend on. Sure enough, when I get there, a car has gone through the junction and hit a van coming across it smack on the offside wing. The van's on its side in the hedge, and the car has been pushed down the east-west road and is now facing back towards the junction on the wrong side of the road. Significant debris field. Both vehicles are badly damaged, but the van driver is out and sitting by the side of the road, and apart from what turned out to be a busted nose, and a lot of blood from that, he seems OK. So I go to the car. There's a woman in the driver's seat who is groaning a bit but is completely *compos mentis* and doesn't look too badly injured. The impact has pushed the engine block back a fair way, and that in turn has pushed the steering column and dashboard back onto her. She's basically pinned in the wreckage. She says her tummy hurts a bit but she seems OK. It looks to me that if I can get at her I should be able to move her seat back and free her. Unfortunately both doors are jammed, so that's a no-no.

I radio up for the brigade, turns out they're already on their way, so I say to the woman, 'Don't worry, the fire service will be here in a jiffy and get you out.'

She says something about her husband being mad about the car, it's his and she only borrowed it because hers is in for its MOT. She says, 'I was on my way to pick the kids up, can you call the school and let them know I'm going to be late?'

Turned out they were at the same school as mine – her youngest was two years above my eldest, so we had a minor chinwag about the headmistress and that. I gave the school office a call, took a few details from her while she was sat there, started thinking about taking a statement from the van driver, and then she suddenly says, 'I don't feel very well.'

I look at her, she's gone as white as a sheet. I've already called for an ambo, I call up again, they're five minutes away. I say, 'Hold on, love, the ambulance is going to be here any minute and they'll sort you out. You're just in shock, that's all.'

She starts crying, and she suddenly says, 'I'm going to die, aren't I? What about my kids?'

I says, 'Nah, what you talking about? You're going to get a bollocking off your old man for wrecking his car, but you're gonna be fine.'

I reached my hand in through the window, which was obviously broken, and held her hand. She looks at me, vomits, and I can see blood in the vomit, and then she closes her eyes and relaxes. And I just knew in that moment that she *had* died. Weird. It was so sudden. From talking to me five minutes earlier, to that. I tried to get at her to perform CPR [*cardio-pulmonary resuscitation*] but because of the way the car was damaged, I just couldn't… I just held her hand until the ambulance and fire arrived. Her kids waiting for her three miles away.

PC, 40, Midlands force

I used to hate getting sent to RTAs [*road traffic accidents, now more often called RTCs*], I had that butterflies feeling in my stomach. *What's it going to be like? God, I hope there's not too much blood. I hope it's not kids.* I only had one person die on me in five years and I did what I could for them, kept telling them they would be OK, the ambo is on its way, all the while knowing they were on their way out, but I always had that feeling of, *Could I have done more? Was there something else I could have done?* In the end, a big part of why I transferred to CID was because I didn't like the roadside. For some weird reason that I can't explain, I can cope with a murder much better than a road death. Maybe it's the complete randomness, whereas most murders are predictable.

DC, 33, Northern force

I went to an incident where two vehicles had collided head-on. One car still had the driver in it. The two occupants of the other car were uninjured, barring the usual minor grazes from air-bag deployments. I called in the update and then went to see what I could do to help the trapped driver of the first car. The front doors on both sides were deformed and were going to need to be forced open by the fire service, but as far as I could tell he was uninjured. He was on his phone to his wife or girlfriend telling her about the accident and reassuring her that he was fine. I called the control room again and confirmed that there was an ambulance and a fire tender on the way. They were, but they didn't know our exact location so I told the guy he would have to wait a few minutes. He said he'd always wanted a convertible. We chatted for a few minutes and I took his details down in my pocket-book.

It was at that point that I noticed smoke. It was faint, at first, but it soon got stronger. I thought it might be the residual smell of an airbag or of hot rubber from skidding tyres, but then I saw a wisp from the bonnet vent on the driver's side of the car. I told him that it was probably just steam from the coolant bottle or radiator, but I nipped off to the car for the extinguisher just in case. I was only away 20 seconds or so, but by the time I got back the smoke was darker and thicker. I ran back to the car and grabbed the crowbar and set about the door, but it was obvious I wasn't going to get it open.

I heard him say, 'Oh shit!' and I looked round and saw the smallest of flames flickering through the gaps in the bonnet vent. I dropped the crowbar, grabbed the extinguisher, shoved the nozzle toward the vent and let off a blast of powder, and then I moved it to a gap where the bonnet had folded up slightly and gave it another squirt. A cloud of powder rose into the air, but when the fog cleared the flames were still there. I tried again with a bigger blast; which had an effect for a few moments, but then things just went straight back to where they were before. The bonnet was starting to blacken around the vent, and the paint was starting to bubble as the heat increased. I emptied the remainder of the extinguisher down through the vent but still the heat and smoke continued to build.

I got onto the control room to find out how far away the fire service were. I said the car was now smoking and I needed more help at the scene. I could now hear sirens in the distance. The driver could hear them too. I saw his face change; he became a little more relaxed. He said, 'Thank fuck for that, I thought I was going to be toast for a minute.'

I was still going to try to get him out if I could. I grabbed a seatbelt cutter, and hacked his belt off at the shoulder. I tried to reach down inside the car to get to the recline cog at the bottom of the seat. The plastic interior trim had bent out of shape and blocked my hand from getting to it. I could touch one or two teeth with a fingertip, but just could not get enough power behind it to turn it. I suspect it was pinned in place anyway. The sirens got louder. I tried the back doors of the car to see if I could get inside and pull the seat back from there. No matter how hard I pulled, it was not moving an inch.

Just then, I caught a flash of blue lights out of the corner of my eye. Unfortunately, it was the ambulance, not a fire engine. I said something unprintable and the driver knew exactly what I was thinking. I sprinted to the ambulance and got their extinguisher. It was bigger than mine, but it was soon gone and the fire was still building. Flames were now coming out from the sides of the bonnet as well as through the vent, and the driver could feel the heat on his feet. The driver of the other car joined me and the paramedic in trying to pull the door open. We managed to get the top of the door away from the roof, but the main panel refused to budge. The driver was getting desperate. He was trying to write a text message to someone. I don't know what it said, but it was short. The fire continued to grow under the bonnet, and I could see smoke coming from under the wheel arches, and then flames. The driver was shouting now, and he was thrashing around. I took him by the arm and tried to pull him free. He screamed out in pain and I apologised for hurting him, but I soon realised that it wasn't me that was to blame. The fire had broken through from the engine bay into the footwell. We tried everything from all sides and using every ounce of strength we had. The windscreen shattered with the heat. The driver was looking straight at me. I could see that he was in pain, and was so scared. He asked me again to help him. I took my body armour off, I needed as much space and freedom of movement as I could get, and went to the rear seat again to give it another try. Smoke was now starting to pour out from around the dashboard. I came back to the driver's door, trying to pull the door open with my hands again. The bodywork on the car was now burning my palms as I touched it. The driver was screaming in pain, screaming at me for help, screaming at me to save him. I kept telling him I was sorry. I knew what was going to happen, and he knew it too. I was driven back by the heat as the flames moved from the engine bay to the inside of the car. He looked straight at me through the smoke. He was mouthing words but there was no sound.

Two or three minutes later, the first fire appliance arrived and the crew got straight into action, but it was too late. Another police vehicle arrived, and I walked over to them. A road closure was needed, as this was now going to be a long job. I volunteered to take that on and the officers in the car agreed. They didn't know what had just happened and I didn't want to have to describe it to them. I simply said. 'It's a fatal,' and wandered off down the country lane to the junction about 600 yards away.

PC, 28, Southern force

I attended a road traffic collision on a single carriageway A-road in our area, where a motorcyclist had collided with a car. Saturday morning. A car driver on his side of the road had for some reason best known to herself decided to commence a u-turn without checking behind her. An absolutely egregious bit of bad driving. To effect the u-ey, she braked and pulled hard right so that she was across the lane. In attempting to avoid her, the biker had swerved into the opposite lane and collided with a car coming the other way.

Death's like that: one minute you're a 26-year-old chap pootling along the road on your way to work, as he was, the next minute the finger of fate has come down from the sky and selected you, and it's all over.

We were not far behind, so I came upon the scene before it was even called in to find one hysterical female car driver still sitting in her vehicle, one dazed male car driver still sitting in *his* vehicle, and one motorcyclist lying in the middle of the road. You didn't need to be a doctor to see that he was in a very bad way. His body was face down but his head was twisted away at a funny angle and his face visor was just red with blood.

I positioned the car with the lights on on the northern side of the scene and ran with some cones *et cetera* to the southern side, quickly checked the drivers and went to my colleague who was trying to perform CPR on the motorcyclist. It was clearly not going to be of any use, but he carried on until the ambulance arrived, at which point the paramedics took over.

By now, quite a substantial line of traffic had built up on both the northern and southern sides of the scene, and I remember how unreasonable some of those drivers who were queuing were. Some people are extraordinary: there's a young man lying dead in the road not 30 feet away and they're bibbing their horns and shouting the odds about how they've got to get to so-and-so. You want to drag them out of their car and pull them over and shove their noses in it and say, 'There, you wee bastard… Are you still in such a hurry?'

I don't know if it's just my personality or being in the Job has made me like this, but I'm much more patient than most people seem to be. If I have to wait somewhere, I just think, *There must be some reason for this that I don't know about, so let's just wait. It's not a problem. I've got all the time in the world, here.*

PC, 30, Scottish force

My non-police family and friends ask me why I drive so carefully. I'm religious about it – 30mph in a 30mph zone, 70mph on the motorway. I say it's because I'm in the police so I have to obey the law, but the truth is it's because of what I've seen. The people who go around campaigning against speed cameras, saying speed doesn't kill… I don't honestly know how they live with themselves. Of course speed doesn't kill on its own, but a car driven at speed is harder to control, the driver is less able to cope with the unexpected, and the damned thing does a lot more damage when it hits you.

I've been to some horrendous accidents and the thing that always strikes me is, literally 30 seconds before this happened this person was a living being with hopes and dreams and plans for later that day... Not dreaming that he or she was just a few moments away from a horrible death. People think road death is something that happens to other people, and that when it does happen it's sudden and painless. 'He died in a car crash.' Yes, he did, but what happened was he bled to death trapped in the wreckage, or was burned alive with his kids watching outside the car after they managed to get out, or maybe he was decapitated which might be quick but isn't something I would fancy. These are all outcomes I have either seen or investigated.

PC, 40, Northern force

In many forces now, and certainly in mine, the RPUs [*road policing units*], traffic departments as-was, have been cut to the bone. Within the police we have never been very well-regarded, we are the 'Black Rats' who will eat their own, but at least we used to get good cars, we had decent numbers, the importance of the department was recognised, if grudgingly. When I joined what was then the Motorway Unit in 1995, we had nearly 30 vehicles available to us. By the time I left in 2009, we were sometimes putting just a couple of cars on the road. This meant we had people driving half way across the county on blue lights to deal with RTCs, and, when we couldn't deal, untrained response officers were having to step in. Traffic now has cars that have done more mileage than the Space Shuttle, experienced officers with more than 30 years in are being A19-d [*compulsorily retired to save costs*] and not replaced, there's no overtime. People are being pressured to work and take time off *in lieu*, which is illegal. In my time we were cut to the bone, and were constantly hassled over KPIs [*key performance indicators*] for the number of EFPNs [*endorsable fixed penalty notices*] issued, for instance, so that they could justify what little budget was spent on us on their spreadsheets. I have nothing against issuing tickets, but we shouldn't focus on stats-for-stats-sake.

Between 1999 and 2008, more than 32,000 people were killed on the roads in the UK. Can you imagine the resources that would be thrown at it if there were 32,000 murders during that period? If you get a gang-related shooting, CID [*Criminal Investigation Department – the plain-clothed detective branch of the police*] will get bodies coming in from everywhere for a Major Incident Team and they'll all be taken off the books to deal with it until it's cleared up. Yet if there's a four-vehicle RTC with three dead, investigation-wise it's a couple of traffic lads dealing with the whole thing, with little or no recognition. Not a single box ticked, no KPIs hit, and it probably won't even come up at the daily management meeting. As someone who has attended more than his fair share of fatal RTCs, I think it's weird. You're still dead, whether you were stabbed or hit by a car.

And it's not like that's the only reason traffic is important. For some reason best known to them, some criminals – even when transporting high value consignments of drugs, or weapons, or anything, really – have an inbuilt resistance to things like tax and insurance and MOTs. Me, if I were a drug dealer I'd buy a two-year-old Mondeo, check the lights and the tyres and get it insured. But they prefer to tool about either in cars with ludicrous spoilers, blacked-out windows and noisy exhausts, or in the sort of thing that might get you 50 quid at the scrap yard. If you have cars out and about, you can stop these people, you know you've got them for no insurance [*police can check insurance status on a vehicle before stopping it*], you have a look in the boot, and lo and behold, what have we here? We've all had some great results over the years. Cut back the traffic patrols and you just allow the criminal better freedom of movement. It all puzzles me. But then, I only drive a car. The people who drive desks, and have chauffeurs to drive them on the roads, clearly have a better understanding.

PC, 46, Midlands force

Not too many of the high-fliers go through traffic, and the end result of that is we have a senior management structure, throughout the police service, who don't really have much of a clue. I spent some years as a family liaison officer attached to traffic. This is to me a very important role. You deal with the families of victims of RTCs, and that includes everything from the simple but emotionally-demanding tasks of sitting with them and being a shoulder to cry on, to updating them as to the investigation, and any subsequent court case, to dealing with the coroner and the inquest, to sometimes dealing with the media a bit for them… I've worked deaths of mums and dads who have left widows and widowers and kids, and it is both important and difficult work. It doesn't take a genius, or even someone especially familiar with policing, to see that.

Unfortunately, there are no targets to hit, unlike, say, for the number of detections. So it came to my annual appraisal, and my inspector pulled me in and bollocked me for wasting too much of my time with relatives. The modern police is run on KPIs and statistics and targets, whatever Theresa May says about it, and there's no way of measuring the worth of time spent comforting a couple who have just lost a kid. Like there's no way of measuring the negative of how many problems are prevented by having traffic cars out and about. How many FPNs have you given out this month? That's what they're interested in. *That* we can measure. It's a number in a box, which we can compare against other months, and forces, and officers. But how long did you spend with that family? That's more amorphous, you have to rely on your officers' discretion, and they don't like that.

PC, 40, South-western force

While most of the officers interviewed have asked to remain anonymous, Metropolitan Police Sergeant Ali Gibb wanted the following story to be told, and would obviously have been identified by his son's details. Sgt Gibb also passed on the victim personal statement which was written by himself and his wife for the court case, and which is reproduced below.

I'm a serving officer in the Metropolitan Police TSG [*Territorial Support Group*]. My son Daniel followed me into the force and then to TSG. We are the only father and son to have done this.

On Friday 5th March, 2010, we had an early morning start for a central London demonstration. His team were making up the numbers on mine, due to a shortfall. He failed to arrive on time. I rang his partner, Rebekah, also a serving PC, and she told me he'd set out in good time on his motorbike. I rang his mobile… No reply. He lived in Bedford. I rang the Beds control room. The question I asked was whether there had been 'any accidents on the motorway'. The police officer answered me truthfully and said there had been none. Unfortunately, there had been an accident not on the motorway. He was aware who I was, and what unit I was attached to. He contacted New Scotland Yard, and my unit Inspector broke the news to me in his office. 'Come in and sit down…'

He didn't have to say any more. I've always tried to put myself in the shoes of those receiving such messages, before delivering them. It is without doubt the most difficult thing a police officer has to say to someone and there is never any easy way to say it. I knew how difficult that was for Gordon. At 5.15am that day, as Daniel was riding his motorcycle to work to join me, the driver of a minibus gave way to two cars on the A507 waiting to turn right onto the major road. He then pulled out in front of Dan. There was no time for him to take avoiding action and he was killed at the scene.

The case against the driver fell short of dangerous driving, and the charge was one of death by careless driving. This is a relatively new offence, which can now be tried summarily or on indictment. The driver elected trial. He was told by the presiding magistrate that to do so would mean that any subsequent plea of guilty fell outside of the leniency terms afforded to those who plead guilty at the earliest opportunity.

Ten agonising weeks passed whilst the defence carried out their own investigations and the CPS file was prepared for committal. On the committal date, a new lay bench were in place. They accepted a change of plea to guilty from the driver, and referred the matter to the probation service for reports. The absolute minimum recommended sentence is community service.

Further weeks passed, and in October 2010 we listened to the magistrate tell the driver that it was a momentary lapse and 'There but for the grace of God…' He, the driver 'had suffered enough', and any monetary penalty would be an insult to Daniel's name. He was working six days a week, which negated any community service as 'it would breach European Working Time directives'.

They took no notice of what had been said at the first hearing. Prior to Daniel's case being called, we listened to a speeding matter before the same bench. They handed a speeding driver, 50 mph in a 30 mph limit, a fine of several hundred pounds. In Dan's case, the sentence handed down was 12 months' disqualified, which is mandatory in law, and a conditional discharge for two years. There was no fine, and no requirement to take another test. No consideration that the driver might be required to take time off or forego some holiday in order to carry out community work. It was far too lenient but there is no recourse to appeal. Prosecuting authorities may only appeal against sentence handed down by a crown court, not a magistrates' court.

The justice system stinks. It always has. The vast majority of those in the legal profession who appear in court are there to fill their own pockets. It is a complete lottery as to how any crime will be dealt with. Different police forces have vastly different standards of how to investigate allegations of crime. They have different priorities, different means of resource allocation and different attitudes to methods of disposal. The CPS [*Crown Prosecution Service, which decides on charges and prosecutes offenders*] similarly will offer vastly differing standards of advice from one representative to another, even within the same office. I had warned my son never to take the sentencing of a court personally. It has always been advice I give to young officers. Little did I think.

Time doesn't heal. I've read people's accounts of the pain involved in losing someone close. Words don't accurately describe the emotions. The passage of time allows us to become accustomed to the pain, the void, the longing for contact, but there is no healing. Significant dates are difficult – Friday mornings, birthdays, *et cetera*. His favourite music, the music played at his funeral, every motorbike on the road… All are a constant reminder. We spent last Christmas, the first without him, renting a house so as not to have his empty place at our Christmas dinner table. We are in a dilemma as to what to do this year. Christmas dinner will not be at home.

Sandi [*Daniel's mother*] and I very quickly found we were grieving in very different ways, especially initially. She needs to continually look at his photographs, whereas it was painful for me. She needs to keep him involved in conversation. 'Daniel would have done this, or said that,' whereas it is painful for me. We have had to compromise… It has been difficult for us both. We have 'slap in the face' moments where insignificant events, things said, observations, stories involving the loss of a child or the death of our service personnel all now cause us to cry. I never openly cried before Daniel's death.

We both have tried to speak to Jamie [*Daniel's younger brother, an Army officer*] about 'where he is'. He blanks it, and is dealing with it in his own way. Maybe that's the Army training. We worry about this.

Helpful processes are things like the fact that my work teambuilding day now has a competition for the 'Dan Gibb trophy'. Raising funds for the charities that help the bereaved, like the Road Victims Trust [*http://www.roadvictimstrust.org.uk/*] and UK COPS [*Care of Police Survivors, http://www.ukcops.org/*], which brings together the surviving relatives and partners of police officers who have died on duty… There's a yearly memorial event at the National Arboretum, and we have a plaque there in Dan's name. Attending police memorial services. Visiting 'his tree' at the crematorium. But these are moments of respite from the always-present cloud.

Sgt Ali Gibb, Metropolitan Police

Victim Personal Statement of Ali and Sandi Gibb

We planned Daniel, and within three months of our wedding Sandi conceived. Towards the end of pregnancy in July 1984, the hot weather made the last few weeks extremely uncomfortable and, true to his character, Daniel decided he would arrive when it suited him. The birth was traumatic. Sandi was in labour for over 24 hours, the numbing effects of the epidural were sporadic and eventually she became exhausted, so with the help of an obstetrician who performed an episiotomy, and the use of forceps, Daniel arrived shortly after midnight on 26 July 1984. He weighed in at 10lbs 1oz. At 5ft 3in tall, it's no wonder mum needed help. Sandi was unable to move properly, unable to lift Daniel; unable to prepare him for feeding, change him or do all the usual things new mums do for about six weeks. I was allowed time off work to help and together we muddled through. Daniel suffered from colic and consequently we suffered from a lack of sleep more than most new parents.

Daniel was our first child, a difficult birth but he was worth it; he was the talk of the hospital, the biggest baby on the ward. Like all babies, he cried a lot, fed a lot and needed nappy-changing a lot. As a toddler, he loved playing with his Matchbox cars. He took great care of his toys. He would hate it if they got scratched or broken and this carried on throughout his life from his GameGear, iPod, computer, car and motorbikes. When he was two-and-a-half, his baby brother Jamie arrived. He was very protective over him. They played well together as children. In the teenage years they both had different circles of friends but, over the last five years or so, they had both got settled into steady relationships with girlfriends and they had started to go out and do things together. They had similar interests, they both drove motorbikes, had the same cars, played the same PlayStation games and would often play each other, at times miles apart, via the internet. They were always competitive and loved making fun of each other. Jamie was proud of Daniel when he passed out at Hendon police college and Daniel was proud of Jamie getting accepted into Sandhurst, and we as a family were looking forward to all being at Jamie's passing out Parade in the April.

He was a timid toddler and acquiring new skills always needed special encouragement from us both. Despite this, he did well at school. He managed a few appearances for the football team and was an accomplished swimmer. He never caused trouble and was a model pupil, a model son, a son to be proud of and we are. After school he had the choice to go to university or begin to earn his keep. He had taken up a part time post at Sainsbury's whilst at school. The personnel department quickly recognized his people skills and approached him to become the store trainer. Daniel decided to follow his dad into the police force. In the meantime, whilst waiting to be recruited, he followed in mum's footsteps and became cabin crew for just under a year, flying around Europe with easyJet. He joined the Metropolitan police in 2004 and served out his probation in Kentish Town. He undertook driver training at the Met's School of Excellence in Hendon and was granted status of police response driver within three years. He took pride in his driving skills, being careful to avoid the pitfalls of busy London streets, particularly when driving to emergencies with blue lights and sirens. He never had an accident.

He had a sharp sense of humour, lifting his colleague's spirits, even in the most tasking of their duties. He met Rebekah, his partner, at the Met's training school. They didn't hit it off at first and for a time they were rivals to see who could score higher in police exams.

He took great pleasure in outscoring her every time, because she was the one with the first class degree. He again outscored her in the promotion to Sergeant examination in 2008 when he passed in the top 100 in the whole of the UK, in competition with some 5,000 officers. It was with immense pride to his dad that he decided to join in the Territorial Support Group and they were unique in becoming the only father and son to do so.

Daniel had been living in Bedford for about three years but often, if he was on an early shift or finishing late, he would stay at our house. He and Rebekah would come most weekends to ours and stay. We saw Daniel twice, both briefly, before he died. The morning we arrived home from New York he was at our house. He hadn't lived at home for about the last three years, so it was a lovely surprise to walk in and see him there. He had gone to work the previous day on his motorbike but had not finished work until late; the weather had turned for the worse, heavy snowfall, so he made the sensible decision of diverting to ours and staying there. That morning Ali took him into work in the car and the bike stayed in our garage for a week until the weather improved.

The last time we saw Daniel was on Wednesday March 3; he had called and asked to be picked up to collect his motorbike. We hated him on that bike, but he reassured us he was absolutely fine. Our comment was, 'We know you are, but it's the other people on the road that are of concern. They're not all careful.' He was excited because he was off to Rome in the middle of March with Rebekah where he was going to propose on her 30th birthday.

We were very close; he valued his mum's opinion, so he had asked her to go into town with him on the Sunday to choose a token ring for Rebekah, until she could pick her own. His visit was only brief and we never had the chance to talk about New York; we said we'd look at the photos and tell him all about it on Sunday.

I woke up at 6.45 on Friday March 5, 2010 to a beautiful crisp March morning, looking forward to the weekend as I would be seeing Daniel on the Sunday. After getting ready for work, I went downstairs and noticed the front door was open. Ali had left early for work that morning and hadn't closed the front door properly so I sent him a text to warn him he may find himself in a new home for the elderly soon.

This is where the if's and why's start, which have been a big part of my vocabulary since Daniel was killed. If the door had not been left open I would have gone to work and still not known about my boy, but Ali within seconds phoned me and said he was coming home and to stay there. I asked why, he just said, 'I'm coming home.' I put the phone down thinking, *This isn't like Ali something is wrong*, and that's when it hit me, it was my son Daniel. Immediately I called back and that's when I heard him say those words which I hear so clearly in my head every day and are the worst any mother could hear: 'I think he's gone, he's gone Sand, we've lost him.'

My heart had been broken; my beautiful precious boy had been stolen from me. I couldn't believe it. How? Why? It didn't seem real until about 9.30, when the police came to officially tell me. I was told the collision happened at 5.15am and he died at the scene at 5.30.

I just wanted to go to him. I still couldn't believe it until I had seen him. I kept thinking, *They've all got this wrong. I'm his mum, I can protect him, I can make this all better, he's hurt, he's not dead*. We had about four hours to wait until we could see him, time stood still.

These are now times of the morning that remain my deepest moments. I regularly wake at exactly 5.15. There is no explanation for this. I just lay there in a deep, dark place that has become my world. He died alone. I should have been there to hold him and have the chance to say goodbye. I don't have to close my eyes to see him, but the Daniel I see is dead Daniel, lifeless Daniel, Daniel in the hospital morgue and Daniel lying in his coffin. Not till I look at his photos which sit beside my bed can I see the real Daniel, and then I still can't believe I'm never to really see him, hold him and have our talks ever again. I don't want to remember him like this and I pray that one day I can remember him for the happy, witty, smiling Daniel with the cheeky grin.

Daniel's younger brother Jamie was away on exercise as part of his course at Sandhurst. He was literally plucked from a field and brought directly home to us. This 6ft soldier in combat fatigues came through the door and flung himself at me, we clung to each other and we sobbed and sobbed. I'd had one child stolen from me and the other child, now a broken figure was hurting, and yet again I could do nothing to make it better.

When Jamie joined the Army I always had the thought that if anything happened to either of my boys it would be him, Jamie, an officer in the Army with the prospects of him going out to Afghanistan. Never in my wildest nightmares did I think it would be Daniel, on his way to work on a March morning, to work with his Dad, Ali, who was proud of Daniel and Daniel who was proud of Ali.

It was my 50th Birthday in February this year both Jamie and Daniel wanted to buy something special and asked what I would like, I asked for something I could keep as I said to Daniel if anything should ever happen to them I wanted something to remind me of them. They chose a necklace which I never take off. Why did he have to die? I have the necklace, it's beautiful and I'll cherish it forever. But I want Daniel here, laughing, joking just being Daniel.

A parent should never have to bury their child, we shouldn't outlive them, never see them dead. Lifeless. Cold. Alone.

I wanted to see Daniel marry, have children. See him become the wonderful father I know he would have been.

One regularly hears the phrase, 'Time heals.' Wrong. It doesn't, we hurt every day, ache to see our Daniel come through the door. Our beautiful son, my beautiful baby. There is a void that will never be filled. A void outside our control. We're so lucky and proud to have had Daniel but now so angry he has been taken from us.

At his funeral, our son's funeral, the church was packed. He was popular with so many people, everyone hurting together, grieving for their friend, their colleague, for Daniel, our son.

Daniel was 25 years old when he was killed. That's nothing. I shouldn't have to write about Daniel like this and wish with all my heart, every fibre, I wasn't. On 5th March 2010 our hearts were broken. It feels like someone reached inside and wrenched out a part of our heart, a part of us died that day too. Our family has been torn apart; we will never be the same again. There's a vacant space at the table for Sunday roast. We've been robbed of Christmases, birthdays, grandchildren, memories that we'll never make or have. Jamie has been robbed of his big brother. Jamie's passing out from Sandhurst was a celebration of his achievements and we were all very proud but the day was also very sad and emotional as one member of our family, Daniel, was missing. Rebekah gave Jamie a gift which Daniel had chosen personally for him; he will treasure this for the rest of his life. The Sunday after Daniel's funeral was Mother's day, I was given a Mother's Day card from Rebekah which Daniel had chosen but had not yet written in and I was also given my present he had chosen. It's a shopping bag, but it's not used for shopping; it now sits in my Daniel memories box. Nothing will take this pain away, a pain we will have to learn to live with. We are trying to come to terms with the loss of our son, we are attending weekly counselling in the hope we will learn to adjust.

You may see us smile, laugh maybe. What you won't see is the pain and the hurt that lurks behind that will stay with us until we die. Our life and our surviving son's life have been altered forever. Nothing will ever be the same again.

As with Sgt Gibb, many of the other officers interviewed condemned the courts for handing down what they regarded as weak sentences.

I'm quite a placid person, but sentencing really winds me up. I've lost count of the number of files, the times I've been to court to give evidence against some PPO [*prolific or other priority offender*] for his 1,000th offence, where he was caught red-handed, and later you think, 'I'll just find out what happened.' And you speak to the CPS, or have a look at the computer, and you find out they've let him back out on the streets with an anger management order or some equal load of bollocks.

For my first three years in the Job, it used to make me furious. I'd go home and be in a bad mood and rant to my husband about it and we'd end up having a row. So then I thought, 'I can't keep on taking this so personally, it's going to drive me insane.' So I tried not worrying about it, and for a while I'd just laugh about it, obviously a bit bitterly, but I'd laugh and say, 'Well, I did *my* bit.' But after a while the anger came back, I just couldn't keep it out. It wrecked my marriage, or was a major factor, but I couldn't help it. You sit with a widow who's had Vaseline smeared on her fingers to make it easier to slide her wedding ring off, or an honest shopkeeper who is struggling to keep his family's heads above water and is in tears at being robbed again, and then you see the people who have been preying on them giving us the finger and smirking outside court, because they've just been let off with some nothing community sentence, because their lawyer told some bullshit story about how they're settling down, and the new woman has just had a baby and they're trying really hard to find a job. And, call me cynical, but when you've heard this story a hundred times before, often about the *very same offender*... We know we'll be dealing with the same people next week for the same offences, just new victims, but somehow there's no comeback on the lawyer or the magistrate. No-one ever says, '*You* didn't jail *this* guy, and *you* smooth-talked *that* guy out of a prison sentence which would have saved 50 old people from becoming victims of distraction burglaries which have wrecked their lives... What have you got to say for yourselves?'

Sergeant, 35, Midlands force

I was on foot patrol in a busy high street, and I signalled for a car to stop. Instead of stopping, the driver accelerated towards me and ran me down. My arse went through his windscreen, and the impact shattered my radio and exploded my CS gas canister. I was thrown over the car. Unfortunately, and I don't know how, I ended up getting caught on the car with my foot jammed on the rear spoiler and my arm dangling through the open sunroof.

The driver, a 30-year-old male called Sean Huntroyd who was unaware at that stage that I was still clinging on, sped away. I alerted him to the fact that I was on his roof, and told him to stop. He refused, and this led to an exchange of punches between us through the open sunroof at about 60mph. All this time, he's shouting about how he's going to kill me and telling me I'm going to die. And to be honest, without making a big London job out of it, I thought I might.

It was a nasty old time on that car for the 60 or so seconds I was there. At one point, Huntroyd even attempted to close the sunroof, realising that this was all I had to hold onto. Anyways, to cut a long story short, after going the wrong way round several roundabouts and flying over speed humps, he did a crazy handbrake turn and flung me off into the street, sparking me out by smashing my head onto the tarmac, breaking my left wrist, dislocating my shoulder and giving me some serious concussion. He then drove off at speed leaving me for dead, before abandoning the vehicle about a mile away. According to the passenger who was in the car with him, he thought I was dead and said to him, 'That takes care of that cunt!'

The CPS contacted me via a CID bobby a few days later after Huntroyd had been nicked, asking if I would be OK with a charge of s47 ABH? [*S47 of the Offences Against the Person Act 1861 is the lesser offence out of the three OAP Act offences most often charged – the others being S20, inflicting grievous bodily harm, and S18, inflicting grievous bodily harm with intent to do so. It is generally believed by prosecutors that it is easier to convince a jury to convict on the lesser charge of causing actual bodily harm – minor injuries such as cuts or bruises; police officers complain that serious offences are often downgraded on this basis, in order that the CPS can hit targets for convictions.*] The answer was, No, I would not. I couldn't believe it. The bloke runs me over, drives off with me clinging to his car at 60 plus mph, tells me I'm going to die and that he's going to kill me… It was attempt murder, all day long. I naturally protested by turning up at the 'case conference' with my CID mate, my arm in a sling and walking like John Wayne due to my injuries. I started gobbing off at the whole room, at which point they apologised and agreed to go with the big one. So Huntroyd gets charged with attempted murder, and loads of other crap... Dangerous driving, dizzy [*disqualified*] driving *et cetera, et cetera.*

I was happy enough with that. But within the time it takes to change a light bulb, the CPS – without discussing it with me, or letting me know out of common courtesy – dropped the charge to GBH. The police and myself – so that's 'we', I suppose – complain till we're blue in the face. Our opinion being that it was a clear case of attempt murder, backed up by the driver's own verbal statements, such as, 'You're going to die,' and, 'I'm going to kill you.' In any case, surely this is for a jury to decide, and not the CPS, who seem to think that they are the judge, jury and executioner these days?

The CPS continued to refuse to up the charge back to attempt murder, and the trial went ahead at the Old Bailey. The judge wasn't happy, and even delayed the trial for a day so he could speak to CPS and ask them to explain their rationale to him. They still refused to up the charges even after this. The judge said in open court, 'I have asked why the CPS dropped the charge of attempted murder. I have been given no satisfactory explanation.'

The driver pleaded not guilty but was convicted and got nine years. Bear in mind that if I hadn't pushed it the chap would've been charged with ABH only, which carries a maximum sentence of only five years. To downgrade the charges without even discussing it with me or explaining their rationale was a disgrace. I felt like it was a case of, 'Yeah we're supposed to discuss these things with the victim, but he's only uniform plod so it's not that bad is it?'

A jury could have found the driver guilty of attempt murder and therefore the judge would have been more inclined to give him life. Yes, he *can* give life for GBH but realistically they don't, do they?

There's a twist to this story, too. About 18 months into his nine years for my so-called GBH, the driver was convicted of his part in a scam by a gang of travellers who were ripping off old people by agreeing to do building work, tarmacking driveways and stuff like that. They were proper scumbags. My man's involvement had been to set up the bank account they used to place the deposits before scarpering with the cash. Obviously, he was well into this caper long before his little escapade with me, but at the time Hampshire Police, who were overseeing the investigation, didn't have enough evidence to charge him with anything. Eventually, they got the evidence they required and charged him with fraud whilst he was in prison.

He denied it but was found guilty at Winchester Crown Court. Here's the bit where you really shake your head and go, 'What the fuck?' For this latest offence against the elderly, vulnerable and weak, and despite forcing those same persons to go through the ordeal of giving evidence at court, he was sentenced to two years and six months' imprisonment. That would have been bad enough, but this was then reduced to nine months because, according to the wise and learned judge, 'He is already serving a nine-year prison sentence.'

Just to clarify, my case was used as an excuse to give him *less* time in prison and a more lenient sentence for his part in conning elderly people out of their savings. You couldn't make it up! It's a sick joke.

The DC involved in the fraud case was clearly pissed off and was pretty vocal about the sentences in some of the media reports afterwards. There you have it: two bobbies let down sentencing-wise on two jobs with the same scrote, but for different reasons – one is pissed off at the CPS, the other with the judge. In other words, everything turns to rats as soon as it leaves the hands of the police and is handed onto the criminal justice system. That's what we're up against every day in this country.

Sergeant, 36, Midlands force

Roy Whiting kidnapped and sexually assaulted an eight-year-old girl. Most decent people would say that a man who is prepared to do that is a danger to *all* young children and should never be allowed to see the light of day again. The maximum sentence he could have got was life: the judge gave him four years, despite a psychiatrist saying he was likely to reoffend, and he served two years and five months. He would have served only two, but he got the extra five months on top because he refused point-blank to undergo a sex offenders' rehabilitation programme in prison. Unbelievably, despite that, they still let him out way early.

A year or two later, he abducted and murdered another eight-year-old girl, Sarah Payne.

If a police officer had failed in his or her duty, and that failing had allowed Whiting to evade justice and go on to commit that murder, that officer would, quite rightly, have been subject to investigation and quite possibly dismissed. What accountability was there for the judge who effectively let Whiting go the first time? Absolutely none. Bit of criticism in the press, but he carried on earning his £120,000 a year and sitting in other cases. Some years afterwards, he came out in the papers and said that the criticism of that original sentence was 'water off a duck's back'. Obviously deeply sorry, then.

Inspector, 42, Northern force

As police officers we do bang on about it – no-one ever gets enough time, they're all laughing at the system. But then, we know what's really going on, whereas most members of the public unfortunately don't. I hope doing this will open people's eyes. So, we had a case involving a guy called Ross Parsons. Parsons was a man with an extensive criminal record, with certainly more than 20 previous convictions for a whole range of offences dating back to his mid-teens. Offences of violence, robbery, theft, burglary… You name it, he'd pretty much done it. Among the most serious offences was in 2001 or 2002, when he broke into a house and made his way to the bedroom of the occupant, a 60-year-old woman, and threatened her with a knife. Bear that in mind.

Late last year, he was in prison for robbery, assault, possessing an offensive weapon and theft, but he was released early. This means that he has convinced the relevant authorities that he is no danger to anyone, despite all that past history. So he has an extensive criminal record going back more than 15 years, involving serious violent offences against other people, including aggravated burglary with a knife, and now he has been let out of jail early.

Just over a week after coming out, in the small hours he breaks into the home of a stranger, a single woman in her early 40s. She is asleep in bed. After taking a knife from the kitchen he goes upstairs to her bedroom. She wakes up, and he says, 'If you make a sound I'll fucking kill you. If you fucking so much as look at me I'll kill you.' He has a bit of a rummage around, and steals her iPod, a camera and some other things. Then he forces her to give him the PIN numbers to her cards so he can empty her accounts, before tying her to her bed, stuffing her mouth with her clothing to gag her, and raping her, without a condom, all the while telling her what he's doing to her. After he's done that, he ties her legs together and leaves to go to a cashpoint, but then he comes back and sets fire to her bed, having started other fires in the house. She struggles, she is terrified, she tries to kick out at him. Parsons starts stabbing her with the knife. The bed is now alight, so he leaves the room. Somehow, she manages to get free and runs out, but he sees her and stabs her again, repeatedly. At some point, he leaves and she staggers outside, half-naked, and the neighbours call us.

At the hospital, they found the tip of the knife embedded in her skull where it had broken off with the savagery of the blows. She had a dozen or so stab wounds including to the face and chest, a punctured lung full of blood, she lost a couple of teeth. She needed half a dozen or more operations, and was left with post-traumatic stress disorder. She has gone from being a confident, outgoing woman with a future, to a shell of her former self.

Parsons, meanwhile, has gone off to spend the money he's stolen on drugs, and is joking with people that he's just killed a woman. He was picked up a couple of days later. He refused to answer questions in interview, but the evidence, including his DNA at the scene, and the statement from the very brave victim, was overwhelming, and he was charged with attempt murder, rape, burglary and arson with intent to endanger life. He pleaded guilty, but then he had no defence so I don't believe he should get any credit for that.

Now, bearing in mind the genuinely horrific nature of the crime, and that he *had* to get life for the attempt murder, what jail time do you think the judge gave him? He got a direction that he serve a minimum of just 12 years. Is that in any way an appropriate reflection of what he did to that poor woman? Can anyone possibly say, given his past history, that he won't do something similar, or even worse when he is released? Has a man like this not reached the point at which society says, 'Sorry, mate, you've had enough chances, we don't accept this behaviour and you are out of circulation for the next 50 years?'

By the way, he refused – refused! – to come to court to hear the sentence passed. I'd have wheeled him in strapped to a sackbarrow with his eyes pinned open and a ball gag in. The victim, meanwhile, will live with this until the day she dies. I would just say to your readers, take a day or two off, go down to your local crown court or magistrates' court, listen to what goes on there. You'll be amazed.

Police officer (rank and age withheld at request), Western England force

I arrested a guy for fraud. Without getting bogged down in too much detail, he'd been ordering things off the internet in various identities. He'd accumulated goods to the value of around £18,000, most of which had long gone [*to a fence*] by the time he was nicked. It was quite a time-consuming investigation and it would have cost a fair bit, too.

Having gone no comment in interview, he went guilty at court and was jailed for eight weeks. Mind, he wouldn't serve eight weeks or anything like it, but even if he did that's still £9,000 a month. Good money. OK, he wouldn't have got full value for the stuff, but you get the point. He was also ordered to pay back at £2 a week. He is on the dole and the judge said it would be 'unduly harsh' to order him to pay back at a quicker rate. I mean, for fuck's sake. This is a guy with numerous previous convictions for fraud, theft and handling. I can only think that because Amazon and other big companies were the victims in this case, rather than Joe Bloggs from down the street, the court thinks it's somehow less of a crime. But that guy was only going to come straight back out and start again. He's a career thief and conman, what else do they expect? These people are not criminals because they are underprivileged – lots of people are underprivileged – they're criminals because they are lazy and greedy and have no morals and care about no-one but themselves.

DC, 32, Southern force

In the last few weeks, I've been in court to give evidence in three cases. There was one with more than 30 previous convictions, mostly thefts from vulnerable people who often won't or can't support, which means many more we couldn't prove, who was convicted again for theft; a second for a series of vehicle crimes, again with a record as long as your arm; and a burglar of sheltered accommodation who asked for nine other offences to be TIC-d [*taken into consideration – a method of 'clearing up' outstanding crimes by a defendant admitting to them*].

Each of the three is very well-known to us, the courts and the defence solicitors, who all, the partners anyway, drive shiny BMWs and convertible Jaguars, have big houses and kids in private schools as a result of repeatedly representing them. Each had a variety of other things on their records – assaults on police, domestic violence, possession of drugs, offensive weapons, assaults, TWOCing cars [*taking vehicles without consent*], thefts from cars. Each had previously breached community sentences, breached bail or been recalled to prison whilst out on licence in the recent past.

Not one of them – not *one* – received a single day in custody. They all got community sentences and the one who was convicted for theft was arrested again the next day for stealing a British Legion charity box from a chippy. I would bet my house on the fact that the other two will also be back in front of the court by the end of next month, barring one of them dying.

You end up with angry victims. You're angry yourself. It's all shite. The only thing I think is, well, *we* do *our* job, we're putting these bastards before the courts time and again… It's the courts not doing their job that's the problem.

PC, 30, Midlands force

Ken Clarke wants to let everyone out of prison, and I can't get people put there, no matter how hard I try. I recently helped put a boy and a girl, both 16, before the juvenile court. They live in supported housing [*subsidised accommodation for 16- to 25-year-olds*] in the town, and they are both ne'er-do-wells, long histories of truancy, very griefy kids… When they were in care, always absconding. Lots of antisocial behaviour. Getting pissed on cider in the park and playing loud music at all hours. The girl I feel a bit sorry for – hardly knows her dad, mum's an alcoholic and amateur prostitute who will suck you off for a fag, literally, or a swig from a can, and is on about her tenth partner since the girl was born. She basically offloaded her into care as soon as she could. The lad comes from a perfectly normal family where they just decided they had had enough of him and put him into care when he was 14. But irrespective of their backgrounds, the pair of them are nasty little shits. History, in both cases, of burglary, vandalism, theft, violence, threatening behaviour. He in particular would steal the teeth from your mouth, probably after he'd kicked them out first. I suspect he will spend most of his adult life in trouble.

Anyway, we put them before the court for the knifepoint robbery of a boy. He was walking home from school and as he went down the alleyway at the back of their supported housing project the lad grabbed him and the girl showed him the knife. They took his MP3 player, his phone, a couple of quid in cash. We arrested them the following day, and recovered the phone and the MP3 player. They pleaded guilty to robbery, and the magistrates gave them Youth Rehabilitation Orders, with a 9pm to 8am curfew and a requirement that they do some community work. I'm like, what the…? I thought knife crime was guaranteed jail time? They can sentence up to two years at juvenile, after all. The kids walked out of court laughing. They will certainly not obey the curfew, and nothing will happen to them when they don't, and if they turn up for more than one session of community work I'll be amazed. If I see them out after 9pm, I'll nick them, don't get me wrong. But it's not like I have the time to go looking for them, and even if I had they are just two of hundreds of people on similar orders… We can't watch them all.

Maybe the mags think they're being kind and understanding, but the *really* kind thing for those kids would actually be to lock them up in, effectively, a school. Help them to learn, give them an education, by force if necessary, do something constructive for them, and, at the same time, make them see that there are consequences. Instead, we give them the revolving door until one day they do something we can't ignore.

PC, 30, Southern force

I enjoy it when I hear people on the radio talking about the barbarity of prison. *The Moral Maze* is a great favourite of mine – lots of posh, educated people who live in London and eat in nice restaurants every night arguing that we should focus on the criminals, not the victims. I listen to the podcasts on my way into work, and shake my head and just wonder. They love to quote 'research'. It's all, 'Research shows…' Or usually, '*All* the research shows…' But most of the research on the subject of whether prison works comes, it seems to me, as a result of speaking to criminals. Researchers visit prisons and half-way houses and hostels and ask these prisoners, or ex-prisoners, 'Does prison work?'

And the answer they get is, 'No.'

'Does it act like a kind of university of crime?'

'Yes.'

'Did you come out more likely to commit more crime?'

'Er…'

'Don't worry, we're not taking names.'

'OK, yes I did.'

'Would more community sentences help more people to not offend?'

'Oh, yes, certainly!'

Hello! These people are habitual liars, folks. They go to prison because they commit crime, and they commit crime because they're criminals. They have to work bloody hard to get into prison, believe me, they've all committed dozens or even hundreds of other offences before they finally get sent down. The idea that *getting* there is what turns them bad is laughable. Call me cynical, but we see them when they are not on their best behaviour. We sit with the victims, we see the damage close up, we see the criminals for what they really are, laughing and joking about the victims, not when they're wearing a suit and being respectful and have a public-school educated barrister speaking for them, or when some earnest young researcher is buying them fags and asking them leading questions which only lead in one direction.

Inspector, 49, Northern force

We send too many people to prison, apparently. How do you define 'too many'? You never get sent to prison for a first offence, unless it's very serious, and then that's very rarely *actually* your first offence – just the first you've been convicted of. The vast majority of people in jail have been through the gamut of community orders and rehab orders and anger management courses and tags and supervision orders and all the rest of it, multiple times. They're in prison, finally, because they carried on committing crime *despite* all those interventions. More of that is *not* the answer.

The fact is, the British criminal justice system has been soft-pedalling on criminality for a long while now. Our jails are fuller than ever, and we jail more people *per capita* than any country in Europe, but that's because we have *a much higher crime rate* in this country *per capita* than in the rest of Europe. There are more than 2,000 recorded violent crimes per 100,000 head of population in the UK. In France, it's a shade over 500 [*504 – 2009 figures*]; it's hardly surprising we've got more people in jail. The USA is supposedly all wrong on crime, too many people in prison. Well, they have 450-odd [*466*] violent crimes per 100,000 population. Less than a quarter of what we do. There is a connection. The problem we have is not that we jail too many, but that we jail too few.

DS, 44, Northern force

We were circulated about the new Criminal Behaviour Orders, which will allow us to seize the proceeds of crime from relatively minor offenders in the same way that we can target organised crime. We'll

be allowed to remove things like phones, iPods, laptops, Xboxes…
All the shiny baubles that young thieves like. Great. Let's not actually
prevent them from stealing these things by locking them up, let's give
them a meaningless slap on the wrist and take away the stuff they
steal, because that will certainly stop them going back out to steal
more phones, iPods, laptops and Xboxes again, won't it?

Then the latest one was, we'll deduct £25 from the benefits of
criminals. Right, good one. I used to honestly wonder whether the
people in charge were genuinely mad, but lately I've started thinking
it's more sinister than that. If you look at it logically, we could lock
up 100,000 regular offenders well-known to the police – after due
process, of course – for five years, and if we did we would cut crime
in this country by 90 percent. In any town, 90 percent of the crime
is committed by one percent of the population. But then, would we
need quite so many lawyers if there wasn't quite so much crime? And
aren't the people in charge generally lawyers? It's when you think of it
like that that it all starts to make sense. Bit tin foil, maybe, but it does
make sense.

Inspector, 49, Northern force

Burglary is not a nice thing. Maybe some people can shrug it off,
but for many it ruins their lives. I've known victims of burglary have
mental breakdowns. Some can't rest until they move house. Others
become paranoid, they don't feel safe even in their own homes.
People have even committed suicide over it. Every time the judges
and magistrates let an active burglar walk away without sending him
to jail, they are basically saying, 'We know there will be more victims,
more suffering, and we don't care.'

You don't do one burglary and then decide, nah, it's not for you.
You break into people's houses at every opportunity until someone
stops you, or you get too old to fancy it any more, or you die of
something. We had a burglar die of something on us fairly recently.
He died of being stabbed by a householder. The householder opened
the door to two blokes, they threatened him and forced their way
inside, a knife was picked up in the kitchen and a fight ensued. During
this fight, one of the burglars was fatally injured. The other ran away.
The case is ongoing as I speak, though I fully expect from what I

know that there will be no charges, but the interesting thing is the list of previous attached to the dead man. He had what the papers call 'a string of previous convictions', going back 15 years. Car theft, violence, robbery, theft and, of course, burglary, multiple counts of on multiple occasions. Never had more than four months inside for burglary, which when you take into account time on remand, automatic discounts and early release on a tag tends to mean about four weeks. What that all tells you is: *we've* done *our* job. We've locked him up. It's the judges who have let him walk.

And short sentences do not work. They keep the offender away from the public for a short time, but they do not assist him in changing his ways. If this guy had been sent down for a proper length of time for one of these offences, perhaps he'd have seen the error of his ways. Then the subsequent offences wouldn't have happened, including the one in which he sadly lost his life.

PC, 39, Northern force

People always complain that we're not on the side of the householder when burglars get hurt, but I can assure you we are. Most bobbies will do anything not to arrest a homeowner who has defended his property, possibly up to and including giving him a few unofficial words of advice as to what he might like to say to us about it, which obviously I don't condone but I'm sure it happens. However, when someone is killed we obviously have to get to the bottom of it. The papers might report it as 'Innocent homeowner kills burglar in self-defence', and that may well be what has happened. But surely people understand that where there's a body in the morgue we ought to try to find out how he got there?

For a start, if there was a complete defence of, 'I found him in my house so I was entitled to kill him', inside a week we would be having a huge number of people being murdered by the simple expedient of rival gang members or rival drug dealers luring or forcing them to houses where they can be done away with. It may be that we wouldn't cry too many tears over some of these people, but that's not the point. So I don't think it's particularly controversial to say, if someone breaks into your house, you can do anything you like to defend yourself, up to and including killing that person, if you think it's necessary to defend yourself and your family, but that later on you may have to ask other ordinary people in a jury to agree with you. And if you are a 20-stone karate black-belt roidhead [*steroid abuser*], and the burglar is a nine-stone teenage junkie, and you chase him out into the street and put a bread knife in him, are you the sort of person we want on the streets? I would suggest perhaps not. But I would say it would have to be that sort of extreme case, or a Tony Martin shooting someone in the back, for it to end badly.

Where I do think we get it wrong is the sheer fact of arresting someone, taking their DNA, sitting them in a cell for x number of hours, interviewing them, then releasing them on bail while the CPS decide as to a charge… I think we should be quicker about it, and understand the trauma and worry that the process alone causes to the essentially law-abiding. There's, in practice if not in theory, no way around the fact that they have to be arrested, because they need to be interviewed in relation to a serious matter, and perhaps we should make clearer that, to an extent, there is no stigma to being arrested, it is in a way just a technicality until you're charged.

DS, 44, Northern force

We had a burglar break into a flat and get battered by the occupant. The burglar in question, who I'll call Tony, and I'll change a few other details for obvious reasons, was very well-known to us, and I personally had arrested him on a previous occasion for burglary. His preferred MO was, he'd target properties inhabited by lone females or elderly people, on the basis that if they discovered him they wouldn't offer much resistance, and go in through a back window in the early hours. Over a lengthy career, he's got away with tens of thousands of pounds-worth of electronic goods, cash, jewellery and other property. It might be insured, but he also takes highly personal effects which cannot be replaced like an iPod or a phone. In the earlier case I dealt with, a widow in her 80s lost her wedding ring and engagement ring. She had always taken them off at night and left them next to her toothbrush, and he had them away along with various other bits and pieces. She was *very* distressed. I asked him about that, to see if we could recover them for her, but he said he couldn't remember who they'd gone to.

I said, 'Look, Tony, if you can help us get these items back we'll make sure the court knows about it.'

He said, 'Whatever.'

It's not like there was even any monetary value in them. The engagement ring was an old ruby worth nothing and both of the bands were worn so thin… You're talking a couple of quid's worth of gold, even at today's prices. If he'd been looking at five years, time-served, which should be the minimum sentence, in my mind, for the upset and distress he had caused this old biddy, but we could have it cut to three for co-operation, he'd have sent us straight to them. But he knew he was getting sweet FA so he couldn't care less.

In court, Tony's sketch, like the others, is he breaks down in tears and blames his heroin habit, and claims he's off the gear now and going straight. Some random woman usually makes a statement to the effect that he's asked her to marry him and that he's a reformed character. If it's really serious, she'll be pregnant and he's just had a job interview. The court takes all this as a given. 'We can't really send him away if he's about to become a father and get gainful employment, can we?' Later, what a surprise, it turns out they've 'lost the baby'. The same with the 'job'. Rarely does anyone say, 'Which site? Working for whom? Can we speak to them please?' Yes, we the police would like to go and check these things out, but it's being said by every scrote in every court in the land every day. It would tie us up forever.

Anyway, the defence briefs present all of this as though they really believe it, despite knowing that the same basic mitigation has been presented a dozen times before. Sometimes, very rarely, Tony might get three months inside, or six, but usually the court will give him another chance. Some sort of community order, a bit more anger management, a drugs awareness course. The next day you see him sitting on the wall outside the Queen's Head, and he grins his toothless grin at you, raises his pint of Strongbow and winks. And you drive on, trying not to think about the widow and her wedding ring.

So, one day Tony made a bit of a miscalculation. He got into a ground floor flat which he thought was occupied by a lady in her 70s but it turned out it was a bloke in his late 20s, who further happened to be a bit tasty. The bloke caught him in the living room and smashed him up, good and proper. Tony had a fractured eye socket, a broken nose and lost a couple more teeth. The occupier then called us, and I attended with a colleague. While my colleague was dealing with Tony and sorting the ambo, I said to the tenant, 'What happened?'

Let's imagine he said, 'Well, I caught the bastard in my lounge and I kicked fuck out of him, didn't I?'

You can see how some officers might have not quite heard him say this, and might have advised him not to speak to them until he'd got a lawyer. In my case, entirely hypothetically you understand, you can even imagine a scenario where I might have said, 'I think what actually happened was, you came across this guy in your lounge. It was dark, you were scared, he lunged towards you, you thought he had a knife and you punched him twice, knocking him to the ground. Once he was on the floor, you let him be, as if you had continued striking him then when he offered no challenge to you that would have been an assault.'

Obviously, I didn't say any of that, because that would be a criminal offence. What I *actually* said was, 'Can you think very hard about it and tell me exactly what happened, please?'

Luckily, he said, 'I came across him in the dark, I was scared, I banged him twice and he hit the deck. Then I called you and guarded him till you got here.'

NFA [*no further action*] against the householder, Tony was off the streets and in pain for a month, eating his food through a straw with the side of his face wired up. That is what we in the trade call 'a result'. Proper fucked up, he was. I loved it. Gleeful, I was. It was a better punishment than anything the courts have *ever* handed down to him.

PC, 49, Midlands force

I had the immense satisfaction of catching one of our nominals [*repeat offenders*] red-handed. It was around 3am, he was leaning into a Cherokee Jeep trying to prise the fascia off with a screwdriver so he could get the CD player out. He tried to do a runner when he saw us, but he's not exactly an athlete so we nabbed him quite easily. There was a bit of a struggle when I laid my hands on him, during which I got a few bumps and bruises, but he was eventually subdued. He had a TomTom from another car in his pocket, and there was a stash of other stuff, clearly stolen from other vehicles, placed behind a wall a few yards away from where he'd first been seen. His prints and DNA were all over everything, and in interview he readily admitted what he was doing.

Jurassic Park, as a great man once said. At court he was bailed, on a curfew. While on bail, he was locked up again for the same thing while in breach of the curfew, but because this subsequent arrest was only two days before his court date the magistrates let the breach of bail conditions ride. Amazing, you might think, but it happens all the time. *Loads* of times people come before the courts for breach of bail conditions and the courts vary them to make them easier to comply with!

At court, he pleaded to seven counts of theft from a motor vehicle, four of criminal damage and one of assault with intent to resist arrest. The result was a £200 fine and 14 weeks' suspended. This is a bloke with 40-plus convictions for similar offences. The message this sends out to offenders and to the law-abiding is, society doesn't really care about your personal property.

PC, 35, Midlands force

The day they announced that you can steal a couple of hundred quids'-worth of stuff from a shop and you aren't getting nicked, that for me was the end. You thought, 'What the fuck is that all about?'

Even more annoying than the fact that you would catch Joe Scrote outside the Alldays with five packets of bacon in his trousers and have to let him go with an FPN was the fact that you also knew that he wouldn't pay it anyway. I remember the minister having to admit that half of them weren't being paid. You think, 'What the fuck is going on here, really?'

Sergeant, 42, Southern force

People commit thefts, simple frauds, get ordered to pay it back at a quid a week. It is no deterrent or punishment to say to a thief, 'Because you stole £100 from a church collection box, we will subtract £1 a month from your dole.' It tells these people that the courts don't actually care. In my admittedly limited experience, the only thing which stops recidivist criminals from committing crime is prison. I think the people at the top know that, but they have taken the view that prison costs money, so as long as the crime rate doesn't get too out of hand among the lower orders, the lower orders can put up with it. It's a kind of tax.

PC, 24, Southern force

I've been through all the phases, from astonishment to anger to resignation. We had a dwelling house burglary on Christmas Eve where the offenders had got in through the kitchen window and had it away with all the presents Father Christmas was going to deliver the next day. The dad was in tears. 'How am I going to explain that Santa didn't come this year?'

We had a whip-round at the nick – everyone who had kids abstracted something from their own pile and we drove it down to the poor guy at the end of the shift, so at least his kids had something.

Meanwhile, the scumbag who did that one had cut himself on gaining entry, so the forensics meant we were able to put him before the court some time later. Of course, all the presents were long gone but you might think, *At least he'll get his just deserts.* He pleaded guilty, not having much choice, and got let out on a suspended sentence with some sort of treatment order. He has *dozens* of previous convictions, so the treatment orders ain't working.

I went back to the family and tried to explain to them that there was a good chance they'd be seeing the bloke in the street, as he'd not been sent down. The father of the house was livid. I had to say to him, 'Look, don't take the law into your own hands,' because for damn sure, if he beats seven shades of shit out of the scrote the courts *will* manage to find space in the jail for *that.* All day long.

He's like, 'But if the law won't do anything, surely *someone* has to?'

In my mind, I was like, 'Fair one,' but I had to advise him to look the other way if he saw the guy. Within three or four months, the same scumbag was before the courts again, this time for stealing pension money off an old lady, who he also battered for daring to try to stop him. For that they gave him nine months. If they'd given him a decent sentence the first time she'd still have her confidence, which has now all gone.

PC, 32, Midlands force

The system is geared to keeping people out of jail. Most people we arrest *are* guilty, joking aside. Where the evidence is strong most of them plead guilty early on. This is because the court will give them a 33 percent discount for an 'earliest admission of guilt', which can be at the police station or at the first court appearance. The people who appear, 90 percent of them, are all frequent fliers who know this, they know the system very well, and if they don't their solicitor does. Their solicitors will advise them, presumably, 'The evidence is very strong this time, chummy, we can't cook anything up here, you'd better go guilty so if you go down at least we get some time off.'

So let's assume a case before the magistrates, something at the very worst end of summary-only offences [*offences triable only by magistrates; more serious indictable-only offences must go to Crown Court; a middle category of offences are triable 'either way'*], the guy's got form for the same thing, the magistrates want him to do six months to protect the public and learn him his lesson. Straight away, he's only doing four. Next, all offenders are automatically released 'on licence' half way through their sentence, to clear prison spaces – little or nothing to do with the supposed 'good behaviour'. So now four months has become two. Then they're credited with any time spent remanded in custody. This can be up to a couple of weeks for the many prolific offenders with whom we deal, so now eight weeks has become six. And when they go inside, once again to clear out cell space and because of short staffing at weekends, the prison governors tend to chuck them out on the Thursday or Friday prior to their week of release – so six weeks has become five-ish. And this is for the offences which allow a six month sentence in the first place – most don't.

You can get better sentences handed down at Crown Court, but then I've seen at least two proper scrotes get a couple of years knocked off on appeal so even if the trial judge is sound there's always the Court of Appeal. Equally, sometimes the mags will send something up to Crown for sentencing in hopes of getting a bit of stick dished out and the judges will be found sadly wanting.

I would make it a legal requirement for all judges and mags to spend a night a month on patrol with uniform, and that they go with them and us to the victims of the assaults and the burglaries and the robberies and all the rest.

DC, 30, Western force

No-one serves the sentence as reported in the news. *X* is jailed for two years? Out in eight months on a tag. The Gary Newlove case, I believe one of the lads who killed Mr Newlove had been released from custody after carrying out another assault earlier that day. He was bailed on condition he stayed away from Warrington. OK, you probably *are* going to get bail for common assault, but what do you get for breaching your bail conditions? Nothing. The youth knew that, they all know that, there is no deterrent, so he went straight back to Warrington, got on the piss and the next thing you know he's using Mr Newlove's head as a football. A father-of-three, dead.

We had a similar case up here, not involving bail but similar. A guy had moved away, started a successful business, nice house, wife, two kids, but unfortunately he lost everything through the drink. He split up from his wife and moved back up here and rented a flat. By now he was middle-aged, late 40s. Before long, lots of our local scrotes had started targeting him, going round to the flat, pretending to befriend him but basically stealing his money and drink and fags and whatever. Eventually, when he challenged a couple of them, they beat him to death in the flat. He had more than 50 injuries on him, including lots of stamp marks. The two who killed him were 19, 20 years old, and from shite families going back several generations. That's the other thing; I'm now locking up the sons of the fathers, and before I go I'll be locking up the sons of the sons.

Now, a year or so before the murder, one of these two had been arrested after smashing the window of a house after an argument with the woman inside it and threatening officers with ammonia and a steel bar. He had to be TASERed to effect the arrest. I think if this moron went round trying to smash his way into Mr Justice Hoity-Toity's house he'd be looking at three or four years, wouldn't you? But that sort of thing never really happens to judges, and I think they see these offences in isolation – a nasty incident, but over and done with in 30 minutes. Whereas they don't think about the general culture in the area that allows a youth to think he can behave like that. He got 66 weeks, and was in and out in the blink of an eye, whereas if he'd done some proper time, a) he would not have been out to stamp this other guy to death b) he might have thought twice about it.

I remember talking to one of our local solicitors, saying, 'You could have predicted this idiot would do something like that one day.'

He said, 'Yes, but this isn't *Minority Report*, is it?'

I said, 'I'm not talking about using computers from the future to read people's minds, I'm talking about the obvious fact, based on his well-documented and extensive previous history, that this was a vicious, feral thug. We already know who these people are and what they're capable of.'

Judges, magistrates and defence solicitors ought to ask themselves of each Johnny Scrote: would I spend an hour alone with this character, without access to a phone? Would I want my wife or kids to? The answer should guide them. We also ought to make any subsequent sentence 50 percent longer than the previous one.

Rank and age withheld, Northern force

We had a regular smackhead leg it from a corner offie with two bottles of Captain Morgan rum. Amazingly, we had officers available to attend, the description was good, he was very well-known to us and he was caught within 10 minutes, getting back into his flat. He still had the rum in his possession. Unfortunately, the shop CCTV wasn't operational but never mind, we have the shopkeeper's description, we've got the bloke, we've recovered the rum. I was confident he would cough it in interview. Instead, he claimed that his girlfriend had given him the rum for Christmas, he'd been on his way to a party and had forgotten something, was on his way back in to his flat to collect whatever it was when we pounced on him. Well, it's a story, of sorts. The CPS authorised a charge. Gets to court a couple of months later, and, surprise surprise, he doesn't turn up. Warrant issued, he's brought in, claims he had diarrhoea and has been on the loo all morning. Terribly sorry, your honours. Magistrates accept this explanation, rebailed for a new date four weeks hence. At court, the shop-keeper gives evidence, he's sure this is the guy who nicked the rum.

Defence brief: 'Are you *absolutely* sure? Because you wouldn't want to lie to the court and my client has witnesses that he was nowhere near your shop.'

Shopkeeper, now some months on: 'Well, I'm as sure as I *can* be, but obviously I'm only human, I can't say 100 percent beyond *all* doubt...'

Result: acquittal. The world's gone mad.

PC, 31, Midlands force

One of our officers came across a thief trying to break into a car. He challenged him and grabbed the suspect after he tried to run. In the ensuing drama the PC was punched in the face, and rendered temporarily unconscious. He came round on the floor with the suspect kicking him. The PC managed to struggle to his feet and chase the suspect again. As he caught him, the suspect threatened to stab him. Despite this threat, and with basically no thought of his own safety, the officer closed with him and CS-d him. This had no visible effect, because CS is often a waste of time, and the suspect again made off. Again the PC gave chase, and this time he laid hands on the man and effected an arrest. In closing with him this time, he was badly bitten but he restrained the suspect until one of his colleagues arrived to assist.

He got six months' suspended, 150 hours of community service and a compo order of £500 to the PC, which last I heard he hadn't paid.

Sergeant, age withheld, Southern force

There's nothing wrong with community punishments, as long as they are rigorously enforced, for young, first-time offenders, unless the offence clearly warrants a custodial sentence. We all make mistakes, be it youthful hijinks or whatever. Jail is, to my mind, for persistent offenders, the people who have been through a number of community sentences and basically it has had no effect. And the main function jail actually performs there is not really rehabilitation, it's public protection. Some people's lives are really blighted by hard core offenders, and I joined the police to protect them.

Let's say Billy Burglar is a professional housebreaker. That's his daily bread – it's like, you and I go to work in the morning, well, he breaks into an old man's bungalow and steals the stuff he's worked 50 years for. He steals old ladies' handbags which have a picture of their late husband in, and 50 quid, 50 quid being all she has to live on for the rest of the week, but which Billy will spend in a few minutes on the gear.

Do we want him to do this? No. Have repeated community sentences stopped him? No. So what will? In my experience, only two things actually rehabilitate the persistent criminal. One is age – he hits his mid- to late-20s, meets a half-decent woman who won't put up with any of his bad boy shit. She has a kid. They have a flat. So now there are consequences to him being involved with the Old Bill. He might lose the job, the flat, the woman, the kid. I know he's never been interested in his other kids, but now he's older, hopefully a little bit wiser. The other is really long prison sentences. I have seen a small number of hardened offenders receive substantial prison sentences, I mean a dozen years or more, where they know they are going to serve a proper six- or eight-stretch. Believe me, their shoulders slump, they go pale, they start crying. They start to wonder whether their kids will know them, who'll be shagging the missus, this is the best years of their lives they're wasting here… They deal in fear, and now *they're* afraid, it's an emotion they understand. And you know that *those* blokes – if they get some help and support when they're on the inside, which, again, I'm not against, and if we can keep them off the gear inside – will not be troubling us too much when they get out.

But it has to be long sentences. What prison does not do is magically convert serious scumbags into upright citizens through the medium of occasional stints of two or three months away. A short break, the deprivation of liberty is a pain in the arse, but his bills are paid, he's doing a stretch so he looks good to his mates, the other half's out of his hair for a bit, he can get his drugs inside if he wants them, he's got his porn, he's got a PlayStation and the telly and that, half his mates are in there with him, and he's king of his little world, giving the screws the runaround. He is absolutely *not* going to stop robbing the old ladies because of *that*.

So to my mind, we need to decide: are we prepared to let the Billy Burglars of this world rob old ladies, because we feel a bit squeamish about depriving them of their liberty, or are we going to say, 'No, Billy, off you go to think about this for a long time.'

DS, 40, Southern force

I've read that it costs £50,000 a year to house a prisoner. I don't believe that. I think it's put out there by people like Clarke who are ideologically opposed to jailing criminals. If you include the capital cost, maybe you get close, but since we don't rebuild a prison every year the real costs are upkeep, clothing, medical and dental care, power and heat, laundry, food and staff. These are not insignificant, but I've seen figures suggesting it's more like £20,000 per year per prisoner.

But even if it *did* cost £50,000 a year, it would make financial sense. If you are arresting the same person five times a year, the costs of the investigations and the court appearances and the community sentences can easily be far in excess of £50,000. That's without even taking into account the cost of increased insurance premiums, replacing damaged or stolen property, people who miss work because of assault injuries and so on. Plus they don't get their Jobseeker's Allowance and other benefits while inside, so you offset that. From an economic point of view it's a no-brainer – prison saves much more than it costs. So why are they so opposed to it? Lots of politicians are lawyers, and if you take the criminals off the streets that's like taking food out of their mouths. Lots of the bleeding hearts and the quangoes, I'm not saying they don't believe what they say but some of them are also making a nice living out of it along the way. *The Guardian* only exists to sell papers to the bleeding hearts. And what they all have in common, is that they are not themselves the regular victims of the repeat offenders they want to let out of prison. The victims are basically *Sun* and *Mirror* readers on the estates.

Inspector, 42, Midlands force

My officers arrested a dealer for PWITS [*possession with intent to supply*]. He had admittedly fairly small quantities of amphet, crystal meth and coke. He had something like 150 ecstasy pills. He had bin-liners full of weed. He had packets and packets of prescription drugs, Tramadol and Zopiclone. He had scales and baggies [*for weighing and parcelling-up drugs*]. The whole thing was worth several tens of thousands of pounds. No question, he was bang at it. The maximum sentence for intent to supply class A drugs is life imprisonment and an unlimited fine – albeit that clearly I accept you'd have to be bringing in tonnes of the stuff for that. He got 12 months, *suspended*. We were flabbergasted, to put it mildly.

He stood there in the dock and claimed that he only got into drugs because of some family problems, he said he'd done the rehab and was basically clean now and that he just sometimes sold drugs 'at cost price to other users'. Which will have any normal person shaking their heads. The judge gave him credit for pleading guilty, or maybe it was his fucking cheek, I dunno, but I'm like, with all due respect your honour, how do you *think* he's going to plead when we catch him with all that shit? It's an open and shut case, they should start with the basic sentence and then hammer him with a bit more for wasting the court's time if he goes not guilty. For the life of me, I cannot get inside that judge's head.

Rank, age and force withheld

Prison is too soft. If you don't believe that, why would bagheads [*heroin addicts*] smash a window and wait to be arrested so they can get in and on the programme? You get people who've been kicked out of hostels who want a bed, you get vagrants who obviously want to get nicked. No-one wants to do 30 years in Winson Green, no doubt, but you'd have to kill about six people to get that. Do they want a nice little three-month stretch to get a bed and some scran and the bills paid and a rest from the missus? You bet they do.

Sergeant, 43, Midlands force

Two blokes in their 30s attacked a 60-year-old chap in a pub in the town I work. He was loosely related to bloke A in some way – grandfather to one of his kids or something – and there had been words earlier. So bloke A went and got bloke B and they went back to the pub, whereupon bloke A smashes the old boy on the head with a spirit level and bloke B follows this up with a hammer. Terrified people everywhere, the old boy is knocked sparko, has to have his scalp stapled back together and now apparently suffers from mood swings, sleeplessness and daily headaches.

Bloke A who started it all has 27 convictions for 48 offences, which means he's actually probably committed several hundred offences he's never been nicked for, and a few days before this all happened was in court for ABH, at which he received a community sentence. The jury found him guilty of wounding with intent, affray and having an offensive weapon, at which point we've done our job and the 12 good men and true have done theirs. And the judge let him walk with a four-month curfew and a three-year supervision order.

The judges are able to hide behind the sentencing guidelines. Say you have a bloke who punches someone to the ground, unprovoked, the guy smashes his head on the pavement and nearly dies, emergency brain op, never quite the same again. To me, that's a solid s18 wounding with intent, but the CPS will charge these as s20 woundings, for which the maximum sentence is five years. You might think that five years for irreparably damaging someone else's brain – ruining their life, it wouldn't be too strong to say – was maybe too lenient. But then read the sentencing guidelines. If the defendant doesn't have a criminal record – which is not the same, of course, as the question, 'Has he just not been convicted before?' – and if he can get the proverbial girl into court to say she's having his baby and if his brief says he's just got a new job and he doesn't take crack any more and if they can persuade someone to give him a reference to the effect that he once helped an old lady across the road, and he's just signed the lease on a flat, he could easily walk out of court with a suspended sentence. I mean, chances are he'd go down for a year and serve whatever fraction of that, but there are plenty of cases where people have been convicted even of s18 and have walked out of court.

Sergeant, 38, Midlands force

Very few people get up in the morning and go bricklaying or digging ditches for fun. Likewise, criminals make a risk/reward assessment: If they do 100 burglaries, the reward can be sizeable, whereas we don't catch many of them and where we do it tends to be a community sentence or maybe a suspended. I come back to what I always say, which is that the people who make the laws and hand down the punishments don't actually understand real life. In most cases, they are quite privileged, they went to nice schools, they live in nice areas, they have nice friends. They're also older, for obviously good reasons. But the downside of that is that I do think they are living in the past, to an extent.

71

My ex-wife is a barrister, and through her I was invited to the retirement party for a circuit judge. I got a few moments chatting with him and he asked me how judges were viewed by the police. And I said, 'To be honest, most of them as a soft touch… I wish you'd have come out with us on a Saturday night ride-along a few times, then you'd have seen your customers in action.'

He said a few platitudes, but he was basically there to drink a bucket of claret and have a good old nosh. Ironically, a dozen cars were screwed in the car park that night, mostly belonging to local barristers and solicitors. Which made me chuckle.

Inspector, 48, Southern force

I arrested a Polish driver who was dizzy driving [*driving while disqualified*] with excess alcohol, having been a repeat customer on that offence. It was a very high level, which would potentially attract a three-year disqualification and six months' custody, and he had his three-year-old daughter in the car with him. She was unrestrained, not in a car seat. He had already been disqualified twice before, and jailed once, and had continued to drive.

Now, fair play to the mags, they sent him down for six months with no credit for his guilty plea – despite an attempt to intervene and gain some leniency from their clerk [*magistrates are assisted by a professional legal adviser, a qualified lawyer*]. They also disqualified him again for five years. That's the good news. But it is clearly not enough. For this offence, the mags can't send to Crown for greater punishment, that will only be possible when he kills someone and is charged with death by dangerous, which will be traded down at court to death by careless by the CPS, who invariably go for the easy option where they're more likely to get a jury to convict. This guy will be out in a couple of weeks and he will continue to drive. He'll be stopped again, he'll go to jail for another few weeks, but eventually he *will* kill someone. Sure as eggs is eggs. Hopefully it will be him and not an innocent driver, pedestrian, or his young daughter.

By the way, despite having been in this country for five years he was 'unable' to understand English and had to have an interpreter in court – paid for by you and me at £60 per hour. Try repeatedly and blatantly driving drunk in Poland and demanding an interpreter.

PC, 37, Northern force

Prior to the formation of the Crown Prosecution Service in 1986, most decisions on whether to charge suspects rested with the police, usually at Inspector level. Now that decision is taken out of the hands of the police and made by the CPS. In serious cases, the CPS brings in high-powered outside lawyers to work with the police in planning investigations; for many matters, however, the decision to charge is made by less experienced, employed staff – often making their decision over the telephone, having had files faxed to them. Police officers made many complaints about this end of the CPS.

We do all the arrests and interviews, but the decision as to whether they get put before the court is not in our hands, it's up to the CPS. The CPS have their targets for successful prosecutions and if they think there's the slightest chance of a not guilty verdict they are loath to run with things. You'll have a strong case and the CPS will knock it back as insufficient likelihood of a conviction. You think, *You what?*

Then you have a victim saying, 'I live on that estate, I called you, everyone knows I've been talking to you, do you know the kind of shit that can cause me, and you aren't even going to charge him? You are just absolutely shit.' You try and explain that it's nothing to do with you, but they've stopped listening to you by then. As far as most IPs [*injured parties*] are concerned in situations like this, it's down to us.

PC, 30, Midlands force

The CPS have many nicknames. 'Couldn't Prosecute Satan', 'Clowns Pretending to be Solicitors', 'Criminal Protection Service', 'Can't Prosecute, Sorry.' At my level they are almost universally disliked. Some of them are so risk-averse you can forget proceeding on a decent ABH based on witness accounts, or even admissions – they won't authorise charge unless you've got DNA, CCTV, a full suite of forensics and mobile phone mast location data. There are others who seem to operate on the rock-paper-scissors method of deciding whether to authorise.

They don't read files properly, they ask for information which is unnecessary – like, they will demand interview transcripts for utterly trivial matters where no-one has been interviewed in the first place. They lose files in this extraordinary black hole that they seem to have in their offices, and have to have them re-sent, by fax like it's the 1980s, often more than once. Plus they seem to see themselves more as an arm of the defence than of the prosecution. I've known cast-iron cases where they refuse charge. If you argue with them, they're quite ready to go over your head to your boss and complain about you.

In the last nick I worked at before my current one, we had in-house CPS, as opposed to on the phone, and someone stuck a picture on the office door of the fat bloke in the wheelchair off *Little Britain*, with the head of the CPS woman superimposed and the slogan 'CPS says No' underneath it. Quite brave, as the CPS office was on the top floor with the bosses. It was taken down and put back up, and taken down and put back up again, and in the end an email went round from the divisional chief warning people there would be serious consequences for whoever was responsible. There was a rumour going round that they were looking at a RIPA [*Regulation of Investigatory Powers Act 2000, which covers how surveillance is carried out*] authorisation for cameras in the nick, but who knows if that was true? It would surprise me, but it wouldn't amaze me, I think that's how I'd put it.

PC, 38, Northern force

A few years back, a group of us were out in a marked van targeting robbery hot-spots. Shortly following a robbery, we saw two known robbers fitting the description – previous convictions were allowed to form part of search grounds back then, which ludicrously they now cannot – walking away from us. We stopped the van next to them and said we wanted to search them re the recent robbery and descriptions given. They ignored us, as if they hadn't heard us. A colleague tugged on the jacket of one youth to get his attention. They spun round and attacked us. A couple of officers were bitten and one was head-butted. The lads were arrested for assault on police but the CPS refused to charge as – despite full admissions of assault police in interview – the suspects claimed we didn't tell them they'd be searched, therefore they 'were just defending themselves against a random attack by uniformed police officers'.

PC, 35, Southern force

I was called to [*the officer's local hospital*] after a paramedic was assaulted by a drunk brought in by ambulance. The male was an Eastern European who had been found lying drunk in the road, and the ambi had brought him in for his own safety. The two paramedics were waiting at the booking-in station; one was completing his paperwork near the head-end of the trolley on which the male was laying. The male suddenly lashed out with his right arm and struck the junior paramedic across the throat and shoulder, causing him to fall back. The male was instantly grabbed by other staff nearby whilst the clearly shocked paramedic was led away. When we arrived he was still in shock and almost in tears.

The drunk was laughing it off, as were his father and a friend who had arrived to take him home. They stopped laughing when they were informed that he was getting locked up for assaulting emergency staff. Of course, at that point the drunk decided he didn't speak or understand English any more. We then spent two-and-a-half hours taking statements and burning off the security CCTV. The footage *clearly* showed the paramedic getting hit.

The next day we were informed by the prisoner handling team that the CPS would not prosecute as the male had stated that he was drunk at the time and didn't remember doing anything. I kid you not. The male walked off scot-free. We spoke to the paramedic and explained that it wasn't down to us. It's not that he blames us, but the shit sticks. We are the public face, not the CPS. They don't have to answer for their shortcomings – we do.

PC, 32, Midlands force

I can see the sense in having the CPS for serious crime, where they form ops teams with detectives taking advice pre-action from senior lawyers and outside barristers, but they could save a lot of time and money if they returned charging to the custody sergeant, instead of forcing us to take the most cut-and-dried matters to the CPS. You get simple thefts where the offender admits the offence and the property is recovered, but because the victim once went out with the offender it's classed as a domestic and has to go to a lawyer for advice. Equally, you get relatively cut-and-dried cases... For instance, I arrested a male for a shoplifting where the articles in question were recovered from down his trousers, he had no proof of purchase and a very dodgy explanation of how it was these items ended up in his pants, and the CPS NFAd it on the basis that there was an insufficient likelihood of a conviction. I personally think there was a 99 percent likelihood that the mags would convict, in fact the guy would have pleaded. A police sergeant or inspector, I think, would have at least given it a go.

PC, 33, Northern force

There's a male on my patch who tied up and seriously injured another male in a row over a girl. The guy was carved and stabbed. We arrested him for attempt murder, CID interviewed him on that basis and he was charged with attempt murder, kidnap and drugs offences. By a process that I don't really understand, the CPS ended up rolling over on it and he ended up pleading to GBH. The rest of it was dropped.

I prefer dealing with the CPS over the phone because if you don't like their first answer you can ring back and try again and you sometimes get a different person who authorises the charge the first one refused. That seems, at best, odd to me. There are some good ones, they're labouring under the same targets the rest of us are. But generally, me no likey.

PC, 32, Northern force

London, in particular, has been the scene of protest, public disorder and large-scale rioting in recent years. At the time of writing, PC Simon Harwood faces a manslaughter charge over the death of newspaper seller Ian Tomlinson, who died after he was struck and pushed over by PC Harwood at the G20 protests in London on April 1, 2009.

The video of the Tomlinson incident didn't look good. But, and this is a *big* 'but', I wasn't there and the evidence available from that video is very far from conclusive. I don't know what was said to Tomlinson, or what he said to Harwood. I don't know what contact Tomlinson had already had with the police that day. I don't know who was five metres to the left, right or front of the police officers, and what they were doing or saying. I don't know how long Harwood had been on duty – it could have been 15 hours, for all I know. I don't know what stress he was under, or what orders he had been given. These might all be factors. So I won't be making any judgment as to his guilt or innocence. We have a fairly long-established system of justice for that. What I don't like is that all over the internet and in the papers, people *are* making the judgment that he is guilty.

PC, 30, Southern force

I have worked lots of major demos and public order situations, including the G20, and we often need to close roads and deny people access, even to streets where they live – or claim to live. Eventually, if they don't listen, you *have* to force them back. This happens *all* the time. There's an old police adage that if you use force on someone you'd better arrest them as well, but then it's very difficult, and often specifically against orders, to arrest for relatively minor offences in the middle of a major demo, because to do so removes resources from the line. So a guy gets told to move on, he refuses to do so and he gets struck and pushed to encourage him. Big deal. Happens *all* the time. This is the job of the police. If we can't *force* people to move in certain situations, what *do* we do? If we ask people and are ignored, do we ask again, with bows on, or maybe we should all just give up and go home?

PC, 33, Southern force

You think, *Have I hit people with a baton? Not very often but, yes, I have. Have I pushed people to the ground? No, but I could see how I might. Have I manhandled people? Yep. Now, if I do that and someone dies, no matter how justified I believe I was will I be able to convince a court of that in a year's time?*

Increasingly, I think people are starting to think, *No, I'm not sure I could.* Especially if it's a high-profile case which has achieved a lot of media attention. I wish our gaffers would stand up and say that being in the police, unfortunately, we *have* to apply force to people sometimes. You'd think it was bloody obvious, but we need to say it. People sadly do not always do as they are quite reasonably and lawfully requested. Sometimes you have to make them, to prevent crime and disorder, to protect other people or property. It's part of our job. And if you're going to end up gripping the rail because of it... Do I want to run that risk?

PC, 33, Southern force

Delroy Smellie is a Metropolitan Police sergeant who was charged with common assault after he struck a woman, Nicola Fisher, at a vigil in London for Mr Tomlinson. Ms Fisher had been standing in front of Sgt Smellie, shouting and gesticulating aggressively while holding a carton of liquid – it turned out to be fruit juice – and had refused several instructions to step back from him. Eventually, he slapped her with the back of his hand and then struck her once with his baton. Video of the incident was posted on the internet and Sgt Smellie was suspended and then charged. Ms Fisher was later criticised because, after receiving £26,000 from a newspaper for her story, she failed to appear in court to give evidence. Witnesses at the trial said that she had been aggressive and confrontational. Sgt Smellie was found not guilty.

The atmosphere that day was quite highly charged, he wasn't wearing a helmet, he was among a group of officers who were surrounded and outnumbered by angry protestors; things could have got very nasty, very quickly. [Fisher] was invading his personal space aggressively and threateningly, he gave her plenty of warning to back off, and she ignored those opportunities. You have nano-seconds in which to react. You're not looking at it on a slow-motion YouTube video three months later. Delroy Smellie is entitled, in fact required, to protect himself and his colleagues. He did so in a proportionate manner – he didn't punch her in the face, he didn't strike her across the head, he just made her move back by targeting a muscle mass area, clearly intending to cause no permanent damage, and then replaced his baton. All completely justified. It was a scandal that he was charged. We are bloody *trained* to do this! 'She was a woman half his size.' So what? What if the liquid in that carton had been acid? Or ammonia, or bleach? He hasn't got any special powers which enable him to know that this mad woman who was yelling at him wasn't about to try and blind him. It might have been piss. We regularly get piss thrown at us. Would you stand there and wait to find out if it was piss or Sunny Delight? Should *we* have to? Is that what the CPS are saying to us? 'Wait until they throw the liquid over you and you've had a good taste before deciding how to act'?

PC, 31, Southern force

He was tried in an open court and was found not guilty after due process of law, and yet people still get to call him a thug and impugn his good character? Right, I see how that works. We are allowed to defend ourselves. If we're charged and brought before a court, we're allowed to defend ourselves there, too. That includes saying the prosecution witnesses are lying, their case is bullshit, and calling lots of witnesses to back you up and discredit the other side. Smellie had lots of witnesses saying this woman looked dangerous and got at *least* what she deserved. She herself didn't bother her arse to show up in court to give her side. I'm afraid you probably *are* looking at a not guilty verdict. Suck it up, guys! This kind of shit happens to us *every* day. It's like when police officers get arrested and go no comment in interviews, and somehow this is scandalous – we're not playing the game. Er, no. Sorry, we operate under the same law as everyone else. We are innocent until proven guilty, same as you are, and if you want to find us guilty you'd better bring the evidence.

PC, 26, Northern force

I was there that day, though I didn't see what happened with Smellie. I will say that there were an enormous number of violent and aggressive people there who deserved a very thorough shoeing, and it is, in my opinion, testament to the restraint and professionalism of the MPS that that didn't happen. Try walking up to a CRS [*the French Compagnies Républicaines de Sécurité, known throughout the world for their robust attitude to dealing with violent protest*] officer in France and calling him a 'fascist pig cunt', and saying you hope someone is at home raping his wife – both of which happened to me for the crime of having turned up at work that day. I suggest you would quickly find yourself looking for your teeth on the floor, shortly before you enter one of their vans, head first.

Sergeant, 48, Southern force

There was video footage of the assault and they *still* found him not guilty! It was *obviously* a cover-up. OK. But if you want to convict a man on the basis of 10 seconds of video footage with no context or live evidence from the alleged IP, then *we* get to use that level of evidence in all the cases *we* bring before the courts. I suspect the very same people who were outraged by the acquittal of Delroy Smellie would soon be up in arms about that.

It took over a year for Smellie to be cleared. He could easily have been looking at losing his job, and maybe his home. At 47, that's not an easy prospect. Most of the people we arrest face none of that stress. Most of them don't even *have* a job. So we're punished twice.

I hope he knew he had the support of the vast majority of his colleagues, up and down the country, and I hope he can move on. These incidents are never a good experience for officers. No-one high up wants to know you while you're under investigation, and even afterwards it rarely helps your career. I don't know him, but looking at him and knowing the kind of work he does, and having grown up black in London in the '60s and '70s with a surname like 'Smellie', I imagine he's a pretty robust character, so he's probably OK. But I'd like to buy him a pint.

PC, 27, Southern force

All police are Level 3 trained [*to a basic public order standard*], but Levels 2 and 1 involve a lot more training and expertise. Level 2 and 1 officers wear the blue NATO helmets and carry the long shields, and are called in after the Level 3 guys dressed in those nice, flammable yellow jackets and flat caps have had the shit kicked out of them for a couple of hours, because the gaffers think helmets make us look confrontational and would rather we took a kicking.

Level 1 are full-time, they're constantly training, they eat petrol bombs for breakfast, whereas the Level 2 guys train twice a year and obviously aren't quite as expert. The reason for having the two levels is there aren't enough Level 1 officers, especially since the nation apparently deciding that rioting was its favourite sport, to keep order, so they are supplemented by Level 2 as and when needed.

What a lot of people don't understand is we volunteer for this. No-one can force me to turn up in my helmet at a riot, I do it because I like the overtime. But after Smellie and Tomlinson, and all the shit we take generally, a lot of people are talking about handing back their PSU [*Police Support Unit, public order teams*] tickets. Like, 'No thanks, if we're going to have trial-by-media based on a YouTube video edited by someone who hates the police, I'll go and join a Case Management Team.'

If they try to force us to stay with it, we have a fitness test, you have to run 500 metres carrying a long shield in less than 2 min 45 sec. Those shields weigh getting on for 8kg – we're all getting older, bit of a bad back, it wouldn't be a shock if you didn't quite make it. I wouldn't like to be the senior officer who told a patently unqualified officer that he had to go and police a riot if that officer then got injured. It would be a field day for the lawyers, I'd have thought.

Sergeant, 38, Southern force

My mate's favourite expression is, 'My bag of give-a-shit is empty.' But then cops are always moaning and threatening to do this sort of thing, it's part of the Job mentality, and we never do. Maybe there are some examples. But I enjoy it, if I'm honest. If I didn't have a sense of humour, I shouldn't have joined, as they say.

That said, I do believe we could get to a world where the police are ineffective, because we're paralysed by fear of a negative outcome to our actions, or we end up seeing more use of TASER and even baton rounds and other stand-off options, which don't involve closing with and rolling around on the floor with people. That would be ironic, wouldn't it?

PC, 32, Southern force

Jenny Jones [*Green Party activist and member of the Metropolitan Police Authority*] was quoted as backing community bobbies and saying at the same time that riot police needed cutting back. I don't know if she realises this, but community bobbies and riot police are *the same people*. In fact, often the *very* people who man the PSUs are SNT [*Safer Neighbourhoods Team – neighbourhood or beat bobbies, rather than response*] officers, because riots happen at weekends when shift officers are tied up dealing with run-of-the-mill crime. You'd hope that members of the MPA might know this.

PC, 30, Southern force

These disturbances were followed by more violent scenes in the capital, when riot-trained officers battled with students protesting at the Coalition Government's plans to increase university tuition fees.

We arrested a male not far from the RBS building. He was a nasty little shit. After we got the cuffs on him, my colleague and I moved him some way off to be dealt with. All the way, he wouldn't shut up about how RBS was owned by the people and that the bankers were leeches and parasites who had stolen the people's money, and we were just fascist tools.

Eventually, I said, 'What do you do for a living, chief?'

'I'm a student.'

'How old are you?'

'27.'

'Ah, you're a mature student, then? What did you used to do before you became a student?'

'I've always been a student.'

So let me get this straight: I'm being lectured about leeching parasites by this herbert who's never done a tap of work in 27 years? It's like, you haven't contributed a penny piece, mate, you don't own so much as a pen-on-a-chain inside RBS… In fact, *everything* you have has been given to you either by your mum and dad, or the taxpayer. They have never grown up, and they have such a sense of entitlement.

'We speak for the oppressed majority!'

'No you don't. All you're doing is making a fool of yourself, smashing up the place and preventing people from getting to work – the very people who are paying for your extremely extended education.'

PC, 30, Southern force

A young woman about seven or eight metres from me was hit over the head with a metal bar. Unfortunately, I couldn't see who had hold of the bar, though to be honest I doubt we could have arrested them anyway because of the violent and volatile nature of the situation. She immediately fell to the ground and a colleague and I ran forward to help her. She had blood pouring from her scalp and was very disorientated. As we were trying to help her, people were yelling abuse, spitting at us and trying to kick us. A woman with pink hair was shouting, 'Don't let them touch you! That is an assault – she hasn't given you permission to touch her!'

Meanwhile, this girl could easily have had a fractured skull. You wonder what planet these people come from.

PC, 31, Southern force

I find all the conspiracy theories quite amusing.

The police are always covering their faces to hide their identity! Er, no. We wear flameproof balaclavas because you idiots insist on throwing flares, fireworks and, in extreme cases, Molotov cocktails at us.

The police are always removing their numbers to hide their identity! Er, again, no. They just fall off because you lot keep trying to fight us, and if you had any idea of the sheer shoddiness of our kit this would not surprise you at all. Not to mention, our helmets have identification numbers on them, anyway.

The police put 'bait vans' out to entrap us into wrecking them! If you mean we pitch up in liveried Transits, park them somewhere handy and then you can't help but smash them up then, why, yes we do!

The police are in the pay of the government and the banks! I've got news for you – we hate the banks as much as you do, and we don't much like the government, either. The reason we're arresting you is because you can't protest like adults, you have to go mental, and going mental like that is against the law.

PC, 33, Southern force

The students wound me up something rotten. It's all bullshit. State oppression? Fuck off. Try that one in Iran. Police brutality? We're as soft as shit. I was on a stag weekend in Magaluf a few years back, and fuck me, *those* boys don't mess around. The whole fees protest, it's *all* bullshit. None of the students really care about fees, they're just a bunch of teenagers who want to get laid, showing off. It's alright, we've all been there, done that. I just wish we didn't have to take them so seriously.

My wife has just left the police to go to university to fulfil a long-held ambition to study medicine. Her original A level results were a decade ago, and to get the specific set of results she needed to get to med school she took a year's unpaid sabbatical from the Job to study for three A levels, in biology, maths and chemistry. Part of this entailed paying her way onto lecture courses at the local higher education college. The stories she tells... Arrogant, lazy, abusive, disrespectful students, blatant cheating and plagiarism, persistent truanting – this from kids who have *chosen* to be there. Persistent drunkenness and drug-taking, in the sense of cannabis being smoked quite openly on college grounds. People playing computer games in lessons, surfing the net or texting their friends, noise and disturbance in lessons. Lots of threats to throw people off courses, but they never did. In the end, my wife effectively taught herself from textbooks and online.

Now, comes the day of the riots, the college hired two buses for them and 100 of these kids went down to London to protest about the increase in tuition fees! It was just about the only time any of them got off their arses all year. My wife was seething. I appreciate this is only anecdotal, but that is the story of a major college in a major city. I see no reason to imagine that it was much different elsewhere.

Sergeant, 43, Midlands force

One lad came up to us and said something along the lines of, 'Next time, filth.'

My mate says, 'Next time what?'

He says, 'Next time, it's petrol bombs.'

My mate says, 'Blimey, you do know it's £1.30 a litre? I thought you was all skint?'

Which rather cracked me up, though the student didn't share my amusement.

We arrested another young lad for threatening behaviour, and of course he immediately started with the, 'I pay your wages!' thing.

'What do you do for a living, then?'

'I'm unemployed.'

'So, actually, *I* pay *your* benefits, then?'

Another guy was, 'I bet you were bullied at school, weren't you?'

I go, 'No, actually, I was a bully, terrible I was. I used to hang people like you out of windows by their ankles.'

They love that sort of banter, they really see the funny side.

PC, 30, Southern force

I am perfectly in agreement that people should have the right to protest. I am a policeman, but I don't want to live in a police state. If we can't protest about the government, we don't live in a democracy. But what annoys me is the lies. 'I was beaten up by the police just for protesting!' No, you weren't, you were throwing things at police officers, they lawfully arrested you and you resisted arrest. In the process you got a few scratches and stuff. That's what happens if you thrash around on the pavement, dude.

Sergeant, 40, Midlands force

I get fed up of people being taken seriously when they complain about police brutality. There wasn't any. You have scores of TV cameras and reporters and tens of thousands of people on the streets, all of whom have mobile phones with cameras. How many actual incidents of police brutality were brought forward and resulted in a charge? None. Believe you me, DPS [*Directorate of Professional Standards*] are watching us in action very keenly, and filming us themselves, and they *and* our senior officers *and* the CPS would *love* to do our legs, but they can't because it hasn't happened.

But everyone glosses over the violence directed at police officers. How many times do BBC reporters get spat at for doing their jobs? We get it all the time. How disgusting is that? Yet that is never reported.

I also get fed up with experts talking about how 'complex' the situation was, when it wasn't. If you want to protest peacefully and in a lawful manner in a lawful area, the police will help you. If you want to protest illegally in an unlawful way, they will prevent you from doing it or arrest you. I cannot for the life of me understand why the supposed intellectual cream of the country find this so hard to understand.

PC, 26, Southern force

Speaking as someone who has in the past been on secondment to the CRS and who has worked as a spotter [*gathering intelligence and identifying known hooligans*] at football matches across Europe, I can say that people accusing us of brutality simply have no idea. *No* idea. We are highly reactive, rather than proactive. We wait until officers have been injured, and even then all we really do is herd people into one place and make them stand there for a bit. In other countries, they would have used tear gas, baton rounds, water cannon, armoured vehicles, mounted charges, dogs. I'm talking about nice, liberal places like Sweden. In Gothenburg in the 2001 [*EU summit*] riots, the police actually open-fired with live ammunition on demonstrators, and shot people. In Italy, at the G8 protests in 2001, people were shot and killed. So let's have a bit of perspective.

We have a police service which goes out of its way to facilitate peaceful protest, even up to and beyond the point where the protest turns violent and police officers start being seriously injured. The irony of all of the complaints about containment is that they will drive us more towards things like baton rounds and gas. Because, if you accept that we can't have mobs of people smashing up the place, and you don't want them contained, what *are* your options? You either have to wade in with sticks, which the media do not like, or you have to sit back and disperse them with baton rounds. I think the time is approaching when we will need as a society to decide on this.

Inspector, 44, Southern force

We're up against people who are quite happy to act as *agents provocateur*, who are quite happy to lie about us, who are quite happy to seriously injure us, and yet rarely do we respond in kind. And yet every allegation against the police is taken ultra seriously and given hours of media airtime. I genuinely do not understand it. I also don't understand, when complaints are investigated to the hilt by PSD [*Professional Standards Department*] and found to be spurious, and when it is clear that they were made falsely in the hope of ruining a police officer's life and career, why the complainants are not then prosecuted to the full extent of the law?

PC, 30, Midlands force

I saw officers with nasty injuries, one semi-conscious, one with a bleeding facial wound. What has any of that to do with fees? Our medics also treated a large number of protestors for injuries to the backs of their heads, where they had been hit by missiles thrown from behind them. One kid had blood pouring from the back of his head and was claiming he had been hit by a police baton, but after he was cleaned up at an aid station – by a police officer, I might add – I was able to show him some CCTV footage and you could clearly see masonry landing on people from behind. They were crouching down and launching stuff, like mortars.

Sergeant, 46, Southern force

Alfie Meadows [*a philosophy student who suffered serious head injuries, and later required brain surgery, at a university tuition fees protest in London in December*] became a real *cause célèbre*. There are thousands of references to him on Google, most of them stating that he was hit on the head by a police baton. *The Independent* ran a piece saying, unequivocally, 'a 20-year-old student was left unconscious with bleeding on the brain *after being hit on the head with a police truncheon*'. There's a Facebook site called 'Justice for Alfie Meadows', which states, also unequivocally, 'Alfie was *struck by a police baton* on the head around the Westminster Tube'.

Then Alfie's mother said that the evil police tried to deny her son access to casualty. *The Observer* reported her saying that it was only because an ambulance worker demanded Alfie got urgent medical treatment that his life was saved.

Big IPCC investigation launched, the police are brutal thugs, *et cetera et cetera*. Except, it turns out the bit about the police refusing to let Alfie get treated, that was bollocks, not that the *Observer* reported the fact as far as I know. The stuff about the truncheon, that's all gone a bit quiet. As far as I am aware, there has never been *any* evidence produced, *anywhere*, by *anyone*, that proves Alfie Meadows was, in fact, hit by a police baton. My strong suspicion is that it will turn out that in fact he was hit by a lump of concrete thrown at the police by other protestors somewhere behind him. A 'drop-short', as we used to call them in the Army. A 'blue-on-blue'. Still, whatever happened, I'm sure young Alfie is philosophical about it.

Inspector, 44, Southern force

I love the Alfie Meadows Facebook Site. There are 8,000 members, and you should read the anti-police bile on there. There are a few posts from sensible people, but most of it is just nuts. [*Calls up site on iPhone.*] Like this post from someone saying, 'I am attending the demo on Saturday [*March 2011*] with my child, like Alfie's Mum. I believe that we should raise our children to do what is right, to understand that our rights were fought for and won and that we should not take our liberty for granted. See you all there. x'

To which I say, are you insane taking your kid to a place where petrol bombs and lumps of masonry are in the air? And exactly which hard-won rights and liberties are you fighting for? The right to demand the other people pay for stuff you want? Or the right to demand the taxpayer *stops* funding projects you *don't* want, because I've seen exactly the same people on both sides of that argument? Or the right to assemble in London and make your point peacefully to the government? Because, don't worry, you already have that right. The police managed it when we marched over our pay in 2008, and we did it without swinging on the Cenotaph, staging sit-ins at Topshop or pissing on any statues of Churchill. Lots of people manage it, all the time. But if you're demanding the right to break the law, sorry, but that's not on.

PC, 30, Southern force

They're all against discrimination and lumping everyone together – unless it's lumping the police together. Apparently we're some homogenous group of people entirely distinct from everyone else. It's like, we're all grown somewhere in a secret factory and harvested by the government to do their evil bidding.

At first, I'd try chatting to some of these kids and I'd point out that I'd been to university myself, that I have a son there now, that a lot of my colleagues, certainly the recent joiners, went to university. We have a lad on the relief who read Maths at Oxford and another with a PhD in biochemistry. As we also have people with five GCSEs. The point I'm making, we just reflect the wider community. We are *from* the community, we live *in* the community, we vote, we shop at Sainsbury's, we go to the pub on a Saturday night if we're not working... We're just normal people with the same fears, money worries, hobbies, family problems, hopes and ambitions as everyone else. All we do is stand there in a line and try to stop the place being smashed up.

Eventually, I gave up. They didn't want to hear it. The thing that makes me proudest of being a police officer actually is the contrast between our behaviour and that of these demonstrators. I have colleagues who hate this government and their cuts every bit as much as the students and anyone else, and yet we stand there and defend the line.

Sergeant, 46, Southern force

The media said we didn't inform protestors of the route, or tell people that they were supposed to continue up Whitehall and rendezvous at Trafalgar Square. But we did tell them all this stuff. We had carriers situated at at least two points to my knowledge, including on the Parliament Square side of Bridge Street, continually repeating that Whitehall was open and asking them to keep walking through to Trafalgar Square. The message was, 'You are free to move on, this is not a containment.' I must have heard that 100 times, somehow the media didn't.

But the fact is, an awful lot of the protestors had decided that they would rather get into Parliament Square, and so instead of moving on, as agreed with the NUS and as clearly requested by the police, they started lobbing bottles and bricks at the police officers and then they ripped up the fencing keeping them off Parliament Square. We could have stopped them doing all of this, but we are too soft for that sort of thing nowadays, sadly. We had people attacking the Treasury and the Supreme Court and even then we didn't go in hard.

PC, 30, Southern force

I came across a kid of 11 and there were lots of others in their early teens. There were also people in their 40s and 50s from the anarchist fringe, which I actually found really funny. Anarchists demanding more government spending – somehow, they don't see the irony. And we had a lot of the usual suspects who came up for a spot of pickpocketing and mugging inside the crowd. Quite a few nice, middle class kids who spent the afternoon chanting abuse at the police suddenly found themselves converted to the side of law and order in the evening. Let's get this straight. You think I'm a fascist scumbag, *but* you want me to go and look for those rough boys who stole your mobile? Hmm.

PC, 39, Southern force

We had a bloke come up to the line with his son, a young boy of about 12 – the lad was dressed in an 'anarchy' t-shirt, which dad obviously hasn't bought for him or anything, it clearly reflects his own mature and considered view of the political and societal character of the west in the early 21st century. The dad was yelling at us about how we were scum and we needed to let them out, it was a breach of their human rights. He kept saying, 'You have no right to keep us here!'

All I could think was, 'What the hell are you doing bringing him to a demo like this? And why didn't you get away while you could, because it was very obvious for some time beforehand what was going to happen.' Arguably, I should have arrested him for neglect. We had supposedly intelligent people saying that the yobs who were throwing stuff at us were 'forced into it' by our tactics. Forced to throw metal barriers at police lines? Forced to pull police officers from horses? Forced to injure the horses, or throw ball bearings on the ground in front of them? I don't think so.

PC, 27, Southern force

One guy was asking why we needed to dress up in all our 'aggressive clothing' which was 'provoking people'. It's mad, but we do hear this a lot, and often from our own senior ranks. Quite how me wearing a helmet because people on the other side are throwing half bricks at me is provoking them, I've never been able to work that one out. The hat and the shield, they're just tools of the job. I'd much prefer never to have to use them.

PC, 33, Southern force

I had a woman stand in front of me screaming at me, over and over again, 'How do you feel? How do you feel?'

You don't engage with them. Staying silent and just looking at them annoys them all the more. But the answer was, awesome, thanks, though a bit tired of you and quite keen to get home to my wife and son without being hit in the face by something heavy. I think that was how we all felt. There were odd moments of *oops*, but basically I was never really worried. The student protests were not really riots, and that's not said with the benefit of hindsight over what came later. I arrested a guy for assault. He said he was involved in 'the liberation struggle'. I'm like, *Yeah, yeah*. It was all a bunch of soft, entitled, largely middle class kids whining that they couldn't have what they wanted, and getting spanked when they got out of order. It was behaviour that was not dissimilar to my three-year-old in Toys 'R' Us after he's had too many sweets.

Sergeant, 34, Southern force

I had a great day out down in London, earning lots of lovely overtime with my mates, so for me the protests were an absolute boon. I also did manage to have a half-way sensible conversation with one guy early in the day, before it all turned sour. He was asking why there were so many of us there and suggesting that the 'police presence' would exacerbate things. I pointed out that it is entirely possible to police 10,000 people with two police officers – it just depends who the 10,000 people are. Go and watch my local club, Leicester Tigers, in the rugby Premiership, and then go to watch Notts Forest in the Championship. Both will have 15,000-20,000 fans there, but only one will have riot vans outside. He said it was all about the 'anger'. I said, 'Hang about, 20,000 furious cops marched in London after we were shafted over our pay, and there was not one bit of trouble. We made our point, we went home.' He said, 'Ah, but you didn't change anything, did you?' He was right about that, but then would it have changed anything if we'd smashed up Westminster? I rather doubt it.

PC, 33, Midlands force

We had a mum approach us outside our cordon complaining that her student daughter was on the other side, and we wouldn't let her out. She was going, 'She's phoned me to say she's cold and tired and she wants to go home now!'

I explained the reasons for the containment, I pointed out that we had had vehicles wrecked, officers injured, serious criminal damage done, fireworks and bottles and stones thrown at us and others, and that we were containing people for their own safety and ours until we could release them in an orderly fashion.

The woman kept saying, 'But this is ridiculous, in a grown-up society they have a right to protest. My daughter's just a child!'

So her argument is, treat them like adults because they're just children. Hmm. Interesting.

Sergeant, 46, Southern force

It makes me laugh, this stuff about 'kettling'. We've been doing it to football supporters for decades. Where are Liberty and that bloke in his wheelchair when we're keeping Liverpool and Arsenal apart at Euston? For some reason, when it's working class yobs who are being contained, that's not a problem. But when it's Student Grant and his mates, all of a sudden it's a disgraceful abuse of civil liberties. I have policed the EDL [*English Defence League*] and we've cracked a few heads there, believe me. Not a dicky bird about that from *The Guardian*, the BBC and the rest of the lefties. Same when the Home Secretary bans the EDL – and rightly so, in my opinion, they're a bunch of thugs looking for trouble. But the hypocrisy annoys me. Some people's freedom seems to count more than others. The Notting Hill Carnival costs us millions each year, takes thousands of officers to police, always ends in a load of arrests for violence and robbery and drugs, and a nice few stabbings. But if we tried to ban that we'd be racists who don't understand the cultural significance.

[*'That bloke in his wheelchair' is activist and leading Twitterato Jody McIntyre, who complained that he was dragged from his wheelchair and assaulted by police; officers countered that they had temporarily removed him from the chair to move him more quickly for his own safety, as a mounted charge was about to take place.*]

PC, 41, Southern force

I don't know what people think we're putting in containments for? Do they *really* think we're all bullying maniacs who just get a kick out of hitting people? I'm just the son of a welder from Essex who only joined the police because I was on the dole and liked the sound of a varied job. I don't like hitting people. I wish they'd just behave, then we could all enjoy a nice day out. My biggest interest in life is playing five-a-side footie for the village pub and going metal-detecting and bird-watching with my lad. Bit sad, but that's me. I must have missed the bit where I signed up for the Stasi. Maybe they cunningly switched the papers when I wasn't looking.

Sergeant, 35, Southern force

In a large group of people, the dynamic can change quite quickly. The kinetic power in a sizeable group – particularly young people who are hyped up, possibly drunk, possibly on drugs, and carrying banners on wooden poles – is considerable, and if you allow them absolute freedom of movement then you can very quickly have people seriously injured. So we contain them in one place to stop that kind of dynamism building, to protect ourselves, members of the public who are not involved in the protest and the protestors themselves. Plus, there are also fewer opportunities for groups of them to split off and cause damage to property. But that's actually a secondary consideration, really it's mostly about public safety. Not that I personally care if a few dozen of these wankers trample themselves to death, but the subsequent inquiry could take years.

There *are* other methods of controlling crowds – for starters, they could control themselves. Clearly, that's too much to ask. We could use things like baton rounds, water cannon and CS gas. But despite these being regularly deployed in notorious military dictatorships like Norway and Belgium, and for that matter in Northern Ireland, we are not allowed them on mainland UK. Theresa May says no-one wants to see water cannon on British streets. We 'police by consent'. I'm sorry, Theresa, but pretty much all the police below inspector rank, and plenty of people who are just irritated at seeing young thugs run amok on their TV, would *love* to see water cannon deployed. And as for policing by consent, sure, but the other side are not actually consenting. Perhaps she hasn't noticed.

Sergeant, 34, Southern force

For some reason best known to the dream warriors in charge, they let Liberty [*the civil rights pressure group led by Shami Chakrabarti*] in the control room. Liberty later wrote a report, which said there were frequent problems with comms between the Special Operations Room, Bronze commanders [*usually inspector-level*] and police officers on the ground, which often led to confusion. Radios did not work effectively, and officers had to resort to using mobile phones. Sounds about par for the course – our radios often don't work, and it actually suggests we did a very good job in extremely trying circumstances.

They clearly know as much about policing as I know about the Large Hadron Collider, but we're supposed to take them seriously. They criticised us for removing banners and signs which had offensive language on them. They said that this was done without any justification, and foul language on placards was not an offence. Well, Section 5 of the Public Order Act 1986 makes it an offence to display any sign which is threatening, abusive or insulting, within the sight of a person likely to be caused harassment, alarm or distress, and since we're told that most of the protestors were just ordinary decent people trying to protest peacefully about spending cuts, how can Liberty know that they wouldn't be distressed by foul language on signs? Either way, doesn't it make you proud that we have come this far, where people like Shami Chakrabarti are prepared to go to the line to defend the right to carry signs around with the word 'Cunt' on them?

Sergeant, 34, Southern force

People say, 'Why can't you just ignore the peaceful protestors and just deal with the violent minority?' How? What happens is, blokes you can't even see lob bricks and darts and coins and plaggy bags of shit and bottles of piss or ammonia or bleach at you from 10 deep in the crowd. Do they think you just wade in, and the crowd parts like the Red Sea and they hold their hands out and say it's a fair cop? The crowd opens up, either deliberately or just because these things are always in flux, and someone pops out, smacks you on the head with a stick or a hammer, and then disappears. And they change their appearance as they go – they pull the cap off, take their coat off. Again, how do you get to them? It's hard enough just distinguishing the violent people who are shouting and chanting and waving their arms about from the peaceful people who are shouting and chanting and waving their arms about.

It's not even that simple – in any big crowd, there are some people who would never *dream* of attacking a police officer, or smashing a window. There are people who would *mostly* never dare do that sort of thing, but may do it when the opportunity presents itself and they feel the safety of the crowd. There are some people who don't give a stuff about the ostensible protest and are really *only* there to attack police officers and smash windows. There are some who will actively try to help a policeman if he's on the ground getting a shoeing. There are those who will look the other way. There are those who will not actively get involved in the assault but who will shield the attackers, or stand in the way of officers trying to reach their colleague, pretending that they don't know what's going on. It's a lot more complicated than it seems on paper.

PC, 37, Southern force

I was standing not far from where the infamous fire extinguisher landed. [*A-level student Edward Woollard was among a group who forced their way on to the roof of the Millbank building which houses the Tory Party headquarters in London. He dropped a fire extinguisher onto police ranks below from seven storeys above, narrowly missing officers.*] I've been drenched in urine, had sandwich bags full of human excrement thrown at me. I've had used tampons and batteries and half-bricks and syringes thrown at me. I've been spat at. I've had young students screaming at me that they hope I and my children die of cancer… All because I'm daring to stand in front of them when they're trying to burn down the Treasury. And you just think, 'You'll probably go off to university, get nice jobs and forget about all of this, because to you it's really just a game.'

But then, the idiot who threw the extinguisher doesn't think it's a game any more does he? I was so pleased when he was sent away. [*Woollard was jailed for 32 months.*] I would like to think that hearing that was the moment when he finally realised that there *are* consequences to your actions. Because my short time in the police has opened my eyes to the fact that we are breeding a generation of kids, in the richest homes to the poorest, who really don't understand that.

PC, 28, Metropolitan police

It can be hard to make arrests on the day, which is why CCTV and photography is such a useful tool. But the frustrating thing for me is not that quite a few nasty people get away with it but that even if they're nicked, not much happens to them. There was a 14-year-old who threw a petrol bomb at officers during one of the student protests. He was given a 12-month referral order. For throwing a petrol bomb at other human beings, his punishment is having to turn up to occasional meetings with the do-gooders of the Youth Offending Team and talk about how sorry he is. I would give him six of the best and his summer holidays in a cell with no TV, no video games and basic food. *That* would be a punishment.

Cameron said the 'full weight of the law' would be brought to bear. Either he's a liar and he knows you get nothing for throwing petrol bombs, or he's an idiot because he really believes this bullshit. There is no deterrent. Community sentences? They don't bother turning up, look at the figures. Fines? What's the use of fining a student? The parents pay it if they've got jobs, and the rest of us pay it if they haven't. I don't think we'll have any impact on these people until we either start jailing them or we take away their benefits. If you're on Jobseeker's Allowance, what are you doing rioting? You should be seeking a job.

PC, 33, Southern force

I think students *should* pay more. I resent the amount of tax I pay already and I resent them dipping their hands deeper in my pocket to pay for their Mickey Mouse degrees. Half of them are going to end up earning more than me, and the other half will never have to pay the loans back. So am I angry at their behaviour? Yes, I bloody am. Does that 'anger' mean that I can turn up to Clare Solomon's office [*Solomon was president of the University of London Students' Union at the time of the protests, and a fervent proponent of organised protest against the fee increases*] with a couple of hundred of my mates and smash the place up? Can I throw petrol bombs at Clare Solomon while shouting that she is fascist scum if she tries to defend herself? The problem with a lot of these protestors is that they want to live in a westernised democracy and enjoy all the benefits of it, but they don't want to think too hard about how it gets to be like it is.

PC, 37, Northern force

Within months, officers were back on the streets in riot gear when first London and then other cities erupted in serious disorder following the shooting dead by Met officers of Mark Duggan.

One of the unmanned nicks in our area was set on fire, and we had to provide a protective screen for the fire service who, like us, were being showered with petrol bombs, bottles of urine, wheel nuts, lumps of concrete. The sheer hatred was what surprised me. I encounter aggression and general 'anti-ness' all the time, and obviously I'm aware that people dislike us, but the concentrated, furious, howling, hatred of the mob, that was disconcerting. There were credible intelligence reports that they were hoping to kidnap and rape a woman officer, and I was in no doubt at all that if they could get their hands on a male officer and get him away he would be killed. I was only three or four years old when Keith Blakelock was killed, but the image of what happened to him that night was very present in my mind. They were burning cars and bins and setting up barricades, and while I never felt that at any point we were in danger of being overrun and things going really bad, it did feel slightly like being in that old Kurt Russell film about New York under siege.

[*A large number of officers referred to the death in the 1985 Tottenham riots of PC Keith Blakelock. PC Blakelock was part of a serial of 11 officers tasked with protecting a fire brigade crew who were dealing with a fire in a newsagent's which was threatening to spread to nearby homes. The fire was a 'come on'; the policemen were ambushed by thugs carrying machetes, knives, bats and iron bars. In retreating, PC Blakelock tripped and the mob fell on him. He was hacked and stabbed to death; other officers were also badly injured.*]

PC, 33, Midlands force

I went down to London on Aid [*the system by which forces reinforce each other in times of need*]. It was shocking. You would be fighting almost for your life in one street, against a big gang of youths, quite scary when you don't know the ground. And in the next street people would be coming up to you and asking what they could do to help. They'd say, 'We ain't happy with what's going on, we're behind you guys 100 percent.' People were bringing over shopping bags full of Ginsters pasties, bottles of pop, Mars Bars… I'm more of a Dime Bar man, myself, but it's the thought that counts, and it was all very well-received by the lads and lasses. Our own snap was either horrible or non-existent. The support, from many sections of the community, was actually very moving.

PC, 30, Midlands force

At first we couldn't really do much more than hold our line. We had to allow blatant and very serious criminality to go unhindered, and that really sickened me. What kind of a police force are we? But we just didn't have the numbers. And when we did get let off the leash, you would find yourself running down a cut-through in the pitch black after a group of youths, trying to snatch one or two. There's maybe half a dozen of you and 30 of them, and I'm sure I'm not the only one who thought, 'What the *hell* am I doing here?' You couldn't see the people you was chasing, except fleetingly, you didn't know if they was leading you into a trap, you couldn't see who was coming behind you, you didn't know what was round the corner. Just about the only thing you did know was that if you got ambushed it was going to be a very long time before you got some back-up, because the air was literally full of calls for support, officers injured, requests for assistance.

PC, 29, Midlands force

We got a lot of stick for responding slowly. I think there's some truth in that, but it wasn't for want of trying. When I joined in the mid-1990s, the shift I went on to had an inspector, who got out of the nick every day, two sergeants and 24 PCs. We put out eight or 10 officers on foot patrol, we had five pandas, an area car [*more powerful vehicle with a roving role for quicker response to developing incidents*] and two and sometimes three vans. Moreover, this wasn't just my shift on my borough – *every* borough had these sorts of resources floating about. If it kicked off in Haringey, officers from Camden could very quickly move across. Not saying it was foolproof, but we had numbers and mobility, in hand and ready to go. Since then, people have been taken off shift to work in offices, to neighbourhood, to all sorts of other non-response roles, and the result is we now have – I won't give exact numbers as it might identify my borough, but fewer than half the response officers we had 15 years ago.

PC, 39, Southern force

Our van went down the streets where I grew up. We got absolutely smashed. I had visions of the vehicle conking out and rolling to a stop outside my mum's house, and eight coppers seeking sanctuary inside. The camaraderie inside the van was outstanding. It reminded me why I joined the police. These days, it's all single-crewing and we rarely get in the van; to spend time with colleagues in an atmosphere where it seemed the world was against us – you can't buy that feeling.

PC, 30, Midlands force

My inspector was widely regarded as a bit of a tool, for all the usual reasons of obsessing about stats, moaning at you if you're not wearing your hat, stupid emails and that, but on the second night of the rioting I saw him leading a charge against a large mob of rioters... Him with his stick out, leading half a dozen bobbies into the fray and then getting stuck in, laying about him like a bloody Viking. It was very inspiring. And my opinion of him changed somewhat, though he still insists on sending me emails. Actually, quite a few of our senior officers were out and about on the front line, against expectations. I heard tell of a superintendent making an arrest, though that may have been a malicious rumour.

PC, 39, Southern force

There's no use denying it, we lost the streets for a while, and I think we were very lucky with what happened. There was a significant period when there was no law in parts of the UK, and given that there were knives and guns in use, and that fires were being set, and people were drunk on it all and completely out of control, it is pure luck that we didn't have a serious number of fatalities. If you'd said to me, a hundred people will end up dying in these riots, I might have settled for that.

We were always going to get back control eventually, but to have anarchy like that and come out of it with only a couple of fatalities and mostly property damage, albeit serious, is surprising. Next time I would think perhaps we won't be so lucky.

Inspector, 50, Midlands force

We'd had a very difficult day, when at times you felt you were on the set of a Hollywood film. Helicopters overhead, smoke everywhere, people chanting and throwing stuff, and it was very tense. Then some lads from a northern serial started singing *We Gotta Get Out Of This Place*, like the US soldiers in Vietnam. It cracked everyone up, and I remember the faces on some of the people we were confronting, obviously thinking, *What are this lot laughing about?*

PC, 30, Southern force

We were part of a mini convoy of three or four carriers and cars sent to deal with looting attempts in our borough's main high street. At that stage, early on, we didn't really know how bad it was going to be. Obviously, we had lots of calls and radio messages, but I don't think I was mentally prepared. At the back of your mind you think, *It can't be that bad*. Well, it *was* that bad. We stopped at the junction of the high street and the A-road that intersects with it, and all the way down the road ahead you could see chaos. It wasn't dark but the smoke was that thick that you could see the flashing from our blue lights and the fire brigade's wagons in the sky all around. Helicopters overhead, a lot of noise, you couldn't even hear your own radio properly. That's another thing – people were sent out with flat batteries for their radios, which was fucking scandalous. I'd best not go there.

With the racket and the helmets, you had to shout to the bloke next to you. Just making sure you stayed in contact with your nearest oppo was a big task. The streets were full of people, I could see just in the immediate vicinity they had already set a shop and a couple of cars on fire and as soon as we appeared you started hearing that 'Thunk! Thunk!' sound of objects bouncing off the carrier. We get people lobbing things at the vehicles, but normally it's one person, they'll chuck something and be gone before it even lands. Here, they were standing out in the open with handfuls of rocks and bottles. It reminded me of Palestinians and the IDF [*Israeli Defence Force*] on the news.

There was obviously some question as to what we were going to be able to do. Certainly, we couldn't arrest people at this stage – there were too many of them and too few of us. The skipper told us to get out of the van and form up into a line to try to move people back, so we could at least reclaim some of the ground. I was pretty nervous. My mouth was dry and my hands were probably shaking a bit, but you try not to show it. I've been in the Job quite a while, I've had a fair few rucks and roll-arounds. I've done Millwall, Chelsea, I've done EDL v UAF [*Unite Against Fascism*], I've been to major fights. But this was different. For the first time, I actually thought my life might conceivably be in danger. That's a very strange feeling when you're wearing riot gear and there's 30 of you!

You don't want to get out of the relative safety of the van, but you've sort of got to. The first thing that hit me was the smell of burning petrol and rubber from the cars. The second thing that hit me was a bottle of something, I assume urine. Actually, it only landed at my feet and splashed me a bit. So we start moving down the street towards the mob, and they did start moving back. But they were not intimidated by us, not one bit. They were taunting us, throwing masonry, bottles, anything they could get their hands on. I think every shop along the street had been smashed up, even charity shops. At the front, it was mainly younger kids – I would say many were in their mid-teens. But at the back, you could see little groups of older men, not doing much, just watching and waiting. I got the feeling that we were being tested, that there were people in charge who were sort of probing us for weaknesses. I know that's not really like it was, because I don't think anyone was in control. As it was, they didn't break us, we stood and took everything they could throw at us for six or seven hours, much as I hated it, and then for days afterwards, and eventually we won. But it was touch and go.

PC, 30, Southern force

I worked 11 days straight through. Some people worked a lot more. I only saw my wife and son for a couple of hours a day. On the third or fourth day, my little boy said to me, 'Don't let the bad men kill you daddy,' which basically broke my heart. We were trying to keep him away from the news, but inevitably he'd seen some of it and probably heard me talking to my wife. When I think about the sheer malevolent glee of the rioters, and their joy in just mindless damage and violence, and look at my little son and how worried he was, it makes me so angry. It's the wantonness, the pointlessness, of it.

PC, 32, Southern force

The main problem in the police is that our leaders are almost always people who have never really policed at the street level. They do literally a few months of real policing, lots of attachments to teams and squads here and there and then they retire to Faulty Towers on the 4th floor and you never see or hear from them again, except by emails. They are people who have been there and *seen* that, not *done* it. And so as a result we've got commanders who think it's a good idea to deploy people wearing yellow hi-vis nylon clothing in streets which are basically ablaze. Either these people are so incredibly stupid that they don't know that nylon, burning petrol and human skin make a bad combination, or it is a very long time since any of them have ever been anywhere near the street, or they don't care. They are so hot on health and safety when it comes to making a cup of tea in the nick. I mean, don't even dream of using a kettle that hasn't been checked and approved by an electrician from the force estates' office.

PC, Midlands force, 30

The best thing that happened in the riots was that both the BBC and Sky News outside-broadcast lorries got hit. I believe *The Guardian* and BBC staff were sent home early, too, as it started to get a little close to home for them. Unfortunately, no Chief Constables or high court judges or government ministers were petrol bombed, but we live in hope.

Our tactics infuriate me. You stand in a line and take whatever they throw at you, occasionally running forward to try to disperse them, and now and then we stumble across someone and nick him. But, by and large, we sit back and hope to mop them up later from CCTV and so on.

On one level, I understand that we simply don't have the bodies to deal with mass disorder erupting at various locations across London. But then, it's the very fact that we do nothing which leads to it erupting everywhere. When everyone's got a mobile phone, it's the work of moments to text your mates that the Old Bill aren't doing anything. I mean, it's on the *telly* that we're doing nothing. So people elsewhere chance their arm. Whereas if we said, OK, it's kicking off in Tottenham, we'll go in extremely hard there and nick hundreds of bodies, I think that might have nipped it in the bud. On the telly, hundreds of cops battering the living daylights out of rioters… That would send a message. Mind you, of course then the media story would have been 'violent cops disgrace in London'. We really are damned if we do and damned if we don't.

PC, 29, Southern force

Initially, they were holding off because we just didn't have the numbers to get stuck in. Then when we did, we didn't have the numbers to nick them… It's all very well arresting someone, but then transporting them back to the nick, booking them in, interviewing… Yadda yadda, you know the story. If there are live rioters smashing the place up in front of you, the first thing you try to do is contain them. If you compromise the containment by removing officers through arrests, then suddenly you have lost control, or lost control to an even greater extent. It looks shit, and it is shit, but it's not down to the officers on the ground, believe me.

I don't know why – when they finally got the numbers to deal with it all properly – that they still didn't steam in. I think they were put off by bad press of people getting sticked, of officers in court on assault charges *et cetera*. It was utter shite. One thing is for sure, we are woefully short of Level 2 officers. No-one wants to do it – on my team of 30, only four are Level 2. It's not hard to see why... the Sergeant Smellie and PC Harwood cases have had a major impact.

PC, 33, Southern force

We coped, as we always have, by bussing officers in from other areas. What was different this time was the co-ordinated nature of the riots. It was the first time in the 21st century that this has happened, and it posed some very interesting questions as to how the police are going to operate going forward. When it's a big event, a protest, organised in co-operation with the authorities, and with agreed routes and rally points and so on, we can deal with that very successfully. When it's dozens of semi-spontaneous events springing up miles apart, that's a very different matter. Despite the scenes of destruction we saw on the news, I thought that, under the circumstances, the Met did reasonably well. However, what does interest me is what happens if it's going off in seven or eight locations in London and then it also starts in a big way in Tonbridge, Brighton and Southampton. Straight away, Kent, Sussex and Hampshire have problems of their own, so they are not sending carrier loads of officers to London. OK, so they get aid from TVP and West Mids, but then they start burning cars in Whitley or Southcote in Reading, and up in Coventry... Luckily, for us, the rioters were not that co-ordinated; they were largely opportunists, and they had no overall command and control. They had no-one sitting back and thinking, *OK, the police are busy here, here and here, and badly stretched there, so why don't we get people out and* x, y *and* z. But even without that kind of overarching planning, they were able to run us ragged. If they ever do get their act together it could be extremely interesting.

Inspector, 42, Midlands Force

We had an enormous number of officers injured. I am fortunate in that I've never been to a war zone, and we didn't have any fatalities and let's not exaggerate, but we had a lad with his nose split in two and missing teeth, we had people pouring with blood from head wounds, we had officers lying on the floor moaning. My question is, who are these kids? They're basically ordinary kids who joined the police to make a difference in their community.

We got control this time by looking at how they were communicating and organising and reacting to it. However, it will happen again. The genie is out of the bottle. It is high time we were given the tools we need to deal with mass disorder... Tear gas, baton rounds, water cannon, armoured vehicles. I would say perhaps 50 opinion formers in key media and political positions do not want to see this: the rest of the country understands that these are criminals bent on destruction and wanton violence and that they need dealing with.

Because there are those opinion formers wittering on about 'human rights' and 'policing by consent' and 'heavy-handed police tactics', and getting hugely disproportionate coverage and influence, thousands of police stand by and watch. Hundreds of officers and members of the public are injured, homes and businesses are destroyed and hundreds of millions of pounds-worth of damage is done.

Sergeant, 33, Southern force

On the second night of rioting, at about 3am, I found myself at a large cash-and-carry-type store in North London that sold everything under the sun. It was basically a huge warehouse with a car park out front, half-lit by yellow spotlights. In the car park were a selection of police vehicles; about four Astras, a van and a BMW 325, all parked at odd, oblique angles like kids' toys scattered across a living room carpet. We'd been called to the warehouse by store security. They'd seen about eight lads in the usual burglar's uniform of black, hooded top and face-covering climb in through a forced fire exit.

There was moonlight, but it was hidden by clouds or smoke from the fires burning nearby, and I remember being struck by the silence of the dual carriageway nearby. This is usually a main artery into London, it's busy with traffic 24/7, every day. But it was now still and silent. I suppose people were staying in to defend their homes, if necessary.

We had all turned up quietly, cars at low revs, no sirens, and we'd not done the usual police thing of leaving the blue lights on when stopped. We were trying to avoid scaring the thieving little shits off. We'd spent all night chasing them off, and now we were pissed off, tired, and sick of playing games. After 24 hours of being restrained by the caution of managers making decisions over radios and in front of TV screens, the view was, this lot are getting nicked, no matter how much they fight.

Before they'd locked up earlier, the security guards had piled an eight-foot-high pallet of mineral water bottles up against the back of the fire exit to make it harder for the looters to break in. Of course, now it stood in our way. It was like a huge plastic-wrapped iceberg with a small gap at the top which the looters had wriggled through.

I had already flopped face down a pile of stock in another shop, and I had no intention of repeating that. 'No way am I climbing over that,' I said. We managed to push the bottles forward and reduce the mineral water mountain to about waist height before we clambered over it and into the shop. As each officer entered and we fanned out across the building, I remember the 'Fff...tik, Fff...tik' of batons being locked out. One guy shouts, 'Come out, come out, wherever you are!' Brilliant. It was dark inside, just a bit of emergency lighting. The whole shop floor was lit in a grey gloom – it reminded me of the computer games I used to play when I was younger. I was half-expecting a zombie or an alien to jump out from behind the racks of supplies around us.

Suddenly, something caught my eye, fluttering high up in the rafters of the store, turning over and over in the gloom. *A pigeon?*, I think, and then, as I focus on it, I'm confused as it doesn't seem to make sense, it doesn't look right. Then, *Oh shit!* 'Bottles!' I'm yelling, as 75cl of something red and probably quite tasty hits the floor to my right. I hear an officer swear in the darkness, and then go sprinting off into cover. I take cover behind a plinth to my left. Immediately to my side are racks of Tag Heuer watches in glass cases.

'The silly sods have gone for the wine instead?' I say. I couldn't help but laugh.

'Either good taste or stupidity,' says the girl next to me.

The lads are now launching cans of baked beans, and whatever else they can grab, at us, in the hope of driving us back, but there was no chance of that. The way they had broken in, they had effectively trapped themselves. We now had control of the only entrance and exit from the place, and there were a lot more of us than them. Due to the Met not issuing decent torches, most of us fork out for our own

Surefire or LED Lenser flashlights, and now we were illuminating the aisles and racks in a systematic clearance of the front of the store. Some groups of officers were moving faster than others, and the ones that had reached another section of the store suddenly sent a radio message. 'They've got knives from butchers' blocks.' We were all breathing a little harder now. 'Same for the baseball bats here, mate,' says someone else. Although it was cold inside the warehouse, I could feel the sweat under my body armour – the skin on my back was really clammy.

Then another message: 'Golf Zero TOA.'

The dog van had arrived, and now we all felt a lot better.

'All units withdraw and we'll send the dog in,' said the skipper over the radio. Just then, I heard, 'Wait! There's one! POLICE! STAND STILL!' and in the light of my torch I saw a black-clad youth sprinting left to right at the rear of the store, hotly pursued by two coppers. I couldn't help but have the image of Benny Hill being chased by a group of scantily-clad girls in my head, accompanied by the comedy music. They got him, and he started with the screams of, 'Get the fuck off me!', accompanied by much protestations of innocence and teeth-sucking. Someone shouted for help, so I ran to assist two officers struggling to arrest a youth. He was quite stocky, and was resisting them attempting to get him into handcuffs by kicking out with his legs and thrashing his arms about. I dropped onto his legs and held them in a prone rugby-tackle type position, as they eventually wrestled his wrists into cuffs, and he was marched down to join the other prisoners at the front of the store, bumping his gums with various allegations and threats against us.

Another guy was cuffed and trussed like a Christmas turkey before being carried to the front of the store and plonked down on his arse. Swiftly followed by the rest of his fellow looters.

Then it's all, 'I ain't done nothing wrong, though.'

Like they were just there for a bit of late night shopping, or had nipped out for an evening constitutional. Knobs. We put the arrested looters into vans and police cars and whisked them off to the various stations where they'd be processed by the exhausted, hollow-eyed detectives and prisoner-processing teams who had been at work for what seemed like days.

I was quite proud of what we did that night. Until they had seen how many of us there were, they had been prepared to use bats and knives against us. We found dropped baseball bats *et cetera* on the floor of the store, where they had obviously thought better of it. And after the threats, the violence, the looting, the bricks and bottles on the street, the red wine and baked beans in the warehouse, the allegations of whatever 'ism' fit a given criminal's background, after all that and more there had been no extra-judicial beatings, there'd been no 'stick therapy', no stitch-ups. Just whereas before we may have spent a long time reasoning with and trying to 'talk down' each individual criminal whilst he was emboldened by the attention he was getting, boosted by knowing we'd be painfully aware of his rights and desperately trying to avoid any reason to trigger a complaint against us… this was different. We had neither the time nor the inclination to tiptoe round these lawless vermin. We simply grabbed them, nicked them, cuffed them and locked them up. The only problem was, every time we did that, there were less and less of us for the next one.

PC, 33, Southern force

I find it funny how the trouble is always caused by 'outsiders'. Our local MP said he'd overheard youths phoning people saying, 'When are you coming to [*the Borough*].' I'm not disputing that he heard this, I'm sure he did, but by the same token, we were arresting people who we arrest all the time, and those two things don't really compute, do they? Really, it's not surprising, because who comes out to smash up shops and steal trainers when they get a chance? Criminals. But I think a lot of community spokespeople and MPs like to imagine it's not 'their' people doing this, hence this 'outsiders' thing. I'm not saying some people didn't travel, but I'd bet my house that most of the people arrested were nicked within a quarter of a mile of their home address. Fundamentally, these people have no get-up-and-go, even when it comes to rioting.

Also, I was listening to a Radio 5 Live phone-in and people were calling in to lament this business of the rioters burning shops down in their own area and I was like, What the fuck is that all about? Does it somehow make it any better if they're smashing up shops in *other* people's neighbourhoods? The fact is, it was better that they did it on their own patch, because then we got some actual support from the local community in identifying the perpetrators. We had people who normally would cross the road to avoid us coming up and saying, 'Listen, I ain't a grass but…' A small part of me wanted to tell them to go away, because if the people in question had been trashing another borough then no way would they have been wanting to help us. It was like, 'Ah, now you want us to help you? Very interesting…'

PC, 34, Southern force

Hearing Bronze commanders literally screaming into radios for more officers as they had officers hurt was not only morale-sapping but also embarrassing. At one point, some slag stole an Airwave radio from an officer and started copying our call-signs [*radio identifiers*] and locations, and then shouting 'Officer down!' over the radio. After a while it was obvious by the giggling that it wasn't real, but it still clogged up our comms. Despite all the wonderful technology, it still took a long time to get the radio number and have it blocked.

PC, 36, Southern force

I'll just go against the grain slightly and say that I loved the riots. I didn't like the fact that we were stood around like spare wotsits at weddings for so long, but once we got the numbers on the ground, it was just great fun. It's what I joined the police for. Any policeman worth his salt will enjoy battering the fuck out of proper, evil shite, and basically that's what we did. I came across some people I know very well, who 364 days of the year I pretty much have to accept calling me a cunt to my face… Now I had pretty much free rein, within the law, to give them a bit back. They are so used to us treating them with kid gloves, I think when the gloves finally came off they were more than a bit surprised. It very quickly went from, 'You fucking pig scum!' to, 'Help, I want my mummy, you can't do this!'

The other reason I liked the riots is because it allowed the country at large to see the kind of human filth we deal with. It was there, in colour, on the TV, it couldn't be ignored, or forgotten, or swept under the carpet. These are the kind of people we the police keep away from you the law-abiding public, and this is what will happen if they ever get the upper hand. Think on that.

PC, 34, Southern force

The equipment was shit, the leadership was shit, the rioters were shit, but it was the best fun I've had in ages. It beats going to shitty domestics in the same block and trying to get the same morons to turn their lives around, day after day, year after year, like an uncomedy version of *Groundhog Day*. Plus the overtime was ace. I'm off to Cancún for Christmas, while the shite are still festering in their own shit, albeit that they do now all have new Reeboks. So, cheers, rioters, you made my year!

PC, 30, Southern force

You had reporters complaining that the streets were under the control of rioters and that the police were nowhere to be seen. But the same reporters have spent the last 20 years of my career complaining about stop-and-search, looking in microscopic detail at every arrest the police make, complaining about police brutality, agitating for shorter prison sentences. It's like, I've got news for you, if you make it harder for the police to take weapons off people, more people will carry weapons. If you put doubt into the minds of police officers when they are confronted by violence, if you say to them you will be dragged through the mill if you dare to go hands-on, they may think twice and step back and bad people will be more violent. If you make it harder for the courts to jail criminals, they will be bolder, and more of them will be on the streets. It's not hard to see this.

And where is the media accountability? The media carried a lot of stories suggesting that the riots were a response to a 16-year-old girl being beaten up by the police. That was made up, it never happened! The BBC had someone from 'the community' on saying that the whole thing was started because this non-existent girl had gone to the police station to protest at the 'murder' of Mark Duggan by the police. The journalists don't correct this, they don't say, 'Er… *Murdered? Really?*' They just let these idiots rant on unchallenged, and the next thing you know it's being tweeted and blogged around the world that the police murdered Duggan and then beat up teenage girls who protested about it, and it's almost fact. Was it Churchill who said that a lie could travel round the world before the truth has got its trousers on? [*Mark Twain: A lie can travel half-way around the world while the truth is putting on its shoes.*] Blatant lies become accepted as fact and are used as justification by the rioters and their apologists. If we make a mistake, quite rightly we get investigated to the *n*th degree, internally by our supervisory structure, management and PSD, and externally by the IPCC, the courts and the media. When the media allow blatant lies and untruths to circulate, who holds them to account?

Inspector, 44, Southern force

I saw lots of stuff in the aftermath of the riots where journalists said that it had all started because the police 'didn't respond quickly enough' to demands by the family of Mark Duggan for information as to his shooting. I don't really know where to begin with this.

Firstly, I didn't realise that you could turn up outside a police station, demand information about a serious ongoing enquiry and then [other] people could start trashing the place when it's not immediately forthcoming. I didn't realise that. No-one told me.

Secondly, as every journalist knows, and ought to be making clear, once a person dies in a police shooting the matter is handed over to the Independent Police Complaints Commission. Blimey, if a person who has asked a policeman the time of day dies within 24 hours of having done so, it will be handed over to the IPCC, as a 'death after police contact'. So once Duggan has been shot it immediately becomes an IPCC matter, and it is not within the Met's remit to start making public statements to anyone about it. A guy has been shot dead, there are investigators looking at the incident, they are independent... Of course, we feel sorry for the family, they're just lost a son, a brother, but do we really want information about the shooting leaking to anyone, family included? Let's wait until they have finished their work, and *then* we'll talk about it. Don't worry, we'll spend the next 30 years talking about it. People have made a lucrative career out of talking about the Brixton Riots. I agree that the IPCC takes far too long to investigate things. Any police officer who has been investigated by them and has had his or her life put on hold for a year or two while it happens will tell you that. But that's just the way it is. You'll have to live with it, folks. We have to.

Thirdly, anyway – who *says* this supposed failing 'caused' the riots? If it's the rioters who said it, why do we believe the word of people who are prepared to burn down shops with occupied flats above them, as though the words they speak are the gospel truth? We think these people are willing to commit arson without caring whether they endanger life, to put the best possible gloss on it, but they wouldn't *dream* of lying about their motivation? And if it's so-called 'community leaders', who told *them*? And if it's so-called 'experts', how do *they* know? It's all a little bit suspect, to me. But it gets repeated over and over and over again by reporters until I almost believe it myself.

Fourthly, even if in some sense it is true that thousands of youths from all over the country who had never even heard of Mark Duggan *after* he was shot, never mind *before* it, decided to rise up in a spontaneous outbreak of righteous anger against the police, how in fuck's name does robbing plasma tellies and trainers from Sports Direct fit that picture? How does stealing the clothes off the backs of innocent members of the public fit that picture? The answer is that it does not, in any way, fit that picture, and the media should never have accepted it as any kind of an explanation for what went on.

The simple fact is, there are people in this country who *like* smashing things, stealing stuff and hurting others, and if they get half a chance they will do it. They want shiny new trainers. End of. It goes no further or deeper than that, and the newspapers and the TV news people ought to be ashamed of themselves for allowing other considerations to obscure the true picture. That was a glimpse of what the country would be like if there were no police.

Sergeant, 37, Southern force

I find the media and 'community' response laughable, to be honest. People need to understand that *CSI* is entertainment, not a documentary. You cannot just rock up to an event like the Duggan shooting, type some stuff into a laptop, take a couple of swabs, have a full report on the Commissioner's desk and then be home for tea. We – by which I mean, British investigators on major incident teams, including those available to the IPCC – are very good indeed, and we *will* work out who fired which weapon how many times, and which rounds struck where, but it is not an instant thing. It's painstaking work. You cannot riot just because the answer is not forthcoming in time for *Hollyoaks*.

But it's all bogus, anyway, all bogus. Mark Duggan is shot dead by the nasty police officers, and the country burns. Thirty young kids a year are murdered in London in gang violence *every* year, and no fucker could care less. Where's the fucking riots over that? The fucking outrage bus never leaves the fucking depot over that, does it? The country just shrugs its shoulders and says, 'That's just one of them things.'

Duggan gets slotted, and suddenly the telly is full of so-called 'community leaders' having a go at the police for racism and stop-and-search, because taking carving knives off youths outside McDonalds is certainly fucking racist. I mean, what do we expect? Of *course*, they're going to riot!

When a 16-year-old girl gets murdered in a takeaway in Hackney… Answer me this, if these community leaders know what's what, and they are such authority figures with the gunmen that they can presume to know their motivations and speak on their behalf, why didn't they stop Agnes [*Sina-Inakoju*] being killed? And where were they after? If I were a community leader, surely I'd be saying to people, 'We need to put a fucking stop to this. I'm going to *lead* this community and put a stop to this. Let's work with the police, here are the guilty men, here are their associates, here's where they stash their drugs and weapons.' But no, it's all, 'Don't talk to the police. The police are raaaayyyciiiists.'

PC, 31, Southern force

Reporters talk about the 'anger' in the 'community'. Anger is *never* a justification for rioting, unless you live in a dictatorship. We live in a democracy, and these people ought to get their arses down to the ballot box and vote if they want to change things. But it's just a smokescreen. They don't want to change anything. Things are just fine for them. They live in the moment, they can't think ahead, and things are just fine. They've got their spliff and their drinks, they've got their cribs and their food. They've all got nice trainers and Xboxes, and they get to get up at midday and do sweet FA all day.

They've got a girlfriend, but she's pregnant. 'Oh, well, not my problem, innit. Someone else will take care of that.'

'Ooh, we need to find jobs for these people, the unemployment...'

Jobs? The *last* thing they want is a job. Let's, please, just have a bit of truth about this.

PC, 34, Southern force

I have policed the Broadwater Farm area [*where Duggan lived*], so I have a fairly sophisticated knowledge of the area, its problems and its people. I'll stand corrected but I don't *think* any journalist who reported on the riots for the national media either lives there, or works there. So I think I can confidently say I'm better informed than they are. The vast majority of the working people in that borough, black, white, any nationality or race, have no problem *whatsoever* with the police, except they don't see enough of us. *They're* the 'community', ordinary people who do their best to put food on their kids' tables, bring them up as best they can in difficult circumstances. But the media don't interview *them* about *their* anger. They're certainly angry, but their anger is with the parasites who basically rule the estates by fear. These are scum who deal drugs to kids, rape young girls and stab young lads as a means of enforcing respect, threaten and beat people into staying silent, claim they own the streets. And it pains me as a police officer to admit this, but it's the truth – our writ does not always run on some of these estates. I mean, if there's a murder or something else serious, we're all over it, but as for day-to-day policing, to keep those streets as safe as, say, they are in Mayfair, or even Islington, it's really not happening.

In the media, you have lots of generally white, middle class, liberal journalists who don't live anywhere near Broadwater Farm and don't really know what's going on there, and they either romanticise the struggle of the people who do live there, or they feel guilty about their own good fortune, or are just nice, well-meaning but naïve people, or are straightforwardly quite hard left or extreme right and want to foment some sort of revolution. Add in to this the general approach to anything that involves race, and what you have is a set of quite gullible but influential people who are cannon fodder to the vested interests on the estates. The message they are getting, and which they faithfully regurgitate, from self-described 'community leaders' is that we don't want heavy-handed policing, we don't want stop-and-search, we don't want a highly-visible police presence, the police are all racists, the police just want to fit up our boys – arguments I very rarely hear from the honest victims of crime on the estates, who say categorically that they want *more* stop-and-search, they want *more* police on their streets, for longer hours, they *want* a heavy hand to be used against the gangs.

On the other side of the equation you have a whole generation of senior officers who, almost to a man, have swallowed this rubbish. Or if they haven't swallowed it, they pay lip service to it because they all want the next rank, and you don't get the next rank by being named as the man who ignored the voice of the 'community' and let it all go pear-shaped. 'Not on my watch, mate.'

So you get a kind of hall-of-mirrors policing. We adopt a light touch. We don't have cops in twos and fours patrolling, 24/7. We attend – sorry, 'engage with' – 'partnership forums' and meetings with 'elders' and 'leaders', and we grovel to them so they'll say nice things about us and won't kick up a fuss. Things you would certainly be arrested for in other parts of London, we turn a blind eye to. And it is so frustrating. I, a lowly PC, could seriously end gang violence in Tottenham inside a month. We all know who most of the players are. If we lifted them, and then swamped the streets with Old Bill and stopped and searched everyone, made three or four hundred more arrests, searched a lot of flats and cafés and minicab offices and lock-ups, and really threw the book at anyone caught with a knife or a gun or drugs or money they couldn't explain… I mean, jailed for five years, off you go… We could end it all tomorrow. It wouldn't even be hard. You wouldn't even have to pay overtime, most of the cops I know would be queuing up, because they are sick to death of letting the honest folks down, of seeing criminal scum who are hurting and preying on others, swagger down the street laughing at the law.

But it won't happen, because the commentators and journos, whose kids would have to be *extremely* unlucky to be stabbed to death over a turf issue, and who can walk to that nice Italian on the corner at night without worrying too much about whether they'll be shaken down on the way there, or find burglars in their house when they get back… Those people simply do not give a fuck. Better to have some nice headlines complaining about the racism of the police than confront reality. The best thing about the riots is it brought reality just a bit closer to those people. We managed to keep it from getting too close. Next time, who knows? And I'm not sure I'd be too upset if one or two of them got a bloody good hiding, as a man once said.

PC, 34, Southern force

I'm sorry, but I'm not losing any sleep over Mark Duggan's death. The fact is, London is a safer place for the majority population without people like him. It would be better if he was alive and in jail, but then he chose to go onto the ground carrying a gun. You reap what you sow.

I'm personally fed up with the suggestion that these things happen because we are racist. Macpherson* couldn't find any actual racism in the Met police, he had to invent something called 'institutional racism'. What is that? I deny its existence. But it has big effects. I stop and search a lot of black youths, not because I'm racist but because I know there's a good chance, in each specific case, they will be carrying weapons or something else they shouldn't be. I stress, it's not a random thing, unless it's Section 60 you have to have reasonable grounds [*Section 60 of the Criminal Justice and Public Order Act 1994 allows the police to search without suspicion in certain circumstances*]. And lots of white youths carry as well, don't get me wrong, and we stop them as well, and I'm also sure some of them, black and white, are carrying out of self-defence. *I'd* probably want to carry a knife if I had to live where I work. But that's another argument. The law says you can't carry knives and guns, that's all I can really focus on.

Now, if I stop a black kid I really try to be open-minded about it, but at the back of my mind I know what's going to happen, and it's pretty much always: 'You racis' man, innit? Man, why you always stoppin' us? You gonna lose your job for this one. Man, I'd love to fry some bacon, innit.'

With all the bolshy shoulders and teeth sucking and throwing gang signs and that. Some of them are highly arrogant; they think they're untouchable, they think that the law should not be applied to them. I just say, 'I'm not stopping you because I'm a racist, I'm stopping you because I have reasonable grounds for whatever.'

'It's just because I'm black, innit.'

116

'No, it's because you match the description of a suspect involved in X. Witnesses have told us he was black, it would be silly me stopping a white boy, wouldn't it?'

I just stay calm and patient and firm.

PC, 36, Southern force

In 1993, a black teenager, Stephen Lawrence, was murdered by a racist gang in London. The Metropolitan Police failed to build a case against the killers (just before publication, two men were finally convicted and jailed), and this failure led to a public inquiry led by the retired judge Sir William Macpherson. The inquiry's findings, published in the Macpherson Report, alleged that the police failures came as a result of 'institutional racism'.

I have no problem, personally, with most of the rules on stop-and-search. We have to tell people who we are and why we want to search them. Fair enough, I'd expect that myself. We have to be reasonably courteous and we can't take all day over it. Again, no complaints here. Somebody has to show these kids how to behave. What I *do* disagree with is, we're not allowed to stop people purely on the basis of what they have done before. This is drummed into you at training school. It's insane.

I'm not saying you commit one crime and we're on your case for the rest of your life, but if we see Jimmy walking down the street, who we know is a prolific burglar with 100 precons [*previous convictions*], then we know nine times out of 10 he's either on the way to or from a job, or his dealer, or his fence, because he spends the rest of his life wigged out in his flat, and in my opinion we should be able to stop him and have a look in his pockets. Obviously, basically this is what any decent street copper does anyway, and there are always some reasonable grounds you can find... You speak to someone and if they are evasive or aggressive or furtive, which they always are, then you have grounds. But it shouldn't be like that. We shouldn't have to 'find' grounds to search scumbags, it's a basic requirement of protecting the innocent members of the public.

If you make a habit of breaking into other people's homes, or ripping up cable, or pushing crack, part of the decision you make when you cross that line should be to accept that you have put yourself outside the protection of the law. They should make it part of the sentence, certainly for community sentences. You will do six months' community work, and for the next 12 months any police officer who sees you will have the unfettered right to have a look what's in the boot of your car or make you turn out your pockets.

I think it would be pretty uncontroversial with the general public, maybe even a bit of a vote-winner. Harassing and interrupting these people is absolutely what the police should do, it's our best tool for disrupting their criminality and protecting honest people.

PC, 26, Southern force

I wasn't surprised by the riots at all. Generations of kids have no dad at home. The fathers have been allowed to spawn kids and then move on. There are consequences to that – a woman simply cannot control a headstrong 16-year-old boy. I've heard it from their own mouths, hundreds of times. 'What can I do? He don't listen to me.'

But even where the dads are around, there's often not much they can do. Pretty much the only language these kids understand, I'm sorry to say, is physical violence. How do they sort out their own beefs? How do the gang leaders keep their juniors in check? Not by discussing their feelings. But if a father tries to discipline his son and leaves more than a slight reddening on the skin, regrettably we intervene, because now we, corporately, don't believe that parents should physically discipline their children. Society, or at least the opinion-forming parts of society, has decided that this is wrong. There are consequences to this.

Add to this, there is no discipline in schools, and these kids are, broadly, uneducated. They can't write, they can't spell, they can't read. They have never heard of Charles Dickens, or Shakespeare. They don't know what a quadratic equation is, or how many inches there are in a foot. They don't know how many centimetres are in a metre. They can't add up without using their fingers. Back when I was a bobby, I spent some time in a community outreach role. I engaged with boys in their mid- to late-teens, and I'd get talking to them sometimes. I used to have control questions I'd ask.

'Do you know when the Second World War was?'

'We never done that at school.'

'What's the capital of France?'

'I dunno.' Or, even, 'What's France?'

Obviously, this is tragic on just a basic level, but it also means they are unsuitable for any work except maybe labouring. But even then, could they follow instructions? I'm not sure. To be honest, lots of these kids, I don't think I'd want to buy a burger from them. McDonalds would be beyond them. I left school after doing my A levels in 1983 and went straight into the police. I never experienced that thought of, *What on earth can I do?* But we have tens of thousands of kids in London, hundreds of thousands across the country, with no hope of ever working. I don't even know how that would feel. There are consequences to all of this.

We've gone in 50 years from a nation that believed in families, and the strap and the cane, and where kids were forced to learn their times table and read, to a nation that believes in nothing and reaps the consequences. As a Christian, perhaps I would be expected to say these things, but it's got nothing to do with religion, for me.

Sergeant 43, Southern force

Mark Duggan's death had nothing to do with the riots, just like Cynthia Jarrett's death in my opinion had nothing to do with Broadwater Farm in 1985. [*Mrs Jarrett collapsed and died during a police search of her home.*] We knew back then that the riots were on the way several weeks before they happened, and by logical extension several weeks before Cynthia Jarrett's unfortunate death. Milk bottles were being nicked, white spirit and paraffin was being stolen from hardware stores, there were a lot of rumours in the air. All they were looking for was an excuse. It wasn't a reason, it was an excuse.

Retired Inspector, 58, Metropolitan Police

I was at Tottenham on the night of October 5th 1985 as a young policeman. I heard the radio messages begging for an ambulance for Keith Blakelock and Dick Coombes, and the fact that they could not get ambulances to them. I couldn't sleep for several days afterward, and I have never been able to get those messages out of my mind. I didn't know Keith but I knew people who knew him, and I knew Dave Pengelly [*the sergeant who was leading PC Blakelock's serial*] vaguely. The general view was that he was a gentle man, a decent man. Married with kids.

After PC Blakelock was murdered, Bernie Grant, the leader of the council, goes on the telly and says that the police got a good hiding. And then two years later the people of the area elected him as their MP. That says it all. When these latest riots erupted, my overriding feeling was, *I hope they burn the whole place down.* There are lots of good people living in these places, but there are a minority who, if they all died it would not be worth the life of one policeman or fire-fighter.

Retired PC, 55, Metropolitan Police

The strange thing is, in my nearly 30 years of service I have seen the police and society pass each other travelling in different directions. When I joined, there were some real hard nuts in the Job and the work itself, conversely, was not actually all that dangerous. I could count on the fingers of one hand the number of times I was *really* scared in the first decade of my service, i.e. maybe once every other year. I remember a really big fight at a gypsy camp once, I remember a massive brawl in the town centre with some squaddies where officers ended up in hospital, a couple of pub fights. But we were able to get the upper hand on these people on each occasion. If you wanted to fight us in our town, you had better be prepared to feel the pain because chances were, you were going to end up minus a few teeth. So we just didn't get much physical grief from people. Most of the time, the sight of a couple of big cops hoving into view at the bottom of the street was enough to make people desist.

Now, most of the old school, 6ft 3in ex-Guardsmen are long gone, and we get grief *all* the time. Our force is full of loads of women and skinny laths of lads of about 5ft 9in, who have their place I'm sure, but they are very much not about the projection of force. I don't advocate bobbies going around cracking heads willy-nilly, but I suspect there is some correlation here, between the softening and the feminisation of the police, from the change from a 'force' to a 'service', and the increasing violence in our streets.

I spend a lot of my time now dealing with officers complaining about stress. I had to deal with a female PC and a very young-in-service male PC who had been in a relationship, and then split up, and the female officer then formed a new relationship with another officer on shift. Or maybe she went over the side first. I can't recall.

Anyway, the male came to me in tears about this. He said it was making him stressed, and asked me to sort it out. I had to point out to him that as long as they were not actually shagging in the front office there was nothing I could do about two adults forming a relationship. His doctor signed him off! There's not a lot you can say about it, because you'll be accused of bullying but, in my opinion, he should not be in the police. I don't like the buzzwords, but he doesn't have the necessary resilience. How is he going to deal with the kind of thugs my lads and lasses face on the streets?

I will just add that I am not rose-tinted about the old days. They were days when there *was* corruption, when people got away with things like drink-driving by showing out [*flashing their warrant card*], when people did fall down the proverbial steps into the cells from time to time and when I know, because convictions have been overturned, that some people were fitted up. It was a time of masons, and the Ways and Means Act, and sometimes a very loose interpretation thereof. Again, not saying that was all bad, either. Shades of grey. Horses for courses.

Inspector, 49, Northern force

In the wake of the riots, the cuts to police budgets – biting hard, despite the government's claims to the contrary – are exercising many frontline officers.

To listen to the government, you would think it was them out there being shot at and fire-bombed. It got on my nerves listening to Cameron and May talking about how they'd got a grip of the situation, when they weren't even in the country when it started. We had officers working shifts of 24 hours' duration, working weeks solid, grabbing a kip here and there, a Mars Bar here and there. Then there's David Cameron on the telly boasting about how the government repelled the rioters. The government did *nothing*. *We* did it. We locked up hundreds of offenders and made the streets safe again, and we did it under the threat of losing our jobs, of our pensions being slashed by the very same David Cameron. Then Theresa May came out and said that policing needed urgently reforming… Astonishing. Successive governments have taken the world's best police force and slowly and systematically destroyed it.

Sergeant, 40, Midlands force

You'd hope that the government would look at what happened and think again about cutting the police. But our force is infested with management consultants trying to show how we can sack everyone but still keep the streets safe. Our response teams are being cut in half. These people don't understand the elastic nature of demand for our services. We're not production line workers who made *x* number of widgets yesterday, and will make the same number today and tomorrow, we are at the whim of the fates, as such. Two officers in a car covering 100 square miles and 50,000 people is fine as long as nothing happens. It's arguably bloody *overmanning*, if nothing happens. But things *do* happen. We're the police, we have to have that elasticity, that fat, built in to our system. And if that means you drive past two officers sat in a car doing not much – though they'll actually be on a meal break, or doing their paperwork, or both – then that's the price we pay. Or else there's not much we can realistically do when the wheel comes off.

Sergeant, 40, Northern force

I understand the need for cuts, because it's been obvious for a long time that the country was living beyond its means. I just don't think it's very sensible to cut the police, or at least this quick and this deep. I make a distinction between the pension and everything else. The pension, it's a major part of why I joined, and I do resent having to pay more into it for less. I joined on the basis that I'd get *x* and now they're going to give me *y*, with *y* being far less attractive. I've kept my side of the bargain – they should keep theirs. However, with my rational head on – and this is not a popular view among my colleagues, I have to accept that – because it's index-linked and I can take it at 50, and because the payments I make, even when they're increased, could not earn me that income in the normal pension sphere, it is still a very good pension. The latest quote I had, I retire in five years, I'll get £1,400 a month. That's still relatively good, especially in an era of high inflation and when the country is basically broke.

The other side of the cuts is where I have real problems. They seem to think you can cut police numbers without impacting on the frontline. My force has to lose another 90 officers this year and is also losing hundreds of civvies. Nationwide, we've seen figures of 16,000 sworn officers being lost over the next four years. I just do not see how anyone can believe that if you cut 15 percent of the police strength this will not impact on crime?

Sergeant, 49, Northern force

Our pension has been historically a good scheme, in that it's guaranteed by the taxpayer, we get to retire earlier than some others, I agree with all that. Having said that, we do pay 11 percent of our salary into it, and soon to be more. I don't know how much the average person pays into his or her pension, but I bet it very rarely exceeds five percent. Then there's the myth that we all retire after doing our 30 years and get nice jobs somewhere – the truth for most officers is not quite so rosy. It tends to be working in security or a job at B&Q – nothing wrong with that, but it's not big money when most people at 55-ish are probably in the prime of their earning capacity. Additionally, a large number of cops retire with often quite serious medical problems from injuries on duty, and many don't live very long beyond claiming their pension because of the after-effects of stress and shift work *et cetera.*

I love the job, I signed up for all of that, but that's the point, among the things I signed up for was the pension. To be told 20-plus years into your career, 'Sorry, we're changing the rules and you have to pay more for less' is like sending off your last HP agreement on your car and the garage saying, 'You have another 12 months to pay that we didn't mention before, *and* the payments will be bigger, *and* we're swapping it for a smaller car.' And I don't accept the argument that there's no money. We've enough to fund African dictators and the Indian space programme. We had enough for Libya. We've enough for all the wars, and to allow able-bodied men to stay on the dole, and to give unemployed people tens of thousands a year in housing benefit to live in houses and flats in parts of London I could never afford if I worked 60 hours a week, all year round. We've enough to give that fat, stupid disgrace John Prescott £55,000 a year in his pension.

Now, they *could* save money in the police. All the PCSOs who can't arrest people or do anything except make work for real cops – they could take on the good ones as cops and bin the rest. They could turn the central heating off in police stations during August. They could cut down on the bloody stationery they order. They could stop paying expensive ad agencies to design and produce glossy posters telling us all to be nice to everyone and showing us what a victim looks like. We *know* what victims look like – we're the police! They could scrap the chief inspector and superintendent ranks, that would save us all a lot of unnecessary bullshit work and also save millions of pounds. There's 30-odd Boroughs in the Met. Chief inspectors start at £53,000, superintendents start at £62,000. Just getting shot of one of each would save near enough four million pounds a year. We've got dozens and dozens of civvies doing non-jobs on £100,000 a year. Director of Human Resources? We can do that on Borough with a duties sergeant, thanks. Director of Diversity? Nothing to do with policing, really, bye-bye. They could stop paying chief constables massive bonuses for the stupid targets the troops hit. They could stop paying their kids' school fees and family airfares. They could tell them they have to buy their own motors – surely it's not that hard out of £150,000 a year, I manage it out of a quarter of that. I can guarantee it won't stop people wanting to be chief.

PC, 39, Southern force

I work a shift pattern of seven on, two off, moving through earlies, days and nights, which means I get two days off in nine. I get assaulted, both verbally and physically. I've been spat at and bitten and then spent weeks waiting in fear to find out whether I've contracted hepatitis or HIV/Aids or whatever the person I was arresting told me they had – during which time I can't live a normal life with my wife. I've never had any of these assailants prosecuted to the full extent of the law, because it's part and parcel of the job, apparently, and not in the public interest to deal with these people. Don't tell me I'm overpaid and take away my pension.

Sergeant, 34, Northern force

We don't have the option of striking, by law. Trumpton can strike, doctors can strike, police staff can strike, but somehow we can't. I would like that option. Other officers I've talked to would not. I'm not saying I *would* strike, but if we downed tools for a day it would bring the country back onside quicker than if the Tube drivers go off, that's for sure.

I think what you *may* see is people starting to work to rule, either officially via the Federation [*union for police officers to Inspector rank*] if that was legal, or unofficially. The police only runs on the goodwill and enthusiasm of officers and the system would collapse without it. 'Can you get in a couple of hours early for this op, mate? No overtime in it, mind.' Er, no, I can't, sorry. I also can't hang around at the end of the shift doing crimintel reports, PACs [*Pre-assessment Checklists completed by officers concerned about a child*], making my custody and case files and arrest notes nice and Gucci... I won't save up several CRIS reports [*Crime Reports Information System*] till close of play, I'll come back to the nick to do it properly as and when I deal with something. Take out a car with a fault light on the dashboard? Ooh, I dunno. Looks risky to me, I'll do it if you sign my pocket-book, sarge, then it's on your head. It can all stop, if they want.

Currently, I get fucked around something rotten, as we all do, by duties calling me in at short notice on rest days. Very easy for me to have had a wee drink when they call, or just not to answer the phone. Currently, I and most other decent cops get injured and just come into work the next day. Very easy for me to take some time off to recuperate, as is absolutely my legal right. Firearms, they're volunteers. PSU are volunteers. How about if they decide they don't want the additional grief that goes with their roles? And on the other side of the coin, how about if I start doing it totally by the book when it comes to enforcing the law? If I arrest and interview *everyone*? No more tickets, or street cautions. We can have a policy of street cautioning for possession, but I'll tell you I can find a good reason to bring them in if I want to. And then I can take the time to write my files really fully and very neatly, instead of dashing them off at heart attack speed so's I can get back out there as quick as possible, like I do just now.

PC, 30, Southern force

My force has to save £50 million over the next four years. There's been a block on recruitment and promotion, enforced retirement of experienced officers and hundreds of civilians, the Serious Organised Crime Unit is being merged with Major Crime, traffic, firearms and dogs are being shared with Thames Valley, we're flogging off 20-odd police stations… Yet by some miracle, all of this won't have any negative impact on the service we provide. I don't understand how they can have the brass neck to say this to people. If we have to share our dogs with TVP, how can we provide the same level of dog cover as before? And the level of dog cover wasn't all that great *before*.

The government go on about back office functions and that, but if we get rid of a hundred civilians, it's not the same as getting rid of the work they do. In most cases, the jobs still have to be done, it's just that they will now be being done by officers, not civilians. And if I'm in an office phoning people to check whether they were happy with the service they got from the police, or at random to see if they're worried about crime in the area, which it pains me to admit we *do* do, I'm not out on the streets actually delivering the service.

I don't understand why the chief doesn't just say, 'We've been given this shit sandwich by the government, we have to eat it, it's bound to have negative effects but we're going to do the best we can.' I think people would appreciate the honesty, both inside and outside of the force. Instead of which, we're all being taken for fools.

PC, 30, Southern force

What we used to call Headquarters, back when we were a police force rather than a laughing stock, we must now call the 'Centre'. The last 12 to 18 months have been a frenzy in the 'Centre', where they are working out what can be cut, and how, and entirely typically for the police they have actually abstracted officers from theoretically frontline duties to form new teams aimed at 'managing the transition to best value while maintaining public confidence'. This team has 16 warranted police officers, including two chief inspectors, an inspector and three sergeants, and they sit around all fucking day talking about 'core competencies' and 'process mapping' and 'pinch points'. They sent us all emails asking us to help decide our own 'core business areas', and talking about 'new paradigms'. I don't even know what the *old* paradigm was. I don't know what a paradigm *is*! You just think, 'Burn that fucking office down and get you oxygen thieves out on the streets, and that would be a start.'

Only in the police. Well, I say that, but my wife's a civil servant and my sister's a nurse, and they have it in spades, too. Somehow, this bureaucratic management bollocks has infested every part of the public sector. I suppose it's because it's a damn sight easier to send an email demanding that someone else arrests 10 burglars this month than it is to actually get off your fat arse and go and take the bastards out yourself. PC Copperfield's woolly mammoths allegory always stuck in my mind. [*In* Wasting Police Time, *PC Copperfield speculates that bureaucrats have existed for aeons, it being easier to sit in a cave and set targets for the hunting of woolly mammoths than actually to be the person going out to hunt them.*]

PC, 30, Northern force

We get endless emails from faceless drones, all earning good money, and on police pensions, and technically being police officers, demanding new and ever newer ideas for how we can cut crime and save money. If you dare to point out that frontline response are already being absolutely hammered, are being run all over town from one job to another without the time to even *think* about what they're doing, to the point where I seriously believe people's life expectancy is being affected, both immediately and in the long term... If you even dare to *hint* that any of this is a problem you are instantly labelled as 'resistant to change', which is the end of your career in the modern police force. You will go no further.

As it happens, I don't want to go any further, so I emailed back, along the lines of, 'With the greatest of respect, shut down 50 percent of HQ, all the change management and diversity units, close down HR – because that job used to be done by supervisors, basically, why do we need a 50-strong Human Resources department headed by some wanker in a suit who earns £100k a year and drives a company BMW? – and put everyone with a badge out on the street.'

Strangely, I got no reply. I think they see me as a dinosaur. I've only got 12 months to go and to be honest I can't wait. I'm going to go fishing and they can all go to hell.

Inspector, 50, Southern force

Recently they announced that senior officers would be holding a series of localised consultation meetings in all the nicks and all officers on duty were warned that they must attend – irrespective of whether they were planning to do some actual police work at the time in question. At no point do they see the irony of arriving in a chauffer-driven unmarked BMW 7 series to ask for ideas on how to cut costs. I suspect this is because they are actually quite fucking thick.

If the chief, who in our force is actually a good bloke, or was when he was a guv'nor 15-odd years ago, actually ever came down to the nick and spoke to the troops informally in the briefing room, we could and would suggest lots of things to him that would make an immense difference. Some would be politically impossible, I'm sure, but there are things which wouldn't be.

It's not like you can't think of some fairly simple ways to cut costs. We have 40-odd forces all using different forms, different stationery suppliers, different IT systems, driving different cars, ordering different uniforms from different clothing manufacturers. You don't need to go to fewer bigger forces to centralise purchasing, surely? If there are 100,000 uniformed cops, that's 100,000 uniforms. That's quite a serious order, surely there's an economy-of-scale argument there. Plus, we could get rid of all the individual wallahs currently responsible for ordering the stuff locally. Are there back-handers being dished out? I'm not saying there are, but it seems odd to me.

Sergeant, 42, Southern force

They set up a team of about 30 people, headed by a superintendent – who, incidentally, only ever walked the street for about six months and has never actually arrested anyone other than by appointment – and containing lots of sick, lame and lazy policemen, to look at 'business areas' where we can work 'faster, smarter, better' and 'deliver more for less'. There was a huge fanfare in the force edition of *Pravda* about it, how they were going to revolutionise the whole place. This seemed to consist of sending out begging emails looking for ideas as to how to cut crime, put more officers on the street, save money and maintain the public confidence targets which the Home Secretary supposedly has scrapped.

This email is just one of a hundred waiting for me when I get back to work after a couple of days off – a blizzard of shite. Have I read this policy? Did I know that business area needed to be kept 'top of mind'? Am I aware that the BCU [*Basic Command Unit – a division of the force*] is slipping behind on street cautions this quarter? Not to mention the in-tray, where some bozo stat-farmer from the Crime Management Unit has waddled down to the report room and left me a passive-aggressive note to say I haven't photocopied the third, entirely irrelevant page of the attached file, and can I please do this as the file is incomplete and the matter can't be resulted until I do so? You've wobbled past half a dozen photocopiers on the way down here, you fat lazy heifer, how about you do it?

PC, 31, Northern force

I am sick to the back teeth with being told we are going to be doing 'more for less'. That's the mantra in our force: the cuts are an 'opportunity'. We're making something like a hundred million pounds-worth of reductions, we're losing a thousand personnel, and yet we should be able to do – not the *same* job but an even *better* one.

My chief inspector was delivering a briefing on this to us, and I put my hand up and said, 'Ma'am, if it's true that we really can do more for less, doesn't that mean that we were wasting money before? Shouldn't the people who were the architects of that waste now be sacked? How can it be that we are trusting the same people who previously provided *less* for *more* to now provide *more* for *less*?'

She wasn't very happy with me for that, but with three years to go I frankly couldn't give a shit. The upper ranks of the modern police are infested with liars, cheats, charlatans, fantasists, creeps, shysters, cowards and bullshitters, and I cannot wait to be shot of them. I'm going to leave and I'm going up to Scotland to run a b&b in the Highlands and I will never think about the police again from that day on. If you'd known me when I joined, when I was a real keeno, completely Job-jammed, you'd be amazed, but this is what they have done to me.

PC, 49, Midlands force

Our force has a change initiative called the Continuous Improvement Programme, which, if you think it has shades of the Marxist permanent revolution you're not wrong. It's essentially an expensive way of rearranging the deckchairs as the ship slips gently beneath the waves. I don't know anyone of inspector rank or below who doesn't think it's a pile of shit, and I don't know anyone above the rank of inspector who isn't a mad-keen evangelist for it, which should tell you something, i.e. the people who actually *do* the policing hate it and the people who only *think* they do policing love it.

For instance, we're now supposed to be very hot on policing by appointment, i.e. if you make a non-emergency call you will be given an appointment that suits you as to when officers will attend to see you. No, no, no. You should be given an appointment to suit *us*, because, with respect, you are not the only fish in the pond and we know what else is going on. And it's often things we shouldn't even be dealing with, anyway.

Like, 'My neighbour's dog is barking loudly and she won't tell it to shut up.' Yep, that's an ASB [*anti-social behaviour*], we'll send someone round. It's not a crime, mind, but we're the police, we do everything.

'There are kids playing in the playground and they're being noisy.' You what? Isn't that what playgrounds are for? But we'll put it on the list and then go over a few days later to reassure the caller – and they won't be in, despite the fact that the appointment was made to suit them.

When in fact what we should be doing is saying to people, 'I'm sorry, we can't come out to that, it's not a police matter.'

HQ are terrified that people might ring the local paper and complain, but to be honest, so what? It's past the days when everyone paid their bit in and was happy to queue. Most of the people who make the most noise about the police don't even *pay* tax. At some historic point in the past, we the police decided that absolutely everything was a matter for us, even when it wasn't a crime or some sort of life-threatening situation.

Police officer, age and rank withheld, Midlands force

We have this new unit, called the 'Change Team', and its specific role is to think up and implement ways in which the force can change for the better.

The kind of change I would like to see is never going to be within their gift. I'd like to scrap half of the forms we fill out in triplicate and longhand every time we make an arrest, but which are wholly repetitive of each other and entirely unrelated to the issue of a suspect's guilt or otherwise. But the Change Team can't wave a magic wand and do that. I'd like to remove the requirement to interview every suspect, which takes hours by the time they've faked a heart attack, said they're suicidal, demanded an interpreter even though they speak perfect English, and sacked their lawyer twice. In Canada, which is a fairly civilised and advanced country, it's a case of, 'Tell your story to the court, mate, and we'll put our side of it.' But the Change Team can't fix that. I'd like to remove the 50 questions I have to ask every detainee which pander to every minor issue and complaint and far extremity of likelihood that the force lawyers can dream up, and just say, 'You're charged with X, you're in a cell till the morning, here's a cup of tea and a religiously non-provocative sarnie and that's you.' But the Change Team can't arrange that, either.

If you did all of that, arresting and processing a burglar would take one hour instead of four, which my rudimentary maths suggests means a PC could deal with four times more burglars than he currently can. But the Change Team are not interested in this. They're interested in meeting up every fortnight to discuss 'issues around proactive policing' and 'managing our core business more efficiently', while they overdose on taxpayer-funded Jaffa Cakes, and spew out tens of thousands of words about 'new policing models' and 'crime management approaches' which will supposedly revolutionise the way we work. It's heart-breaking, it really is.

Sergeant, 34, Midlands force

I'd mind less if all of these units actually made productive and useful suggestions as to how we can improve, and did so in a relatively short space of time. But they never do; they're set up, more people are seconded to them, they meander along creating paper and emails and 'evidencing their effectiveness' and a year later come up with an idea that, if it even makes sense, you or I could have knocked off in the pub on a wet afternoon.

They did a massive consultation exercise in our force called something like 'Listening to You!' which involved asking us at the lowest levels what we thought. I suggested a trial period in which every single warranted officer was put out on the streets and went round nicking criminals. Revolutionary, I know. Every working copper knows slags in their patch who need hammering, but we are so busy chasing our own arses we don't have time. So my thinking was, instead of having 200 of us at it, why not, for one week, have 2,000 of us? Close the offices down just for a few days, I know we could absolutely smash some of the scum on our area and really improve the lives of the law-abiding people.

To my surprise, I got called up to HQ to meet the chief, he said he was very interested in my idea, could really see it had potential, was going to put some of his best men on planning it.

And if you believe *that* you'll believe *anything*. They never even acknowledged the suggestion. You think, 'Why is that?' Too many people with cushy, 9-5, Monday to Friday jobs and car park spaces risk losing all of that if we proved that actually they have no impact on crime and are in fact a drain on resources. If I tell you that the committee they set up was led by the head of Human Resources and the boss of Force Admin, that gives you an idea.

Sergeant, 47, Midlands force

On the very day that they announced we had to make millions of pounds-worth of cuts, our divisional supernintendo took delivery of his brand new BMW 5 series, costing a shade under £50,000. That replaced his previous one, which was nine months old, had absolutely nothing wrong with it and had never been used in the furtherance of policing, in the sense of being used to arrest anyone or in the solving of a crime – it was simply so he could drive to his office and to meetings. So I suppose, given that he is a weapons grade halfwit, the vehicle has, if anything, been used to *impede* policing. Meanwhile, our pandas are fit for the scrapheap, we have a van that needs bump-starting and CID share one vehicle between them. They did build us a new nick costing tens of millions, but on the downside you can't use the radios inside it and it's all open-plan so if you need to meet to discuss a sensitive op you need to do it in the gents'.

Sergeant, 42, Northern force

The force offered redundo, and people were almost killed in the rush, which surprised the senior leadership team but did not surprise anyone who has made even a cursory study of the effect on people of spending your working lives being knifed in the back by people who are constantly patronising or lying to you. As a result of this exodus, we've paid out millions in redundancy and are now advertising to fill some of the posts that have been vacated. It wouldn't surprise me if in many cases they are filled by the same people we have just let go. It's completely farcical. Meanwhile, some of the jobs which were being done by civilians now have to be back-filled by officers. For instance, our contact management centres – which is a poncey name for people who take phone calls from the public – were denuded, and so we had to take police officers from the frontline and redeploy them to offices, where they sit on their backsides and take calls from people who want to complain about the fact that there are no police on the streets!

A police officer is not a like-for-like swap with a civvy – they have important powers and responsibilities on the street, they have training and expertise and they cost about twice as much to employ. We now have them answering non-emergency calls about dog mess on the pavement rather than responding to emergency calls. Only geniuses can do this.

By the way, it's not like we're superhuman and the civvies are all idiots. There are some jobs they can do that we can't. A PC friend of mine was seconded to the control room, for instance, and she basically sat there twiddling her thumbs because she hadn't been trained to use the computers in there.

PC, 36, Midlands force

My dad was an old-school copper, in the days when every job in the nick bar cleaner and canteen lady was done by a serving cop, and he was always dead against the civilianisation of the police. He always said what would happen is that in times of feast we would take on more and more unnecessary 'luxury' work, along with civvies to do it, and that in times of famine the civvies would all be canned and cops would have to do their work. I used to call him a dinosaur, but he was right. I'm not saying all back office jobs are pointless. There were always support roles – someone has to man the front desk, the phone, the radio, and someone has to make the chief inspector's coffee. But in my dad's day there were a lot fewer of those roles and it tended to be that you'd done your 20 years on the frontline and you got to spend the last 10 doing something a bit less confrontational.

Sergeant, 40, Midlands force

They went round handing out A19s to anyone with slightly grey hair, and then they asked the people they had just binned to come back to work for the force for nothing. I think that's a bit much, when the headshed [*a military-derived term for senior officers*] are all raking in thousands of pounds a year in bonuses, and obviously most people's reply was along the lines of, 'You fucking *what?*' But some people went along with it. I know an inspector who got his A19 and came back to work, doing his old job, as a special constable. Not even an inspector-level special! I mean, what an utter cock. He's making it work for them. But then, you do get these people who can't live without the Job. He's obviously got nothing else in his life. Which, if you think about it, they should do a bit of covert work on people to find out who these idiots are and then sack them but cunningly ask them to work for free. They'd probably all do it. That's a brilliant idea, actually. I ought to put it forward, that's the kind of blue sky thinking can get you a couple of pips [*gain promotion to inspector*].

PC, 36, Midlands force

The worst thing that ever happened to us is the politicisation of the police. In some areas of the country we are hated, and I have to say it's our own fault. I joined in 1984, just before the miners' strike, and in some of the pit villages round by us – and Warwickshire was not by any means an NUM hotbed – people still remember bobbies waving wage packets at miners and telling them that Scargill was building them an extension. People have long memories, and the politicisation of the police during that period has hurt us badly. Equally, we spent the New Labour years bending over backwards to go along with whatever new load of rubbish Blair and Blunkett and the rest were pushing our way. In my opinion, that's why the Tories are now screwing us over.

Sergeant, 43, Midlands force

Why did I join the police? That's a good question. I joined because my dad had been a policeman and my older brother was in the Job, and I used to listen to them shooting the breeze and it all sounded interesting and exciting. The question is, why have I stayed? It's not for the job satisfaction any more, because now we're more like clerks or uniformed social workers than anything to do with upholding the law. We get a call, we drive there and spend an hour writing stuff down that people say to us, then we drive back to the nick and spend another hour putting it all into the computer. I do that half a dozen times a day, and then I go home. In terms of actively getting hands on with criminals, or even really investigating crime, those days have pretty much gone. I know people will say, 'But that's rubbish, because the police do arrest people and put them before the courts.' And, obviously, we do. Particularly with serious crime, I still think we're the best in the world. But at my level, it's mostly about handing people fixed penalty notices telling them they've been very naughty and they need to pay £80.

My dad left in about 1985 and my brother got out in the early 2000s, just as the nonsense was really starting to kick off, so I kind of do feel a bit cheated, like they had the best times and for me it's more about my ability to fill in forms than anything else. That said, I still get a lot out of what I do – I enjoy the banter, the feeling of being in a team, I enjoy helping decent members of the public. I don't like the fact that there is basically nothing we can do to criminals unless they have racially abused someone, or committed a murder.

PC, 40, Midlands force

Thousands of police officers are assaulted each year, some very seriously. Official estimates are thought to understate the problem considerably, as officers do not report all incidents.

I was first assaulted five weeks in to my police career. I was off duty, it was at around 11.30pm one night in November, 2001. I had walked my then girlfriend home and I was walking back to my parents' house when I came across a male breaking into a car. Flushed with the new sense of pride in my job, I got hold of the male and informed him that I was placing him under arrest. Being all full of the training school rules regarding 'reasonable and minimal force', I failed to restrain him fully. The male struggled and, using the screwdriver he was using to break into the car, he stabbed me four times – once in the face near my jaw, once in the shoulder and twice in the left side of my torso.

Luckily I was wearing a thick-weave denim jacket, and all but the facial wound failed to penetrate more than a few millimetres. The facial wound only stopped when it hit my jaw bone. I wrestled the male to the ground and had the better of him, but when I saw my blood flowing freely I thought I had been stabbed in my neck, and believed I needed treatment before I bled to death. I let the male go, and he ran off shouting he was going to get a 'shiv' [*street slang for knife*] and stab me up properly.

I ran home and dialled 999, not having a mobile phone in those days. I was treated and gave an accurate description of the offender, who was a well-known heroin-addicted burglar and car thief. He was arrested that night and admitted the offence. The offender was bailed and 10 weeks later I stood in the Crown Court in my best parade-ground number ones, all shiny with razor-sharp creases. The CPS decided to drop the charge of s18 to a s20, as the offender was pleading guilty. This was despite him fully admitting the stabbing. I learned that he had received a suspended sentence three weeks prior to stabbing me for a string of burglaries and car thefts. With the resentencing for the burglaries, car thefts and stabbing me he received two years in prison. He served 12 months. That equates to three months for each time he stuck a piece of metal into my body, not caring if I lived or died. It was a very big slap round the head from reality.

PC, 28, Northern force

We get a call on a fine weekday morning. Mum has called because her 17-year-old son has gone and sold his four-year-old sister's bike and pinched 20 quid from mum's purse the night before. We rock up, knowing said son is on bail for assault police. Mum is crying, sister is happily playing with her toys and asking me about my uniform and what each little bit does. A bright, engaging kid, she was.

Anyway, up the stairs to wake son, let's call him Steve. 'Wake up Steve!' He's not surprised to see us, but he is compliant. Up he gets. We remind him to grab his phone and bus pass for when we know he'll be released later and will need to get home. I've let a bloke have a fag and a cup of tea with his mum before bringing him in. Anything to keep them quiet.

Anyway, Steve suddenly makes a grab for a razor and the window. This is not good. Fight ensues, and after a few minutes he is subdued. I have a fractured arm and a few razor cuts, but our suspect is secure.

A few months later at court, mum is refusing to give evidence as to why we were there, so we can't pass into evidence the fact that *she* called us. His defence is, 'It was like some unknown person was storming my bedroom, so I defended myself.' We lost because we couldn't say, 'Hang on, your mum called us, we woke you up, allowed you a quick wash and morning necessaries and then you bloody attacked us.'

I hate trial by jury; they always believe what they saw on American cop shows.

PC, 35, Southern force

I've been assaulted several times during the course of a 12-year career to date. If you don't count being pushed and spat at, which basically happens all the time, two of those have been potentially very serious.

On one occasion I entered a business premises with a colleague to search them after a report of intruders. I disturbed a male and he attacked me before I had chance to do anything other than shout. Unfortunately, I had got myself into a bad position and he was able to stab me with a knife or a screwdriver in the shoulder… Basically the blade came in from the side under my stab vest and penetrated under the clavicle. I knew straight away that I'd been stabbed because I lost most of the strength in my left arm and let him go. He then made off, and was never caught, unfortunately. I was very lucky that the blade didn't pierce any major blood vessels, but there was quite a lot of blood. At the time, being a bit of a drama queen, I thought it had gone through my jugular vein and that I was going to bleed to death there and then. I was imagining my poor old dad at my funeral, telling everyone who would listen that he'd never wanted his darling daughter to join the police in the first place, and why couldn't

I have been a teacher or a nurse or something. Though, of course, they get assaulted, too. Then my colleague came over and told me it was basically just a flesh wound. He'd been in the Royal Marines, so I assumed he was right.

The other occasion was when I'd been in the Job for about two months. We attended a report of a pub fight. I was with the same colleague, maybe he's my Jonah. This particular pub is at the arse end of a rough estate on our borough, and we're always getting called there. Usually, to be honest, it turns out not to be all that serious, but on this occasion it was like something out of the wild west. There were at least two men unconscious or semi-conscious on the pavement outside, all of the windows had been put through, a mass brawl was clearly ongoing inside the pub and there were people rolling around on the ground outside in a number of smaller fights, and bottles and glasses and chairs flying everywhere.

We radioed for immediate back-up, and got out of the car. I have to admit that I was very frightened. I've heard people saying that adrenalin takes care of fear, but I was so weak at the knees I could hardly stand. You remember all the things the old sweats tell you about taking control of the situation, being authoritative, talking firmly, so I ran over to the nearest two blokes and shouted, 'Please stop fighting!'

I know. Pathetic.

They completely ignored me. I tried to sort of inveigle myself between them, and one of them just punched me straight in the face. It knocked me off my feet onto my backside, and I banged my head quite hard on the road. Another three feet or so back and it would have been a kerb under my neck, which might have been very bad. My colleague immediately leapt on the guy and had him cuffed in about three seconds flat; it helped that he's about 6ft 4in tall and built like a tank, and the male was incoherently pissed. By the time I'd got back to my feet, other units had arrived and the situation was slowly brought under control.

It turned out that the fight had been between two traveller families over an allegation of sexual assault by a young male from one side on a 14-year-old girl from the other side. They'd met at the pub to sort it out, like you do. I had double vision for a week or so, but I always wonder what might have happened if I'd hit the kerb. The guy who assaulted me, it was his word against mine and that of my colleague, but he muddied the water enough that the CPS refused charge in the end. I was livid about that. I said to the CPS lawyer, 'What would you think if every time your wife went to work someone threatened to kick her head in?' but he just said it was different for the police.

Sergeant, 32, Southern force

Before I joined the police, I found the argument that they – we – should be given special treatment ridiculous. To a certain extent, I still do – why does the killer of a policeman do 50 years, and the killer of a bus driver only do 15? But I do think assaulting police officers should attract a greater penalty than the random victim. I'm not trying to come over all SAS about it, but if there's a fight in the high street, *you* can walk away from it, whereas we need to run *towards* it. We joined for that, not a problem, but if you are asking people to put themselves more in harm's way I don't think it's unrealistic that they get some extra protection. Secondly, slightly more esoterically, when I put on my uniform I represent something more than myself. I represent the law, the people at large, the country itself. If you strike me, you strike at the law itself, and that is the thin end of a very big and unpleasant wedge.

I don't think either of those things are particularly hard to understand or even controversial. But far from giving stronger sentences for assaults on police, the reverse often happens. As a uniformed Inspector, and before that, as a Sergeant, and a Fed rep, I've been involved in a large number of cases of assaults on my officers. The general pattern is one of the CPS refusing charge except in the most egregious cases. In the cases where they do charge, they will accept pleas to lesser offences – so the defendant says he won't plead to GBH but he'll plead to ABH, or he won't plead to ABH but he will plead to common assault. Instead of saying, frankly, bollocks to that, we've got the evidence, let's have a trial, they roll over to keep their own stats up. And then, the courts do next to nothing to offenders. I've had a young WPC bitten and scarred – no jail for that. I've had officers hit with iron bars, chains and bottles, and the offender is given anger management and a small fine. I've had an officer stabbed with a syringe where the offender claimed that he had AIDS, which turned out not to be true but was horrible for the officer. No jail for that. It makes me very angry.

Inspector, 44, Southern force

I've been lucky in that in a long career I've never personally been seriously assaulted, but it's happened often to officers I work with. A while ago, two of my female officers very bravely detained a male for street robbery. During the course of the arrest he broke the nose of one and gave the other a split lip. Both had numerous other cuts and bruises and scrapes. He was jailed for a year for the robbery, and got a concurrent two months for the assault police, which was a sick joke on the part of the judge. Maybe I'm getting soft in my old age, but seeing those two brave young lasses, younger than my own daughter, sitting in the nick comparing their bruises and laughing about it, both their shirts covered in blood… It made me immensely proud. This country produces the worst of people and the best of people, and I truly believe we saw both sides in that one incident.

Inspector, 50, Northern force

I was first assaulted as a relatively new officer. My crewmate had nicked a man outside a club, I was watching his back while he carried out the arrest, and all of a sudden this fat girl is running at me. She pushes me full force in the chest, knocking me off balance. My natural reaction was to grab her arms so I didn't fall over, which caused her to start slapping my head.

I was all over the place. She then moved on to throwing haymakers at the side of my head, and connected with my ears a few times. It ended when I bear-hugged her. There was a lot of woman to hug.

Looking back, I would have been quite within my rights to put her down. She's a woman, but a 14-stone woman throwing punches is dangerous. But I felt like I couldn't put her down, or even really defend myself, for three reasons. The first was that she was a woman. The second was my inexperience – I wasn't sure what I could or should do. The third was that there was a bad atmosphere in the town. The nightclub in question was rammed, and there were a lot of people shouting abuse at me. To be honest, I was shit-scared that the lads in the club would kick the crap out of me. I shook her by the shoulders and shouted in her face, and she sort of calmed down eventually. I should probably have nicked her, but I didn't – the crowd was baying for my colleague's blood, custody was full and all that we could have done was street-bailed her or given her an on-the-spot fine. So just pointless, in other words.

Special constable, 35, Northern force

It's not politically correct to say it, but I personally enjoy the physical side of the job. I like the adrenalin rush it gives me. I have never minded a bit of confrontation and I see it as my duty to confront those who want to throw their weight around. That's what the police are for. We have officers who in my opinion should not be wearing the uniform, who are frankly scared of their own shadows. They do not want to get involved, they hang back, they're always on the fringes. Turkish slippers – they always turn up at the end. Then there are others whose hearts are in the right place, but who are about as much use as a chocolate teapot in certain situations. I don't want to be sexist, but a lot of female officers fall into this category, with the best will in the world many of them are utterly useless if the shit hits the fan. There is a role for them, but it's not outside nightclubs at 3am.

Like everyone else, I've been punched, kicked, spat at, I've had a few nights in casualty, but it's nothing I personally can't handle. I've had worse playing rugby, bar the spitting.

What does annoy me is the lack of support from the CPS and the courts. For instance, I had my nose broken while arresting two males fighting outside a club. There were about two hundred people watching, with a lot of them quite 'anti', and four officers trying to arrest about 10 offenders… It could actually have got quite nasty, but the CCTV control room were all over it and we got some back-up before it got out of hand.

I managed to detain my two prisoners until I could get some assistance, at which point one of my colleagues says, 'Have you seen your face?'

I had blood all down my front. My nose was actually straighter than it had been before, but I could feel it had been bust. Later, we had a look at the CCTV and you could quite clearly see one of the males give me a snidey dig while I was attempting to get the other under control.

We had an independent witness, a cab driver, and two of my colleagues had seen it happen. So the detainee was charged with section 47 [*ABH*], section 38 [*assault with intent to resist arrest*] and various public order and affray bits. I was quite pleased with that – the CPS often refuse charge as not in the public interest. I put a lot of time into my statement. I thought, *I'll enjoy my day in court, we can show the video, we can show the custody video as well, where the guy is calling me a wanker and a pussy and chatting about how he hates the police, we're all scum, this and that.*

As it happened, I got a phone call to say I was de-warned [*as a witness for the court case*] because the suspect will be pleading guilty. I was disappointed, but he's pleading so happy days. Except I later found out that the CPS had done a deal with the defence to get it down to common assault and affray. No ABH, no resisting arrest, and certainly no jail, just a £300 fine. The fact that we had good statements from several police officers, independent witnesses, photos of my injuries, clear CCTV... All that doesn't matter, as long as the CPS tick the box in their figures which says 'successful prosecution'. The morality of the situation, that it isn't even serious to break a policeman's nose... Who cares about any of that?

PC, 34, Southern force

I do think some people attract violence more than others. There's a lad on our section who is always being assaulted. Now, to put it in context, he's ex-Royal Marines, he's very fit, he does the krav maga [*Israeli special forces self-defence system*], he can really take care of himself. He's very confident, he has a lot of natural authority. So, some might say he gets into more trouble because he is more lippy with people than is strictly necessary. Others would say it's because he puts himself at the forefront of things. There's probably a bit of truth in both. Most people, myself included, come out of pub brawls shaking and wondering whether they could transfer to the public satisfaction unit or the helicopter unit or something, he comes out grinning, with a black eye and a chipped tooth, going, 'That was fucking great!' I suppose it's horses for courses. I will say, if I found myself down the proverbial dark alley with half a dozen scrotes, he's the bloke I'd want with me. I'm not sure he'd want me, mind you, but there you go.

PC, 29, Welsh force

Officers are assaulted every day in ways which no other section of society is expected to tolerate. When they defend themselves, the outrage is ridiculous. I'll give you a for-instance from our patch, which was the witch-hunt surrounding Toni Comer and Anthony Mulhall.

[In 2006, PC Mulhall arrested a 19-year-old woman called Toni Comer outside a nightclub in Sheffield. Comer had been ejected by door staff; outside the club, she criminally damaged a parked car belonging to one of the bouncers, and officers arrested her. Some months later, CCTV footage showing the arrest was leaked to The Guardian *and shown on the BBC's* Newsnight *programme. In the video, PC Mulhall was shown subduing Comer with repeated blows.]*

The Guardian did this big piece about police brutality headlined, *Four men, five punches and a boot: A 19-year-old woman is arrested.* No bias there, obviously. The general tone was, 'Ooh, we've obtained this footage' – the word 'obtained' suggesting this is something we, the police, were trying to cover up, when actually we didn't even know it existed at the time. 'The video has already caused concern in Sheffield among those who have seen it,' says the piece. Does this mean local people are horrified that a young woman can behave like a sailor on shore leave? No, the thrust is, 'She was only 5ft 4in, a nine-stone girl, what were they doing hitting her?' She was apparently mixed-race, whereas Mulhall was white. I suppose that meant it was racist police brutality, too. Just for balance, they interview a character called Ruggie Johnson, editor of the highly-respected local publication *Wha'a gwan*, who likens what went on to the Rodney King beating in LA. Let's just say someone's losing the plot here.

Then it went on *Newsnight*, as though this was actually an important news story that demanded the attention of journalism's finest minds, where a bunch of people who have *never* had to detain a pissed harridan outside a Sheffield nightclub pull serious faces, stroke their chins and say things like 'this raises lots of troubling issues surrounding policing'. Given that this sort of thing happens *every* Friday and Saturday night in *every* town in the country, the way these fools behave when they get hammered, you might think that was a bit of an over-reaction.

It was in all the papers and all over the internet then, and the general tone was, again, *Bully cop beats up harmless young woman.* Mulhall was withdrawn from duty, a full investigation was launched by the

IPCC and I think she got paid for an interview by someone. I may be wrong about that. She certainly was photographed in a shoulder brace of some kind, talking about how she hoped the officer who 'assaulted' her 'got what he deserved'. *No-one should ever have to go through this*, that sort of thing. To which the answer is, actually, they won't if they don't get so pissed that even a nightclub in Sheffield won't put up with them, and they then go on to damage a car outside in a temper tantrum. But if they do, they'll be coming in whether they like it or not. But I digress.

Then it all goes quiet for a bit, until, lo and behold, the IPCC report comes out and says PC Mulhall did nothing wrong. The CPS aren't interested either, and there's no internal action. Basically, he was whiter-than-white, if I can say that. He was striking her in an approved and trained manner in order that he could get the cuffs on her, because for some mysterious reason she just would not get into the van and come down the nick unaided. Turns out she preferred kicking him, spitting at him and trying to rip his bollocks off. Strangely, she also hadn't made any allegations about the arrest when she got to custody and in fact she didn't complain at all until she saw a copy of the CCTV footage a few months later. Which you also might think is a bit odd.

Of course, all the papers who'd run big pieces about this then ran equally big pieces about how they'd got it all wrong and *Newsnight* invited PC Mulhall on the show to set the record straight. *Not.* In their piece reporting it, *The Guardian* even quoted Comer's solicitor saying that the decision would fuel further public concern about the police's use of force, and that Comer had never had any confidence in the police complaints system. All you can say is it's hard to win with people like that.

The *real* tragedy of this is that Anthony Mulhall died shortly afterwards after taking six packets of sleeping tablets in Snowdonia. His wife told his inquest that he'd been having trouble sleeping and that she'd noticed a change in his behaviour, that he'd become withdrawn. For these journalists I have nothing but contempt. They are making a living out of producing tomorrow's fish-and-chip paper, whereas Anthony Mulhall was a decent, honest man who put his body on the line to make a difference in his community.

Inspector, 49, Northern force

I had the misfortune to star in one of those videos [*showing an arrest in a busy town centre*] that somehow finds its way on to the internet. It was a standard late Saturday night, early Sunday morning. By standard I mean there were about 3,000 pissed people on the streets, of whom 90 percent were good-natured and looking for a cab home, five percent were violent thugs looking for trouble and five percent were looking to see which way the wind blew. As ever, we were way under strength. There was me, a colleague and one special constable. Pretty much everyone else was either back at custody dealing with prisoners or over at [*a neighbouring town*] where there was a major disturbance going on at a Greek restaurant.

There was a time when I really enjoyed these sorts of nights... I liked the adrenalin, I liked the edginess, I enjoyed the feeling that it could go bent at any moment. But that was 15 years ago, when I was younger and there were more of us about, when there were fewer people out who were less drunk and who had more fear of the police, or at least of the law. Nowadays, to tell the truth, I dread it. One day in the near future a police officer is going to be kicked to death in the street in full view of the CCTV and onlookers in a county town just like ours. Nevertheless, I still turn out and I will keep on doing so until they pension me off.

When you are that low in numbers, it's really for me an exercise in 'not noticing' stuff that isn't deadly important. You let things go that you would prefer to intervene in because you have to hold yourself back in case anything serious happens. So you bimble along ignoring and tolerating things and smiling at everyone, all the while hoping it stays just the right side of mental. Some forces hand out lollipops and free flip-flops to try to keep people onside, which is humiliating but probably makes sense.

Unfortunately, a fight broke out outside a kebab house, it turned out that a lad had innocently walked off with someone else's order, and he was laid out right in front of us. I jumped on the puncher while the special ran to assist the unconscious youth and call the ambo and radio in to control to get the CCTV on it, see if there was any chance of any back-up and that. As always, the first thing that happens is a crowd gathers around you. I always think of them as cows chewing the cud, because of the way they stand there in a circle, munching on their burgers, looking vacantly at you like you were something of vague interest. You think, *It would be nice if someone would help!* Then you think, *Actually, no, keep out of it.*

If we lived in a fantasy world, one nearly 40-year-old bobby and a skinny part-timer with specs and borderline asthma would be quickly able to subdue a raging, yelling, spitting, kicking, biting, 14-stone, 20-year-old man with a couple of sarcastic one-liners and have him cuffed and in the back of the van in no time. But the first thing that happens is you fall to the floor and start rolling around in the gutter, which you hope there's no dogshit or vomit in. You both get punched and covered in phlegm. Then your hat falls off and someone nicks it. Then you get the cuffs on one wrist and the other cuff hits you in the eye as the guy flails around. Then a few of the onlookers finish their burgers and wake up a bit, and start yelling at you to leave him alone. One or two of them start getting a bit closer, so you have to try and keep an eye on them as well. Then you CS the guy, but it has no effect on him because it doesn't seem to do anything to people like that but your own eyes start streaming and your nose is dribbling snot. Then you get an elbow in the balls. Then people start shouting, 'Leave him alone, you bastard pigs!', and you'd like to point to the guy he's just knocked sparko and explain that that's why he needs to be arrested but you can't see the other lad or your colleague because of the crowd, plus you have a feeling they wouldn't be interested anyway. Then you finally get the guy onto his front with his arms behind his back, and he just will not stop banging his head back upwards at you, even if it means he's banging his own face on the road on the down-stroke, and you can't get his wrists together for the cuffs, so you start striking his upper arm to get him to comply, as you are perfectly entitled to do, and about five people whip out their phones and start filming you. And a week later, a 10-second clip from the video's on the internet and there are 1,000 comments from people who were not there calling you a fascist bully and a pig, and absolutely no mention of the fact that the guy was a) responsible for a nasty assault, b) that you tried to arrest him without violence and that the violence was almost all coming your way, and c) that there *was* vomit in the gutter which got in your hair and all up your back but which you ignored because it is your job to keep the public safe from people who smash other people in the face outside takeaways because they accidentally picked up the wrong kebab.

PC, 37, Southern force

Dr Johnson once said that you don't have to be a carpenter to criticise a table, and he was right. But you *do* have to understand what the basic function of table is, to know what job it's designed to do, for your criticism to be taken seriously. If you want to write an article in the paper that criticises the police for being violent thugs, or judge us in court for using violence during an arrest, or write a TV drama about policing for the BBC, that's fine, but first you should try spending a few weekends of Friday and Saturday nights in Grimsby town centre, and stand with us and deal with people as they come out of the pubs and clubs looking for trouble. If you've walked in my shoes, and rolled around in the same gutters, then you have earned the right to an opinion on how I do my job. You can do this – most forces will allow you to accompany officers. It ought to be mandatory for newspaper columnists.

PC, 36, Northern force

We're expected to deal with violent people with intricate ju jitsu moves and deft flicks of the wrist which frankly work about as well as a bus timetable, and when that doesn't work and it takes a bit more, all of a sudden, all policemen are violent thugs. It's right at that point that I remember the line from *A Few Good Men*, when Jack Nicholson says, 'You can't handle the truth… You don't want the truth. Because deep down, in places you don't talk about at parties, you want me on that wall. You need me on that wall… blah blah… I have neither the time nor the inclination to explain myself to a man who rises and sleeps under the blanket of the very freedom I provide, then questions the manner in which I provide it!' Pure class.

Sergeant, 40, Southern force

They were dishing out the new jobs, which they do from time to time, and I asked to be PBO [*principal beat officer*] in the hardest area on the patch. People were like, what the hell do you want to do that for? But my feeling was, I want to work the hardest area. It will be the most interesting. Plus, I didn't like the idea of no-go areas. Law-abiding people have to live there – are we saying the police won't even venture out there?

My sergeant didn't want me going into this estate on my own at night, but in the end we reached a compromise where I would park the car and then patrol around it, basically. I'd never be too far from the car.

And I really enjoyed it. Most of the people were absolutely fine. I mean, they were rough-and-ready, but they were basically decent, and I built up some great relationships. As with anything, one family can ruin a street. They're shits, and they bring their shit friends with them, and it ruins it for everyone else.

Sergeant, 43, Midlands force

Many police now believe that they should be armed – if not with firearms, then certainly with TASER.

I think the time has come for us to be routinely armed, preferably with a sidearm, but certainly with TASER. I am personally fed up with me or my team being sent to deal with a bloke going mad in the street with a samurai sword, and all we've got is a little stick and a tin of Sure for Men. If you raise this with senior officers, they will say, 'We've got ARVs [*Armed Response Vehicles*] and AFOs [*Authorised Firearms Officers*] so this is not an issue, but the fact is that in my force the ARV can easily be an hour away. That is not much good to me, is it?

Sergeant, 40, Northern force

I used to be anti-arming, but things have changed in the decade and a bit since I started in the Job. It wasn't *Dixon of Dock Green* then, but it was less scary than it is now – and don't forget, Dixon was murdered in the end. Hard to put your finger on what it is. We've had a lot of people coming in from places like Poland and Albania, or further afield like Somalia and Iraq. These are people who we don't have the first idea about, we have no antecedents. They are often used to handling firearms, the kinds of sentences and the jails they face here are a walk in the park compared to back home. There's also our own home-grown gangsta wannabes. Now, to me, the arguments against routine arming no longer hold any water.

'The criminals will only arm themselves.' They already *are* armed. I think what you would find is that *fewer* criminals would arm themselves. When they're the only ones with a gun, they're the boss. Facing officers with better training, weapons, ammunition and tactics, they are risking going home in a box, and most criminals are huge bullshitters and cowards.

'Ordinary police officers couldn't be trusted with weapons.' Ordinary squaddies seem to do OK. It's about training.

'It would cost too much.' A Glock costs about £200. My force has just spent £100,000 on artwork for the force HQ. The money is there if they want it.

'Look at de Menezes – loads more innocent people will be shot.' Any innocent person being shot is a tragedy. Yes, police will make mistakes. But the question is, how many seriously injured police officers, even dead ones, do we have to take?

'The public will not put up with the sight of armed police on our streets.' That must be why no-one from Britain ever goes on holiday to France, America, Spain, Portugal, Italy, Canada, Australia, and why they all come back shaking in fear at the sight of all those armed cops. Never mind the fact that when they fly out of Heathrow, the cops are armed there.

'I'm a police officer and I wouldn't want to be armed.' My answer to this is, OK, make it voluntary. You don't have to be armed, but I want to be.

Sergeant, 44, Northern force

People go on about Jean Charles de Menezes as though it was the clinching argument against routine arming. That was a terrible tragedy, but the fact that no officer was prosecuted over it, I suggest, shows that it was an awful mistake, by people acting in a heightened atmosphere engendered by the deaths of 50 people on the Tube a couple of weeks before. To my mind, those officers were heroes. How would you like to run onto a Tube train in pursuit of a man you honestly believed was about to detonate a suicide vest? How would you like to be on a Tube train when a bomb goes off, where the guy *could* have been shot but wasn't because of the potential fall-out?

Plus, the obvious answer is the dozen people who were murdered by Derrick Bird in Cumbria. Unarmed police officers came across him after he'd shot the first three or four of his victims, but they could do nothing about it. Had they been armed, a large number of people who are now dead or suffering from injuries they received at Bird's hands would now be alive. You can name three or four people accidentally or wrongly shot dead by police ever – Bird killed a dozen in two hours. Purely as a numbers argument, there's no contest.

Inspector, 42, Northern force

I have read surveys which say the majority of police officers don't want to be armed, but then these surveys include all the desk wallahs whose biggest risk is a paper cut. If you only asked response officers, who are actually being sent to deal with armed and dangerous psychopaths day in, day out, you would get a different answer. I'm not saying everyone wants guns, I know colleagues who don't. But it should be an option.

I don't understand why they don't give us TASER, at least. It's a less harmful detention option than any of the others. If I spray you, it's going to make you feel pretty shit. If I hit you with my baton, bearing in mind I am only going to do that if I am in fear for my own safety, I am going to give it all I've got and you're going to be at least bruised and in pain for some time afterwards. You may well have broken bones. With TASER, it hurts like buggery for a second but then it's gone.

There's supposedly 'a perception issue', but to be honest the time when I cared about perceptions has long gone. I want to be safe at work. And if the MPs and the Chiefs don't agree with arming, how come everywhere they go they have armed officers with them? If my Chief Constable had to come out with us every Friday night, we'd all have TASER on Monday morning. I know my force has bought enough of them for all of us, but they're locked away in a cupboard at HQ somewhere. Currently, we're not even bringing a knife to a gunfight, we're bringing a stick.

Sergeant, 43, Midlands force

TASER effects remarkable changes in behaviour. It has to be seen to be believed. People who are foaming at the mouth and threatening to kill the first copper that comes near them with the sword they're swinging round their heads almost always become instantly compliant as soon as the red dot appears. If they don't become compliant, they are TASERed, and that's game over, every time. CS and even Captor [*spray*], some people it doesn't seem to affect, our batons are flimsy little things, you could subdue my mum with one but the people you need it to work on are often drunk, aggressive males who don't always feel it the same way. Not to mention that to use a baton you have to get within arms' length of people you would prefer not to be that close to. I love TASER, absolutely love it.

PC, 34, Southern force

The Job is definitely more dangerous now than it was. When I joined in the late 1980s, you hardly ever fought. Now you'll get involved in a proper fight every week, or certainly a couple of times a month. People have no respect for or fear of the police any more. That said, I've only used my baton in anger twice. I have used it a third time, messing around with it in the nick and I caught myself with the damn thing. It comes pretty sharp, I can tell you.

The first time I used it on someone, it worked straight away. The second time, it did nothing at all. We CS-d and batoned a guy and he just kept going. It was a call to the high street where a kid of about 19 had gone mad with a couple of knives. What it was, he was slightly educationally sub-normal, and he was always being teased by the local scum. Eventually, he decided he'd had enough of this and he armed himself with two carving knives – I'm talking foot-long, razor sharp knives – and was standing in the street threatening people. We arrived and, as I say, CS-d him to no effect. We batoned him to no effect. Eventually, we managed to get close enough to him to grab him and take him to the floor. I was rolling around with him, and he was trying to stab me in the head with one of these knives… I could see the damned thing inches away while my mate was trying to get control of the arm.

151

It seemed to take ages, but in the end we did subdue him. I had realised that he was a bit disabled, so once we'd got the knives off him, I just lay there with him in my arms going, 'It's alright mate, you're OK now.' Just trying to calm him down. As we lay there, this bloke pushed his way over. I thought it was one of the scumbags who'd caused the whole thing, but it turned out it was the lad's dad. He had seen us hitting his son, but he understood why and he was very emotional and grateful that once we'd got the thing under control we were immediately concerned for the lad's welfare. I felt quite proud of the way we handled that.

Sergeant, 43, Midlands force

[*After Osama Bin Laden was shot, the then Metropolitan Police Commissioner Sir Paul*] Stephenson came on the telly warning that there would probably be reprisals, that the threat level was severe, yadda yadda yadda. My wife said to me, 'How serious is this, then?' She thinks just because I'm in the police I know stuff.

I said, 'As far as I know, very serious.'

She said, 'What's the worst that could happen?'

I said, 'Oooh... A nuclear bomb, probably followed by nuclear dirty bomb or chemical or biological attack, probably followed by a Mumbai-type of thing.'

She said, 'What's most likely?'

I said, 'I work for [the police], not MI5, love. But probably Mumbai.'

So she said, 'How serious would that be, then?'

I said, 'Well, we've all been trained to deal with gunmen going berserk in Bluewater [*shopping centre*], does that reassure you?'

She said, 'Not really.'

The truth is, the training I've had consists of an NCALT [*National Centre for Applied Learning Technologies**] online e-learning package from the NPIA [*National Police Improvements Agency*] which boils down to, if you see a group of heavily-armed men discharging automatic weapons in the high street, run away, get behind something solid and call in. Then wait for firearms, who as far as I can see could be quite some time away, who may find it quite hard to locate a mobile group of blokes and who may well be outgunned when they do. The MP5

[*Heckler and Koch sub-machine gun used by the police and some Army units*] is a Gucci [*high-quality*] weapon but it's not an AK47 [*which fires a heavier, more destructive round and has a far greater range*].

I'm actually quite angry about it. As I see it, there either will or will not be an attack like Mumbai in the UK.

If Stephenson [*since replaced by Bernard Hogan-Howe*] doesn't really have any intelligence about such an attack, in my opinion he should stop worrying the public, and me, about it.

But I assume he *does* have intelligence, because he must be a reasonably serious man, albeit a slightly orange-coloured one, in which case he should *do* something about it, other than just repeatedly announcing that the threat level is severe. Getting plods like me to look at some fairly unhelpful computer slides and stand around in yellow jackets at train stations to 'reassure the public' does not, in my view, constitute 'doing something about it'. It doesn't even reassure the public, if they're half-way clued-up.

What we need, if this threat *is* serious, is a hugely greater number of armed officers on the streets and in position to respond. I understand that this changes the good old British bobby forever, and that most people and even a lot of police don't want us all armed, blah blah blah. But the world of the good old British bobby is long gone, folks. Wake up and smell the coffee! Derrick Bird was one fat old bloke with a shotgun and a .22. Imagine a team of young guys with some military training and assault rifles, who are on effectively a suicide mission. Hundreds could die in London. *Thousands*, maybe.

I'm talking half the force, armed, full-time. Because if this sort of thing *does* happen perhaps the only chance we'll have of averting an absolute bloodbath is if the shooters are taken out almost immediately, and that will only happen if there are armed cops nearby. I don't personally feel that we should put the lives of hundreds of people down to the luck that one Trojan unit [*in the Metropolitan Police, the radio call sign for armed response vehicles is 'Trojan'*] happens to be nearby and is actually on the ball rather than polishing their weapons and scoping the birds from behind their Oakleys.

PC, 39, Southern force
NCALT was set up to 'assist the 43 Home Office police forces in England and Wales and the wider policing community in adopting new learning technologies'.

The NPIA 'was formed in April 2007 to make a unique contribution to improving public safety'. Some police officers are believed to think that the money spent on these projects would be better used on frontline policing. Both organisations have websites which are warmly recommended to keen jargon-spotters and students of wasted expenditure.

I'd like to be armed, but I wouldn't fancy the scrutiny that would come with it. I have no problem with the police being scrutinised, but I do have a problem with uninformed comment, speculation and stupidity. We are held to impossible standards, and that would only increase if we were all tooled up.

Raoul Moat goes bananas up north, the papers and Kay Burley on Sky News wants him caught *immediately*, and everywhere the bobbies go they're followed by camera crews and reporters basically broadcasting to the world, which at that stage still included Raoul Moat, current operational information. And when, despite this, he gets caught and he's kneeling in the field with the shotgun to his head, they're like, 'Why can't a marksman shoot the gun out of his hand?'

Which you can sort of understand, because that's what Bruce Willis would have done. When the guy tops himself, that's our fault, too. Why don't we use our special secret powers to get this homicidal, suicidal, steroid-chewing, cop-hating maniac, who hasn't slept for days and knows he's looking at spending the rest of his worthless life in jail, to change the habits of his entire lifetime and do the right thing? Because surely we must *have* a box of powers like that somewhere? I've seen Kiefer Sutherland in *24* and he'd have sorted this out in a jiffy.

Sergeant, 32, Southern force

I've had people say to me, 'Raoul Moat's a hero, he's a legend. He should have shot more of you. One blind copper's not enough.' [*Early in his rampage, Moat shot a defenceless PC, David Rathband, in the face, blinding him.*] This is the kind of thing we get. I point out that the first two people he shot were a woman who he'd clearly been unable to satisfy, one way or the other, and the innocent bloke who *was* able to do that. Dave Rathband he basically ambushed. Then he went on the run until we found him and when we did the coward shot himself rather than take us on. So if a sexually inadequate, woman-beating, steroid-munching, educationally-subnormal coward is your hero, your role model, you go ahead and knock yourself out.

PC, 36, Northern force

As ever, we're damned if we do and damned if we don't. A classic case of this is the barrister in London who was shot after repeatedly firing his 12 bore into the street in Chelsea. Imagine you're the officer with him in your sights. If you shoot him, you're a killer, all over the papers, there's a massive IPCC enquiry, the family are giving press conferences demanding heads on plates and answers as to why the evil police slaughtered their completely sane and reasonable son in cold blood. (Answer: he was firing a shotgun into a London street.)

Or, imagine you *don't* shoot him and instead *he* manages to shoot someone. Now you're incompetent, all over the papers, there's a massive IPCC enquiry, the victim's family are giving press conferences demanding heads on plates and answers as to why the stupid police didn't shoot the lunatic when they had the chance. (Answer: because last time we shot anyone they made the officer's life hell, so I'm paralysed by indecision and actually, fuck it, here's my weapon, I'm going back to neighbourhood.)

Speaking as a firearms-trained officer myself, I would say that the officer who fired that shot will have suffered unbelievably, but no-one seems too bothered about that.

PC, 38, Southern force

An ongoing concern for officers of all ranks is bureaucracy.

Since time immemorial, cops have been producing prosecution files on paper. Many years ago, prosecution files were standardised across the country into the MG [*Manual of Guidance*] form series. Pick an MG1, an MG2, and MG3 *et cetera et cetera* as needed, up to MG20, and fill them in. For a murder or serious crime matter, the file would be massive. For a minor summons offence – say no insurance, or urinating in a public place – the file would be a statement off the officer, a front sheet detailing offender details, offence details and witness details, along with a couple of other ancillary sheets of paper.

Summons files could be batted out in 10 minutes parked up in a panda on nights when things quietened off. Not that long ago, my force bought a computer-based file preparation system – I shan't reveal its name, for obvious reasons. The new computer system holds the MG forms and they can be filled in on screen. It sounded like progress, but there was a catch. You could only do electronic files after you had done the two-day training course. So that's two days' training, to do a task that you can already do on paper. I consider myself a reasonably educated man. I can buy house insurance and car insurance online, I book holidays, do internet banking and deal in shares online. I have never had to have a two-day training course for any of these things. Even a spread betting site only involved a 20-minute phone tutorial.

Our case file system, however, needed two days to explain the intricacies and convoluted paths that had been built into it. On one screen, unhelpful boxes pop up to explain a tick box, whilst carefully hiding the same tick box so you can't tick it. On another, when completing your own statement you have to create yourself on the 'witness tree', and, on opening your statement to type it, the first box to complete is your own name. So although the computer knows you, and you have created yourself on the 'tree', you have to tell the computer your name again. On statement screens, when statements are typed into the system it demands a date and time of creation. I'm no computer wizard, but even I know that they have a built-in clock.

Even more annoying, the system does not remember witnesses or phone numbers. Many witnesses are 'repeat witnesses', such as store detectives, cops, fraud investigators and the like. When I go to the pain of putting my office and mobile number against my name and print off the MG9 [*a list of witnesses, addresses and phone numbers*] – yes, you guessed it – no phone numbers next to me, and the system rather impersonally just prints off my surname rather than first name as well. Let's just hope there aren't too many jobs featuring officers with the same surname as witnesses.

And, finally, the biggest joke is that the CPS *still* want signed original copies of the file. They are lawyers, after all. So after the file has been completed electronically, we print it off and send it away to the CPS through the internal post. You would have to be some sort of genius to come up with a better way of wasting police time.

PC, 42, Northern force

After more than 20 years in the police, I no longer regard myself as a copper. What would you call a cross between a clerk, a playground monitor and a taxi driver? After I left the Army I was scratching around for something to do. I dabbled with a few things and nothing really appealed. When I joined the police it was like a revelation. OK, there was always bullshit to work on, but basically when I joined it was all about nicking thieves and burglars, breaking up fights, patrolling. Proper police work.

Now, everything I do is geared towards keeping the bean counters at Force HQ and the Home Office happy. We don't give a toss about decent, taxpaying victims any more. We haven't got time for them. Now, I'm ashamed to wear the uniform. I basically hate what I have become. People may say, 'If that's the case, why don't you jack it in?' I'm 48 years old, we're in the middle of the biggest economic mess in decades and I have a mortgage and two kids just finishing school. I *could* quit and go on the dole, but that wouldn't help.

I remember when I joined in 1990, I used to listen to the old sweats swinging the lamp about how things had been loads better in their day. If I heard 'the Job's fucked' once, I heard it a thousand times. I used to think, 'I'll never be like that.' But the truth is, things *were* better in their day. They were better in *my* day! Most weeks, I see injustices carried out or I come across orders from management or new policies which are utterly political in origin and which will, at best, have no positive impact on crime and criminals. I ought to say something, but I daren't, basically. There's no room for dissent in the police. You get labelled, sidelined, they find ways to get you out. So I count the days to the pension and keep my head down.

PC, 48, Eastern force

We've had people burgled, and the details have been taken over the phone. We're supposed to send SOCO [*Scenes of Crime Officers – usually civilians, who gather forensic evidence at the scene of a crime. Known in some forces as Forensic Scene Investigators, Crime Scene Investigators or Crime Scene Examiners*] but we don't. We might go round three days later, but it's really just to drop off a leaflet. Meanwhile, a call will come in that a couple in their 30s are having a Barney at home, and just because it's classed on the computer as DV [*domestic violence*] we have to get round there on blues and twos, be there within 10 minutes, make sure the Duty Inspector has been notified, spend forever there and probably nick the bloke, knowing full well it will go nowhere because she will refuse to assist. Yes, eventually, one in a million of these ends up in murder, but how many other serious offences don't get dealt with properly in the meantime because we're too busy trying to sort out people's lives?

A row in the street where one man calls the other something rude and the other thinks it's racist… Irrespective of whether it objectively is, this will be recorded as being racially-motivated and immediate-graded, which means we have to get there at the speed of light.

This stuff doesn't really benefit anyone, except the people with the flip charts and the spreadsheets compiling their figures so that they can say at the end of the year, 'We had *x* many racially-motivated or DV incidents on our force area, we arrived at *y* percent of them within the approved time and detected *z* percent.'

In the same year, an old lady who got burgled died, probably the shock of the break-in didn't help, but no-one's counting that. Everyone knows it's bollocks, but we still do it. It gets to the point where you think, *Hang about, we're police officers, grown men and women sworn to uphold the law. Why don't we all get together and tell the senior management to stick their performance targets up their fat arses?* But we never will.

Sergeant, 34, Southern force

[*Officer shown* Daily Telegraph *clipping headlined, 'Police fail to investigate one third of crimes'*]

This is a common complaint – '*What a scandal it is that the police don't investigate every single crime reported to them.*'

I'd like to ask the reporters, how come you don't put *every* piece of news in your newspaper? '*The Daily Telegraph admits it only reported 0.0001 percent of things that happened in Britain yesterday.*'

Answer: because you have limited time, limited resources, even limited actual, physical paper. If you had a million reporters and a million pages, you *still* couldn't report on everything that happens every day in a country of 60 or 70 million people, could you? It would be impossible. So you allocate your resources as best you see fit.

I appreciate there is a difference between the police and the *Daily Telegraph*, in that we are paid by the public purse. I don't have to buy the *Telegraph* but I can't choose whether or not to pay for the police. Ironically, the only people who *can* choose not to pay for the police are prisoners, mad people and people on benefits, and about seventy percent of our time is taken up on policing the squabbles of the benefits classes, and another five percent is probably dealing with mad people because other agencies can't be bothered.

But even though we have a duty to respond to calls from the public, we don't have a duty to respond to *every* call. It would be impossible. So while it sounds bad if you say, in stark terms, the police ignore a third of all calls about crime, what you have to think is, *What are these calls?* No doubt on paper, some of them will be quite serious offences, and the failure to respond will be down to a failing by someone, somewhere, because we're only human, and we should have responded. But in lots and lots of cases, we have to make judgments. Do we go to the street robbery just reported, or some crime which will be, in practical terms, insoluble?

'We've just come back off holiday and someone has kicked a hole in our fence. The neighbours say it happened overnight a week last Wednesday and no-one saw them do it.'

OK, I suppose in theory we could send a team down to do house-to-house enquiries – maybe the neighbours are lying, maybe they're mistaken. We could maybe do footwear analysis on the fence. We could hold a press conference, put up posters, put up a reward. I suppose we could seize CCTV from the shopping parade down the bottom of the road to see who was in the area. But seriously? For a murder or a rape, yes. For a fence? Because while we're doing all of this, unless we increase the size of the police service dramatically, we are not able to go to the street robbery, or other serious jobs where there's a realistic chance of catching someone.

'My brother swore at me.'

'I can't find my phone and I'm sure it was stolen.'

'Someone pinched my bike from round the back of the house.'

All unpleasant, no doubt, and all potentially crimes – assuming the phone wasn't lost. But is there any hope whatsoever of convicting the brother for swearing at his sister? Is that a matter for the police?

And how much does a chain and a padlock for a bike cost? I'm not condoning bike theft – we *do* care about people pinching bikes, if we see them at it we'll nick them, if we recover bikes from houses... Christ, we must have 30 recovered bikes in our yard at work, come and have a look if yours is among them. But there are limits to what we can and should be expected to do.

Where we go wrong is in not treating people like adults. We slavishly record every call that comes in, record as crimes things which are questionable at best, and allow ourselves to be judged against this mountain of figures and stats. Look at the quote from the Met in that *Telegraph* piece: 'A Scotland Yard spokesman said it was the Met's policy to ensure that a "thorough primary investigation" is conducted into all crimes.' 'No crime goes uninvestigated,' says Staffordshire police. Instead of, 'We don't have the time or personnel, sorry. Some of it's very minor, and some of it we have foolishly recorded as a crime when it probably wasn't even a crime, so people can get a crime number and will go away.'

We should be saying to victims, 'No, it doesn't sound very nice that your brother called you a whore, but there are limits to what we can do, and you should steer clear of him, or just accept a few insults as part of life. Lock your bike up. Keep your phone safe.'

The other problem is, we promise the earth. *Working Together to Smash Crime in* x *Town! Detection rates up! Public confidence up!* I'd sign up for a slogan that just said, 'Doing the best we can with limited resources, crap kit and enormous bureaucratic interference to police a country where 50 percent of adults behave like children.'

Inspector, 42, Southern force

Of course we have to screen things out and NFA them. It would be ludicrous if we didn't. It's happened to my own family – my daughter had her phone nicked from her bag at college. We get called by someone from Crime Management... 'Sorry, there's no CCTV and no lines of enquiry, so we'll give you a crime number but there's nothing we can do.'

OK, fair enough, I understand that. But what they then do, which annoys me, is follow that up with, 'But are you absolutely *sure* the phone was stolen, and that it wasn't just mislaid?'

Which lays the whole game wide open − it's all about stats. We don't want crimes reported which we can't solve, because those are unsolved crimes on our figures and we look bad. Screw the public, the chief needs his bonus.

PC, 40, Eastern force

I wouldn't believe the crime figures for a moment. We are world-class at cooking the books. This is the problem with having everything driven by stats, when most of your focus is on the press release you're putting out at the end of the year claiming crime is down on your division or force area by eight percent. Too many shed breaks? Record them as damage due to wildlife. Too many burglaries? Record them as criminal damage. Nothing was taken − it was just a broken window, sir. Yes, still a crime, but much less serious and it's nice to be able to say you've slashed burglaries. If you can get away with it, say it was broken by a pebble thrown up by a passing car, then it's not a crime at all. Attempted theft of motor vehicle? No, that's a criminal damage, too. Someone runs down the street slashing a dozen tyres… That's one ongoing and continuing offence, not 12. But if an arrest is made, all of a sudden that *is* recorded as a dozen separate and detected crimes. Instead of one outstanding criminal damage, 12 detected ones, and that means the Superintendent is getting his five grand bonus this year.

Sergeant, 39, Southern force

TICs are the most obvious one. [*A 'TIC' is where a defendant asks the court to 'take into consideration' other offences for which he or she has not been charged when sentencing for the offence in hand; these other offences are officially recorded as detected crimes.*] In principle, they're not a bad idea − if we have someone in for burglary and he wants to admit to a couple of dozen other housebreaks then why wouldn't we want him to? It means we don't have to spend forever investigating the outstanding offences, potentially have several different trials, so we save time and money there, the homeowners get some measure of relief in that they find out the offender isn't someone known to them, or someone with a personal grudge, he's just random slag, and so on.

So the TIC system is a valuable tool. But the problem is, it's an easy hit. I'm not saying people are induced to take on TICs they haven't done, I have no knowledge of that. But chummy gets to spend the day driving round the estates pointing at houses he says he broke into, with the assistance of a couple of 'tecs to jog his memory and buy him burgers and fags. The court doesn't add anything on for these extra offences and may even reduce his sentence for his 'co-operation', so he doesn't care. We get to tick lots of boxes saying we've cleared up various crimes that were otherwise going nowhere. I can't say that chummy didn't *actually* carry out those burglaries, because only he *really* knows, but let's just say it isn't impossible that one or two of those TICs are being taken on for someone else.

I don't say for a moment that we should do away with the TIC system, I just think that if we're having stats then there should be some way of weighting detections to show what was properly detected and what wasn't. I would also weight the offences themselves.

Inspector, 42, Southern force

The most important of Peel's principles is that it is the basic job of the police to prevent crime and disorder, not to detect it. But if I stop a burglary from happening, how do you measure that? If I can catch a burglar after he's stolen your family silver and ruined your lives, I can tick a box. Senior officer are absolutely cynical about this. They couldn't care less about you or your burglary. Without burglaries, there are no detections, and without detections there are no headlines, no press releases, no promotions and no bonuses.

Sergeant, 40, Eastern force

In my force, it used to be that I could give you formal words of advice and write off a minor matter in that way. Now I have to formalise this as a 'discretionary disposal', which is written down and entered onto the police national computer and counted as a detection to make up for all the crimes we can't detect. What's worse, inspectors are bullied to make sure their teams are harvesting these bullshit clearances, so skippers bully the troops to make sure they hit a monthly target. I'm supposed to produce three of these per month. Targets that the government says have been abolished. If you try to complain about it, you are threatened and denigrated and you could have your career destroyed. Forget institutionalised racism, the police service is in this sense institutionally corrupt. It saddens me to say this, but I believe it to be the case.

PC, 36, Midlands force

I was directed to a street where there were youths collecting money for Help for Heroes. A householder was suspicious because they weren't carrying any ID and didn't appear to know that the British Army was fighting in Afghanistan. They admitted what they were up to, so we took them down the nick where they were reprimanded, which is like a caution for kids. They had only managed to accrue around £6, and could say where it had been obtained from, so the money was returned to the few people who had been taken in. On my way to take it, my inspector said to me, 'Knock on a few doors and find out who else they tried?'

Basically, he wanted me to get statements from every house in the street that they had tried so that we could add in lots of attempted frauds. Victimless crimes, no punishment for the offenders, but good for the figures, you see. Never mind that it would take me off the books for the rest of the day. I was surprised he didn't ask me to do the whole area.

PC, 28, Southern force

You get sent harrying emails if you miss the target time for getting to a call by as little as a minute. No recognition of the fact that we are grossly understaffed, or that we are all run ragged doing stuff that the public would not even recognise as policing. One that really grips my shit is cell watches – we have fully-trained police officers sitting outside cells because the people they've arrested want to strip naked and bang their head against the wall. In my view, you want to bang your head on a wall, be my guest, maybe you'll knock some sense into yourself while you're at it. But we can't have that because if one of these idiots actually hurts themselves, it will be down to the brutal police, not the fully-grown adult themselves, and *The Guardian* and the IPCC will never let us forget it. Fair enough, but this is why we can't get to I-graded [*immediate-graded*] calls within the target time and, more importantly, why the homeowner has to wait for 24 hours for a visit after a burglary – a burglary, ironically, carried out by the *compadres* of the idiot hurling himself against the walls back at the custody block.

PC, 32, Southern force

We should be big enough and ugly enough to say to the media and the politicians, we can't solve everything, all the ills of society, sorry, we're doing our best but if you want us to do more we need to cut *x* and *y* from the load of non-police crap that we have to do instead of catching criminals, or you have to double our budget so we can employ more cops, rather than A19-ing them. It's really as simple as that.

But if we really must measure everything, why can't we have a points-based system? If a detective arrests a businessman for a complex fraud that has taken a team of six detectives a year to crack, that's one detection. Assuming one offence, but let's not get too complicated. If I arrest Wayne for a simple fraud, such as claiming he cleaned the windows in a street when he didn't, that's also one detection. Though, again without getting too complicated, my guv'nor would actually turn this into 40 detections by ordering us to knock on every door in the street so we could get all the attempts, too.

The black and white numbers on a sheet don't reflect in any way the differences in the difficulty and complexity involved in these two cases. So it's not all that surprising if we put more effort into detecting the easier stuff. Picking the low hanging fruit. It works even more the other way. If you are the victim of a simple window cleaner attempt fraud, and we can't find the guy, that's one undetected crime. If you are a widow who is conned out of her life savings by some thieving scum, and we can't find the scum, that is also one undetected crime. But which should we give more weight to? Sometimes I think we put more ingenuity and effort into obtaining frivolous detections or even cuffing [*writing off*] crime than we ever do in dealing with the stuff people really worry about.

PC, 39, Eastern force

I blame the gaffers but I also blame the government, specifically whoever it was who introduced NCRS [*National Crime Recording Standard*] and the HOCR [*Home Office Counting Rules*]. The idea behind these [*to standardise methods of recording and counting crime across the police forces in England and Wales*] sounds like it makes sense, but these people are maniacs. They don't know where to stop. I defy you to read and understand as a layman the HOCR. It runs to hundreds of pages. 'Offences of theft from an aircraft to be recorded as class 49/10 – and General Rule J applies.' 'A theft or unauthorised taking of a vehicle must be recorded as AVT if, at that time, one or more of four circumstances that determine AVT under the Theft Act 1968 Sec 12A applies.'

You can shrug your shoulders and say, 'So what?', but basically some well-paid people have sat down and spent a very long time designing all of this, with steering groups and meetings upon meetings, probably with very nice lunches at nice hotels and conference centres, and drawing up all the flow charts and thinking of every possible kind of robbery and fraud you can get, and then police officers have to be trained on it, which takes a long time and costs more money, and then there has to be constant reference to it, and then we employ internal auditors to scrutinise and re-scrutinise every piece of paperwork for compliance and to send endless hectoring emails to police officers because they haven't entered the right code in the box in the corner of page 30 of some file, and then we're further endlessly audited externally on it to ensure compliance. All, basically, so that we can be sure that Merseyside Police and Sussex Police are writing down their offences in the same way as each other. Not a bad aim, maybe, but it should be massively secondary to the primary purpose of the police, which is stopping crime and nabbing criminals. If we've got that covered and squared away, fine, let's worry about how we record everything. But we haven't. I can't begin to imagine the waste of time and money, but it keeps people in jobs, I suppose.

DC, 36, Northern force

How it works if you phone the police is, you call 999 and you *don't* speak to a police officer. You get through to a call-taker, usually a civilian. They decide, based on the information they glean from you and the state of our resources, whether a policeman needs to be sent out. If they think you should get a bobby, they give the job a code and pass it on to a supervisor, in our force a sergeant, who takes it on from there. They update the computer log with everything that gets done, up to and including what we call 'resulting' the job. In an ideal world, the original detail of the job should be coded with the correct result as laid down by the government in NCRS. This is so that, later on, the force's performance can be analysed using the result codes. Unfortunately, the call-takers and a good few of the supervisors are far removed from actual policing, and geographically the control room is also miles away – it's 25 miles from the town I police. So one of the side effects is we get sent to jobs where the original report is written by someone who doesn't really understand policing, using an unwieldy and complex system to allocate jobs based on their view of what a member of the public an hour's drive away is calling in. Bearing in mind that our callers are often either drunk, mental or highly agitated, or all three. And then the control room expect the reality of the situation to fit exactly what the caller says it was when you arrive, but when you get to the job what you find often bears no relation to what you were sent for. Last week I was sent to a 'robbery' which turned out to be a woman who had collapsed with hypoglycaemia. But because it's written down on the system as a robbery the control room skipper wants it dealt with as a robbery. He doesn't want to take your word for it – his arse might be on the line if he deviates from what the computer says. The pressure they can put you under to conform to the entirely fictitious recording is outrageous – how they can know better than me, who is there on the ground, what is going on I don't know, but they seem to think they do.

Additionally, every log on the system has to be checked later to ensure the right codes were entered, and that the job was dealt with correctly. This is then double-checked by the audit department and ultimately I supposed HMIC triple-check stuff, too. We could save a fortune and work better if we scrapped the civvies and auditors, put that money into frontline cops, and had the phone answered by experienced officers trusted to bat rubbish off and supervised by sergeants and inspectors with the stones and nous to agree that stuff has been dealt with properly.

PC, 39, Midlands force

NCRS and the rest has created some terrible outcomes. For instance, I remember as custody sergeant, a young lad was brought into the station. He was a nice kid whose parents were going through a traumatic divorce. He had gone into a shop and stolen a Kit Kat worth 49p. He stood there in his school uniform – it was immaculate. And I thought, *I didn't join the police to put kids like this on the sheet for stealing a Kit Kat, when their home life is in bits.* I said, 'I'm not charging him for this. Here, go and pay the shop for it.'

And I fished a £1 coin out of my pocket and gave it to the arresting bobby. The problem was, because the offence had been recorded, it had to be cleared up. No two ways about it. My inspector told me to charge the lad, and I said, 'If you give me a lawful order, I'll charge him, but I don't think it's right.'

He gave me the order, so I charged him and the kid was cautioned. This does stay on your record – it's not a matter of, no-one will ever know. There *are* consequences. Since this sort of nonsense was publicised, the wheel has turned and our force has rowed back from it. Nowadays, we wouldn't even have him in the custody block for something like that. We're allowed to use other methods of disposal. Basically, it would be written off as not in the public interest to charge him. I'm not condoning theft, but, bloody hell, who amongst us hasn't pinched a sweet out of the Woolies pick 'n' mix as a kid?

Sergeant, 43, Midlands force

I dealt with a common assault between two employees at a pizza takeaway. Piotr called us to say that Domek had pushed past him aggressively because he had been talking to Domek's girlfriend. Then Domek called and said he had been pushed first. This is the kind of thing we have to take seriously, as a result of the rules – pretty much, if the complainant thinks it's a crime, and the points to prove are there, it's a crime and must be recorded as such. It's why normal people have to wait six hours for us to come round when they've been burgled.

Anyway, so I go to the pizza parlour with the intent of basically banging their heads together. By the time I get there, the heat has gone out of the situation, so they effectively agree to disagree and shake hands and generally keep on spreading the anchovies of love on the pizzas of peace. In any sane world, assuming you think it's 'sane' that I've had to go and tell two men in their 20s to stop bickering, surely to goodness I could write in my pocket-book that the matter was closed, and move on? But no, I have to finalise the crime report as 'Detected/IP declined'. So I do this, only for the skipper to tell me, No, this week we've changed it so we can't detect as 'IP declined' any more, that's all ancient history.

So what are my options now? There is scope for crimes recorded as such in error to be no-crimed, but the call-handlers will flatly refuse to agree that an error was made. Which I suppose in this case it wasn't, in fairness, it was called in. So I either have to find what's called 'additional verifiable information' that the crime was not committed, or I have to arrest them both. Bonkers. If I go back looking for them to make new statements that actually nothing happened, doesn't that mean they were originally wasting police time? If I go back to the pizza place and arrest them both, and then I spend time booking them both in, waiting for interpreters and lawyers, interviewing them... It's like, aaaarrrrggghh! *It's. Never. Going. Anywhere.* The CPS will NFA it, quite rightly. No-one will *ever* be before a court over this, and if they *were* it would be a scandal. It is all just a waste of time. It was never serious in the first place, now neither of them want to know and they both think the matter's closed. What the hell are we doing here?

PC, 26, Southern force

If I go back to 2003, our then chief superintendent was a man intent on going places. He wanted 'performance' and sanctioned detections were the big thing. Every incident that we attended that might just possibly be criminal *had* to have a crime report submitted. Every investigator was encouraged to arrest and detect these 'crimes' by means of charging or formally cautioning the offenders. That was the only way to detect a crime.

We would ask at meetings what to do with minor matters. Can we not just bollock kids graffitiing a bus stop with a marker pen and get them to wipe it off? Problem is, if NCRS says we have to submit a crime, how can we close the crime when we have an offender who has been informally told off but has not had a caution? So his answer was they were to be locked up. Arguing with him was futile. He wanted us spending our hours in the custody office dealing with kids for trivia whilst the real villains continued to pillage.

I recall on one occasion speaking to a few kids larking around with a road cone and chucking mud at each other. They got words of advice off me and that was it. I got a memo from the chief's bagman as to why I had not crimed the matter as a section 5 public order. I considered replying to it but binned it instead. It didn't matter who we criminalised, and at what loss of troop numbers on the street, in detecting this trivia. Detections were the one and only goal. If I was to be cynical, the policy was as a direct result of a bonus culture from the top on detection rates. We might not detect an armed robbery, but get a kid in for stealing apples and you have a 50 percent detection rate. The troops didn't get any bonuses, but the bosses did.

Almost 10 years later, and that chief superintendent is now a rank or two higher in another force. There he is pushing 'RJ', or Restorative Justice. This is the procedure extolled from the Home Office, where we can bollock kids for minor matters and close the crime without criminalising the child for trivia. No fingerprints, DNA taken and a record, but a word with the parents and get the kids to repair the damage. We had been asking to do this when NCRS came out, but no, we weren't allowed.

Almost 10 years later and I am still a PC in the same area. I still bollock kids for minor matters rather than locking them up. I do not let the latest craze or management fad influence my decision to do what is right. I think for myself and do what seems best at the time. I'll let you decide who (1) did the right thing (2) has the greater moral courage (3) earns more than the other. Promotion in the Police above inspector involves being a believer that the latest Emperor's clothes are beautiful.

PC, 41, Northern force

The start of a night duty shift, dispatch comes in and reads, 'Female has called to state that a male gets on the same bus as her every morning and stares at her, can we attend her H/A [*home address*] to get the details.'

I'm gobsmacked. We have four cars out and the night is just starting, this will tuck us up for a while. Get on the radio to speak to communications to question why, first, SNT can't deal at a reasonable hour, and, two, why the Female can't walk the less than five minutes it would take to get from her H/A to the manned 24-hour station office that's on her doorstep, and, three, why is the classification 'harassment'?

To be fair, the operator didn't know either, so after she went back and forth a while, it came back with. 'It's gone on as harassment and the female could be in danger.'

Totally exasperated, we rock up to the address, get past the conçierge on the door and head up to the 7th floor. I know I said 'conçierge', but the only reason they have one is the block we're in was so full of crime and ASB a few years ago that the council installed one years ago, along with full CCTV… Crime rates dropped so much that in the six years I worked the ground it was the one and only time I went there.

All the while, I'm wondering, *OK, maybe I'm wrong, maybe the details given were incorrect or taken down wrong, and this female is in serious danger from someone she knows*. So, after stepping around the peeling paint and cracked floor tiles, I knock on the door, fully expecting a stunning bird in head-to-toe Victoria's Secret to open the door. Door was opened to a fat, 60-year-old woman with tufts of hair missing, a hairy mole the size of a 50p piece on her cheek and the top right set of teeth missing, dressed in a moth-eaten dressing gown and rugby socks.

After gaining entry and a few questions, it was established she did not know this male, had never spoken to him, or he to her, that he didn't know where she lived, and that the harassment consisted of, he got the same bus every morning at exactly the same time that she did, and got off at exactly the same time she did, before they both went their separate ways. I wanted to crack her head open. Instead, I left and went back to put on my harassment CRIS. You really couldn't make it up.

PC, 35, Southern force

Any policeman or woman will recognise the scenario of this week we've got too many recorded offences on the books, so the skipper says, 'If you find people pissed up and bolshy in the town, we are mostly not arresting them for section 5 [*S5 of the Public Order Act 1986, disorderly behaviour likely to cause harassment, alarm or distress to others*], we're nicking for drunk and disorderly.'

Conversely, if we've had too few detections on division this week, the skipper says, 'This week we are mostly arresting people for section 5, not drunk and disorderly.'

The thinking behind this is, section 5 is a notifiable offence, which means we have to record it, but d&d isn't, which means we don't. Exactly the same behaviour can lead to an arrest either way, so if we've had too many people on the books, we nick for d&d, and if we need a few detections, we nick for section 5 – because having nicked them, effectively we've detected the crime. In my area at the moment, there's a real push for d&d, like you'd better have a bloody good reason for section 5, because section 5 is 'officer-created crime' and no crime is better than lots of detections. The bobbies are all up in arms because section 5 is a lovely way to hit your detections target, which Theresa May says we no longer have. Next week, it will be the other way around, though, so it's no biggie.

PC, 25, Southern force

When I joined the police, 28 years ago now, we had some discretion. Not everything was perfect then, of course it wasn't, but we were not arresting juveniles for fights in playgrounds, or arresting adults for insulting each other. Gradually, I have seen that discretion eroded. We had bad apples and idiots, they exist in all runs of life and we still have them, but one thing I never saw was policemen making arrests just because their sergeant told them to, or because a memo had gone round from the top floor demanding more arrests, or because they were below target for detections for the week.

We never *had* detection targets early on: I was sent out of the nick in the morning or afternoon, I patrolled either on foot or in a panda until I saw someone doing something illegal, or I was sent somewhere where a proper crime was happening, and then I made an arrest if I judged it to be necessary.

I know of a sergeant who persuaded a teenage boy to accept a caution for cannabis, a pea-sized lump of resin about enough for one spliff, when for various reasons the evidence that the cannabis was even his was sketchy, to say the least. He implied that if he refused the caution he would be arrested, his house searched, and, by implication, his life made a misery. He went heavy on the line that this was not a criminal record, and that it was basically just a bureaucratic means of writing off the crime which would have no implications, and that it was basically easier for him if we didn't get too formal. All rubbish – we wouldn't search the lad's house even if we knew the dope was his. We've got better things to do. It would never have got formal – if the lad had refused the caution it would have been NFA-d in a heartbeat. And the idea that this will have no implications... There's no fine or jail or community work, but cautions are declarable on a CRB to employers. He'll probably never go to America on holiday or for work, either.

There is bullying in the police to hit the targets we allegedly don't have. I always say to young officers, don't give in. People say they've been bullied, but find a pair or grow a pair – ultimately, they cannot force you to make unlawful arrests or issue wrongful FPNs, and if you accuse them of bullying nine times out of 10 they will shit themselves, because that can be a career-ender for them. If you have a skipper who is putting you under undue and inappropriate pressure, make notes and challenge him, and mention your PACE Codes [*Police and Criminal Evidence Act 1984 Codes of Practice, which dictate, among other things, that a police officer should only arrest after considering 'less intrusive means' and where he or she has reasonable grounds, at his or her sole discretion.*] It's your arse if you make a wrong decision, they won't be queuing up to say you were only following their orders.

PC, 48, Eastern force

It's not just that the public don't know what we do, it's that neither does the Home Secretary. I laughed out loud when she said targets and the Policing Pledge were scrapped and all we should be doing was 'cutting crime'. They're not scrapped at all. They might have told *you* that, love. We still have the same pledge wording. We still have targets for everything. Arrests, detections, TNO [*Total Notifiable Offences*] reduction, response times, victim visits, victim satisfaction, community satisfaction, ASB [*anti-social behaviour*] reduction. You name it, we measure it. And as for just worrying about crime? Thanks Theresa, but who's going to deal with road accidents, coning off broken-down trucks on the roads, suicides, sudden deaths, guarding scenes, looking for missing kids, looking for missing old folks, checking up on old folks behind locked doors who've not been seen for a few days, or who've fallen over and pressed their alarm button – not a police job, but we do it and if we don't are you saying the old folks can go fuck themselves? Or dealing with mentally ill people who should not be in police custody in the first place, watching suicidal people in cells for eight hours at a time, watching people who are not at all suicidal but claim they are because they'd rather have the door open and a bobby to talk to in cells for eight hours at a time, spending whole shifts sitting by the hospital beds of people who suddenly develop alleged chest pains on arriving at the police station, calls to rowdy kids who are just playing football but people still want us there, escaped livestock calls, PACT meetings [*Police – or sometimes 'Partners' – and Communities Together*]. The list is quite endless. She really is clueless. And never mind her, our own senior officers are equally useless. Not long ago, I got called in to see my inspector because I'd had a bad week, in a bad month, and had not met expectations as regards various KPIs.

He said, 'I'm looking at your figures and wondering what you've been doing all week.'

I said, 'Well sir, on Tuesday I attended two RTCs and in each case I had to assist in closing the road for accident investigation and vehicle recovery, which took hours and hours. On Wednesday I spent the afternoon looking for a vulnerable MFH [*missing from home*] and in the evening I had to go to a PACT meeting at such-and-such village hall. Thursday was a training day, so I was at HQ playing around on a computer answering questions about traveller culture or learning how to avoid straining my eyes while reading a screen. Friday I was in court all day. Saturday I arrested a male for fighting and drugs in the town centre and when I got him to custody he developed chest pains so I had to go with him to hospital, and that took me out for the rest of that shift. On Sunday as soon as I arrived at the police station the custody Sergeant pinched me to do a cell watch on a suicidal male, who we'd actually be better off if he did top himself, which sadly he never will, and that was me out of action for the rest of that shift as well. So yes, one arrest isn't a lot to show for six days' work, but I don't know which of those jobs you would want me not to do in order to tick some of your boxes.'

I might have been just slightly less cocky than that, but that was the gist.

He did a double-take, looked down at his spreadsheet and then back at me. It was clear he hadn't considered that I might have been busy doing things which didn't tick any of his statistical boxes. Not that it helped me. I was told that I was being 'unconstructive' and my team sergeant was asked to have a word with me about my attitude, with the hint in the background that I might be put on an action plan. The inspector, by the way, has only been in the police about five minutes, he's on accelerated promotion. I have no doubt that one day he'll be a chief constable. It's quite frightening.

PC, 29, Southern force

Every week I have to fill in a coded spreadsheet for my inspector detailing how many arrests I've made, how many tickets I've given out, the number of stops or searches I have made, how many intel submissions I've made. We all have to do this. It takes quite a bit of time, half an hour at least. Then the inspector collates it all and turns it into multi-coloured bar charts and pie charts and takes it upstairs to the chief inspector, who presumably further collates the spreadsheets supplied by all of his inspectors and takes the whole lot over to force HQ, where he sits in a meeting with all the other chief inspectors and they all show their spreadsheets to the ACC or whoever. If we are not hitting our divisional targets for numbers of arrests or tickets or whatever, all the other chief inspectors laugh and point at our chief inspector, so the pressure comes onto my inspector and then onto me. There is nowhere on any spreadsheet where I can record the time that I spent on a hospital guard, or searching for a MISPER [*missing person – police officers have to deal with thousands each week, the vast majority involving people who are not really missing in any important sense*], or on a cell watch.

I believe that Einstein had a sign hanging in his office at Princeton saying, 'Not everything that counts can be counted, and not everything that can be counted counts.' I'm not saying my boss is cleverer than Einstein. No, I'm really not saying that.

PC, 26, East Midlands force

We're measured on everything. We even get judged on MDT [*Mobile Data Terminal*] use. They actually count up how many times it gets used, and if you're not using it what they feel is 'enough' you're in the shit. Never mind that you can get round it easily just by activating it, whether you need to use it or not. If you do that, just press a random button every now and then, your stats look great – 'Oh, Smith's using his MDT loads so he must be busy, what a jolly good chap!' I think this is what annoys me the most about stats – not that they're collected, so much, but that they are shite.

PC, 26, Northern force

In my opinion, one of the biggest moral issues for police officers is what they do about statistics. If I just want to hit my targets, it's easy – I can just go down to the arcade and stop half a dozen teenagers. There you go, six forms filled in. I might find a little piece of resin, so that's a street warning for possession, which is a detection. But is that right, morally? OK, the cannabis, maybe, but just turning youths over to hit targets? Yet there are officers who do this, because of the pressure they are under. It has nothing to do with the actual job. What I would regard as actual policing, non-response, that is, which is patrolling and nosing around, seeing what's what… We don't have the time for that and if we did we couldn't measure it, so that's not important. Thefts from motor vehicles are up? OK, let's go and stop loads of people. We don't actually catch anyone, but we fill in lots of pieces of paper which the chief inspector can show her boss.

PC, 36, Eastern force

They seem to go out of their way to make life harder. For instance, in a given file I might have to input, say, a witness's name and address several times. Working with MS Word, you would think I could input it once and then cut-and-paste it on the other occasions, but for some obscure reason they have disabled the cut-and-paste function on our computers. They say it's because of our MOPI protocols [*Management of Police Information*] but I cannot see how it can be an issue in the real world if I have copied something I have just typed in, rather than laboriously retyped it, several times? It might only be a few minutes lost each time, but if you think there are tens of thousands of cops, many of whom type up files all the time, it must add up to millions of police hours each year.

Luckily, the IT people are as incompetent as the chiefs, and when they disabled the function they took out the right click on the mouse and 'ctrl x' and 'ctrl v' options, but they accidentally left the drop-down menu at the top intact so you just click on that and away you go. I used to work in IT before I joined the Job and our systems and processes are laughable, that's the only word I can use. All of our IT is so slow and old that it's useless, and, where they have introduced new IT, it doesn't talk to the old stuff or to the stuff other agencies use. If you wanted to design a programme to cost millions and properly fuck with people's minds, it would be a good start.

PC, 27, Midlands force

Not long back our force moved away from paper and went over to a largely electronic file process. They sold it to us as, this will be quicker and more efficient. But it's farcical. We all had to be NCALT-trained which in my case was 10 hours in a classroom. Never mind that we've all been doing MG files for years, and that we're all well-versed in how to turn on a computer because we've all had one at home since about 1990. Then, minor little jobs that used to take a few minutes writing them up in the car, now you have to go back to the nick, turn on the computer, wait for it to warm up, wait for it to crash, reboot it, then type everything in. The best thing of all is once the file's been completed on the computer, then you have to print it off onto paper for signature. So the printer's bust, or it jams half-way through, or the ink is low or... You just think, why on earth can't we just write the bloody thing on paper in the first place?

Training days, by the way, what a waste of flipping time and money. I wouldn't mind if they were something useful, like some new insight into fraud that's doing the rounds, or some new case law relevant to the job, or some training on self-defence or public order, but most of our training is now patronising online packages about diversity and cultural awareness written so that a nine-year-old could understand them and designed purely to cover the backsides of our REMF [*Rear Echelon MotherFuckers – US military-derived term for those who stay well away from the front line of operations*] senior officers, so that in the event that one of us does something wrong, they can say, 'Look, not my fault, they were trained, here's the proof.'

PC, 30, Northern force

The drive to reduce bureaucracy in our force has consisted not of actually reducing bureaucracy at all, but of giving us all PDAs [*handheld computers, or Personal Digital Assistants*] so that we could do all the same paperwork, but do it electronically while we're out and about, rather than being in the police station. It was all part of our 'Visibility Strategy'. That's fine, in theory, but the PDAs are miles slower than a proper computer, they have tiny little keys which means you're always having to re-input everything because 'Smith' comes out as 'Dnurg', so you're sat there staring at this miniscule console and furiously tapping away and any passing member of the public thinks you're having phone sex with your missus.

It's all like a hall of mirrors. The very day I heard Theresa May announce that we were doing away with bureaucracy my boss told me we had to start filling out a new matrix for anti-social behaviour, which is not even a crime. Then they introduced new procedural rules on disposals, so that if we need, for instance, to NFA something minor we have to send an MG3 [*CPS form formally seeking a charging decision*] over to an evidence review officer [*usually a station-based sergeant or civilian*] for them to approve. Not that we need their advice – we often know the score better than they do, and if we need advice isn't that what our Team sergeant's for? – but you can easy wait 90 minutes on a caution approval. I know it's a bit old, but this is time when I'm not out policing and the detainee has to sit around, too. And at the end of this the original file isn't even kept, it's shredded. So how vital is it? Mrs May says they've abolished the policing pledge – well, they've just plastered our nick with a load of new posters about our force's pledge. They're worse liars than Labour.

PC, 30, Northern force

Everything is a 'priority' nowadays. Priorities are the 'growth area' of our 'business'. Mention these words to frontline cops, listen to the sigh and watch the eyes roll skyward. Priorities are decided by support

177

staff and police officers who spend their days sitting in offices and attending meetings, where they trade in the relevant statistics of those priorities. Priorities are as lucrative to some people's careers as carbon credits are to others – not least because they let you patrol a desk on regular 9-5 days. After the meetings, out come the emails with graphs, charts and spreadsheets seeking to identify how the priority is being 'addressed', constantly troubling us for results and action.

My inspector has priorities – usually revolving around reducing anti-social behaviour and all crime detections on our area. My Senior Management Team has priorities. If I was to be cynical, I would say these priorities would be whatever is set by HQ and therefore affects their bonus – usually burglary and violent crime reduction. My local community has priorities, set by local meetings, which are put on the force website. These can range from dog poo on the pavements to burglaries, but usually focus around problems more visible in the community. The force sets priorities, too – usually whatever crimes we are not doing well detecting and the 'hot topics' such as domestic violence and race crimes.

Now, the dictionary defines priority as, 1. the condition of being prior; antecedence; precedence; 2. the right of precedence over others; 3. something given specified attention. The fact is, *all* our work is *someone's* priority, but I'm expected to deal with all of it as… er… a priority. This leaves me with a huge headache. How do I prioritise which priority takes priority over which other priority? When I devote time to catching a drug dealer peddling crack in my area, how can I defend myself when my inspector says that is not a priority? Should I have let the dealer walk away? The community would *definitely* want a crack dealer arresting ahead of lesser offences, but if they don't know that he's up to it does that mean it wasn't their priority? If the dealer also does some burgling, do I still 'tick the boxes' even if I haven't actually *caught* him burgling? How can *everything* be a priority? Did I leave the iron on?

If I was to be cynical again, I'd say 'priority' is a purely defensive management word of no use to street cops. After all – the drug dealer is getting arrested whatever anyone says. I have been and sat in the hot chair at those community meetings where angry residents have a go at the councillors, police and housing associations. 'Priority' is the management shield. As soon as someone complains we are not doing enough about X, the old mantra trots out: 'X is one of our top priorities... blah blah...'

And you can't argue with that. It's a priority because the chief inspector says it is. The public get the feeling and reassurance that x is being dealt with while those of us out on the streets remain confused as to how we can prioritise so many things with reducing frontline numbers.

An enterprising group of cops at a nick to the north of my city have found a solution to this confusion. They have constructed a 'Prioritimeter' out of cardboard in pure *Blue Peter* style. Listed on it are, as the Senior Management Team calls them, our 'key areas of business' and visitors to the office are asked to spin the cardboard wheel to see which priority is the priority for the day. With some assistance from gravity, the notch on the meter often stops at the top where fortunately the priority is 'Brew up'.

PC, 34, Northern force

As an inspector, I am the highest rank in the police which actually does police work. Once you make chief inspector and above, you're off the books, certainly in uniform. Some very good senior officers run murder teams and other major enquiries in CID, but in uniform you'll only make an arrest if you are unlucky enough to have Billy Burglar run into you as he legs it round a corner with a bag marked 'Swag'. Even then, you'll probably have to call a bobby to remind you of the caution.

I consider myself as a bridge between the troops and the dream factory, and I see it that it's my job to shield them from the bullshit from on high. I know what counts in the figures and what doesn't. I will look at an officer who has 25 arrests in a given month. If they're all for shoplifting, then I'll know he's just picked them up from store detectives. Another officer might have five arrests, but if they are what I would call quality he's done a better job. I will stand my corner when the top floor start questioning what we're doing, why our figures are not as good as other teams on other divisions.

Inspector, 50, Southern force

No targets? We have a board in our office about six feet by four feet with, I kid you not, gold stars next to the names of officers who are top performers in a given week. We also have performance figures emailed to us from the Centre on our PDAs. Our force intranet is crawling with information about performance. We have meetings at which the chief inspector tells us that the only thing that matters in our lives is to increase our BCU's detections from x percent to y percent over the next quarter. At the end of every single shift I get asked for my figures. It doesn't matter what I've been doing, and whether whatever it was is, in fact, measurable. You can get hauled over the coals to explain yourself for bad figures if you've been on annual leave for two weeks!

PC, 33, Northern force

I don't really have any non-police friends any more, and I try to avoid talking to members of the public about the Job. They don't understand, so it's pointless. I didn't understand myself before I joined. You'll meet people at a barbecue or on holiday and they'll ask you what you do for a living, but I just make something up. Years ago I used to be an assistant manager at Sainsbury's in Swansea so I say I'm still doing that, and if they ask any questions I can answer them, whereas if I said I was a fighter pilot or a brain surgeon I might get caught out.

I try to pick up the kids from school whenever I can, and some of the mums at the school gate know what I do. One time a woman started berating me because her mam or something had been burgled and the police had been shit. We hadn't caught the burglar, which amazingly sometimes we don't. I think she was expecting me to be apologetic.

My attitude was, 'We were shit? Tell me something I don't know, love. Of course we were shit. All the bobbies are trying to stop Darren and Tracey having a row because one of them has de-friended the other on Facebook, filling in forms about it and then calling Darren and Tracey to check they were happy with the service they received.'

I don't think I swore, really, and I probably didn't call her 'love'. Anyway, she just stared at me, and then she said, 'Yeah right,' or something.

I broke the habit of a lifetime, and actually spent the next 20 minutes explaining to her in minute detail that we really *do* have real police officers investigating nasty comments made on Facebook or texted to people with mobile phones, that this is absolutely not a rare thing, that we really do go round to the houses of the people involved, that in 2011 we really do take longhand statements, we sometimes seize phones and computers over it and send them off for evidential analysis – in fact, the threat of doing this can often make a minor matter suddenly disappear. 'We need to seize your phone to prove it received the message you're complaining about. Be back with you in about three months, is that OK?' 'Ah, OK, I don't want the matter to go any further.' That we make arrests, we fill out reams and reams of paperwork, and then we drop everything the following day because the supposed IP has changed his or her mind.

By the end of it, *she* was almost apologising to *me*. I said, 'If we could say to Darren and Tracey, "Sorry, you're grown adults, if you want to call each other names and threaten to duff each other up that's really your affair, unless one of you actually does it, in which case obviously we'll get involved…" If we did that we could take thousands of police hours, probably millions of police hours a year, and put them on burglary, assaults, car crime *et cetera*.' Why on earth the public, I mean the tax-paying public who keep the whole thing going, haven't twigged and rioted in the streets about it yet, I don't know.

Sergeant, 43, Welsh force

Folk know about the bureaucracy now. I go to jobs and they'll raise their eyebrows and say, 'This will take you a while to write up, eh?' But at the same time, I think a lot of other folk have got bored with it, because they think it's just policemen whingeing. 'Yeah, yeah, yeah, we get it, you have to fill in forms.' The point is, we do a lot less *police*work because we're doing a lot more *paper*work.

They also, I think, don't really understand how mad some of the stuff we do is. For instance, we have bobbies spending half their lives looking for missing kids. Now, I've nothing against looking for a kid who is really missing – say a five-year-old who's wandered off from his mum out shopping. But we get 15-year-olds absconding from care homes *every* day – I mean, the *same* kids do it every day. The care home staff can't stop them walking out, so they walk out and go down town. The care home then has to ring us and report them missing, to cover their backs, and once it's on the system we have to react as if it's a real MISPER, to cover *our* backs. That means getting bobbies to drop the jobs they're on and go round looking for these kids at their usual haunts, the arcades, the back of Sainsbury's, waking friends and family up at 3am… 'Hello, sorry, I know it's late but have you seen so-and-so? OK, do you mind if we come in and have a quick look round?'

When we find them and bring them back, again, we have to fill out a 20-page form about the incident. Often you can be filling in *exactly* the same information about *exactly* the same kid that you did yesterday.

Or dealing with arguments between adults who have fallen out. 'She called me a bitch!' 'I never, she texted me that I was a slag!' Seriously, if you call us to say that your mate called you a slag and you want them done for it, we will probably have to go out and talk to them. If it's two people in a domestic relationship – be they husband and wife, son and father, sisters, whatever – then we're *definitely* going. If one of them is minority ethnic or from some other vulnerable group, again, we're *definitely* going.

We could do a much better job for much less money if we dropped a lot of this crap. If they let us decide which missing persons are really missing, and act accordingly, we could free up so much resource, and if they let us treat domestic arguments on their own merits, as the people on the spot, rather than dictating that we arrest everyone and spend hours filling in risk assessments. True, in some very rare cases things will turn out badly. But my argument is, these things happen anyway – the tick box mentality doesn't solve things, it doesn't stop people killing each other, it just introduces complacency. The police can't do everything, we can't police people's lives for them. We have spent a decade or more proving this, it's cost a lot of money, let's stop trying to do the impossible and focus on doing what we can do better.

If we just had a uniform branch that patrolled and arrested street criminals and burglars, and a detective branch that investigated everything else, that would be about right. Scrap the CPS and let us charge again. *Really* cut down the bureaucracy, so that we don't have to write the same information down on five different pieces of paper for every file we build, so a file takes half an hour, not three hours. Ditch all the health and safety and our obligations to comply with the Human Rights Act and the Disability Discrimination Act, which eats up days and weeks of police time and ends up with concrete wheelchair ramps being built where no-one will ever use them, like at the back of public order training facilities. Slim down the booking-in procedure, so that I can book a prisoner in in 10 minutes, not an hour. Pull out of the MAPPA meetings where idle officers sit talking about strategies all day, eating biscuits. Stop our bosses turning bobbies into stat-bitches who spend half their lives recording and inputting figures on everything to the Centre. Stop trying to use the police as a tool for social engineering and return us to the days when we simply upheld and enforced the law. But these things would all require some guts on the part of the government.

Sergeant, 39, Northern force

MISPERs can do your head in. Morning, get a call from a frantic mother. She's had a text message from her 11-year-old child's school that they have not shown up to school that day. After a few calls I get the mother and she is frantic, her work are driving her home, this has never happened before. Mum is distraught, not least because there had been a few stabbings that month in the area. I'm on my radio updating control and on my own mobile trying to calm mother.

Get to the school, I am told, no, the child is definitely not here.

Back on the radio updating everyone, ASU [*Air Support Unit*], MSU [*Marine Support Unit*] and more units out to start a search. Most MISPERs are crap, but this was the real deal.

Get the head down to speak to us, he is just as concerned, but then he informs me that the text is automatically generated via computer if a box is not ticked from the admissions office. Right, now I want a word with the person who runs that. Meanwhile, I've got people on the radio asking if I want the Commissioner's Reserve [*experienced officers held back for special incidents*] deployed and BTP [*British Transport Police*] informed, slow day for them I guess. I hang fire on that at this time, my spider sense was tingling. Twenty minutes later, the admissions woman walks in. After questioning she tells me her system is infallible, and that we need to be looking for this child. I'm trying to convince her to send someone to the child's classroom just to check, both the admissions woman and the head are against this as it would be 'disruptive'. Heads of school are tricky. Never mind that half the nick are waiting outside for my instruction. Just then, mum arrives. She is proper hysterical, crying, wailing, screaming and grabbing desks and collars everywhere. The head gets the point by now, and dispatches someone to check the classroom.

Lo and behold, five minutes later a terrified child comes in, wondering why his mum is there sobbing into the arms of a police officer half her age, and why he has been dragged out of class.

All's well that ends well, stand down all units.

I stand there giving admin woman and head a dressing down, not so politely, about having got the ASU, MSU and everyone else out. I get a complaint from the schools officer, but mum loves me for sticking up for her re the stupid text message idea. I think it went all the way to the commander, but they backed me on this one.

Sergeant, 35, Southern force

The Macpherson Report in particular led to a huge ramping-up of diversity awareness training for officers, which many resent – along with what they see as a generalised slur that they are racist.

In the last two or three years, my force has won, or been praised by, or short-listed for, the Work Life Balance Awards, the Advancing Women in Public Service award, a place in *The Times* Aurora 'Where Women Want to Work' Top 50, the *Opportunity Now* Diverse Women Award, for our 'work in improving female representation in specialist roles', the Race for Opportunity 'Benchmarking Gold Award' for doing pretty much the same thing for blacks, the Stonewall 2009 Workplace Equality Index for doing the same thing with gays, the Employers Forum on Age Awards, for doing the same thing with wrinklies, the Race Equality Impact Assessment Award (Public Sector), the list goes on.

Now, I'm emphatically not against women or minority ethnics or gays in the police. I'm slightly against the elderly, for practical reasons, but as long as you obey and uphold the law, I honestly couldn't care less whether you're a black gay or a female Asian or a straight white male, I just want the best person for the job. I do object to the waste of resources that must be involved in putting in for all of these awards. I can absolutely guarantee that days and days will have been spent on getting each entry just right... And imagine being from the forces that spent the same amount of time putting in for this shite and didn't win! Not to mention the focus on this rubbish during our working lives.

Sergeant, 39, Midlands force

Sadly, I don't think we can ever get rid of racism. It would be nice if people were treated according to the content of their character rather than the colour of their skin, but I can't see it. People, particularly the less intelligent ones who we tend to deal with more, just aren't built like that, for some reason.

That said, I personally think the anti-racism drive in the police was a good thing. I think it has had some effect. If you lined up 100 police officers and 100 members of the public, I am 100 percent convinced you would find more unpleasant attitudes in the public line. And it's not just from whites, either. The biggest problem in our area is between the Afro-Caribbean and African communities, and between them and the Pakistanis. For some reason, they all seem to hate each other. You might say I'm exaggerating, but how often do you hear of a Pakistani girl marrying a Jamaican? If the answer is 'very rarely', is that down to racism?

PC, 33, Midlands force

I think diversity is important, and relevant. Working in a majority ethnic BCU, policed by mostly white officers, I think we need to demonstrate and prove to the people we serve that we care about them, just saying we do is not enough. As much as anything, I look at it in practical terms, in that it makes my job easier if I have people onside. I do think we have to be careful not to lose that control, we need not to have people taking the piss. I also think some senior officers and probably some entire rural forces with very few BME [*black/minority ethnic*] residents take it too far, because it's the name of the game, promotion-wise. That's the real cancer — not the fact that we have diversity training and we're anti-racist, which is a good thing, but that careers are made and broken on diversity, rather than on catching criminals. It's important, but it's not our primary function.

Sergeant, 36, Southern force

All police forces now are bursting with diversity training. We spend a vastly greater length of time — like 10 or 20 times as much — learning about how to be nice to the various faith groups or sexual orientations or races than we do about how to catch burglars or how to look after yourself in a riot situation. Crime only really matters in a statistical sense. I have attended some quite high-level meetings in two forces and I have *never* heard an ACPO rank officer say words to the effect of, 'My job's on the line if we don't sort out this burglary problem, or catch these scrotes who are conning old folks out of their life savings.' But the mere mention of a problem with someone who might be from a vulnerable group and they are all over it like a rash.

Inspector, 42, Northern force

I attended an annual diversity lecture with the usual series of middle class white boffins and social worker-types who spent the day role-playing, telling us how racist we all were and trying to get us to confess like it was the Truth and Reconciliation Commission. The last speaker was a lady of Jamaican origin who was the single mother to a teenage boy. She started off a bit 'anti', and a bit defensive, maybe we were, too, but as she explained to us how her life worked and the difficulties and limitations she faced — no man around, her boy was twice her size already and basically a law unto himself, albeit not that bad a kid — I started sort of warming to her. And we started discussing PACE and the whys and wherefores of searching.

One of my colleagues said, 'Honestly, I have no interest in whether the people I stop are black or white, and only you can tell me who you think causes most of the street crime around here. But what I can say is that the single most effective tool we have in our armoury to take guns and knives off the streets, never mind stopping burglaries and drug dealing and all the rest of it, is stopping and searching people we believe may be carrying.' Then he described watching a post mortem on a young black boy of the same age as her son.

By the end of the session this lady had come right round to our way of thinking and was saying she wanted us doing *more* searches, not less. Afterwards, one of the white lecturers took my colleague to one side, he was furious, and he said, 'That was a real low blow, that stuff about the post mortems.'

This is the kind of mentality you're dealing with.

PC, 30, Southern force

I arrested a 16-year-old Somali for dealing and carrying a knife. Get him down to the nick, he's swearing that the only reason I stopped him was because he's black and a Muslim. My wife is black, actually a lot darker-skinned than him, and I had no idea he was a Muslim before he mentioned it, but ignore that. I pointed out the real reason I stopped him is because I saw him exchange what turned out to be crack cocaine for money on the corner of the street, and then leg it when he saw me.

His mum was fetched and brought down to the nick to act as his appropriate adult. She said to me, 'Ignore all that rubbish officer, he blames everything on racism and he has been nowhere near the mosque in the last decade.' I could have kissed her.

PC, 31, Southern force

We get sent emails trumpeting our force success in employment of, and working environment for, people from 'under-represented communities'. The force newspaper is filled with it. There's a section on the intranet bragging about it, giving the percentages of VEM [*visible ethnic minority*] officers on all teams and departments. There's only one department with absolutely zero BME officers – the SMT. [*Senior Management Team – officers of chief inspector rank and above, most of whom spend their lives being driven to meetings, drawing up strategies and issuing press releases about carnivals.*] How about two or three of them stand down and make way? Some very senior people have said that the entry standards were reduced to get more VEM officers and women in. [*The government's police reform czar Tom Winsor said last year that a former commissioner of the Met and a serving member of the Police Federation that entry standards were lowered to attract more black and minority ethnic recruits.*] The tragedy of this is that perfectly competent, professional black or Asian or female officers, of whom there are many, walk around feeling that people think they're only in because of a quota. Why do we do this to ourselves? Most nurses and primary school teachers are women, but I'm not aware of any action plans or formal targets to get more men into teaching or nursing? How about just employing the best person for the job?

Sergeant, 43, Midlands force

Every year we have to go through Performance and Development Reviews, PDRs. These apply to all officers and basically set out how we've done this year and what we need to do next year. They take up a lot of time when I'd rather be out trying to catch criminals. My skipper knows I do my job, that should be good enough. If you think that 140,000 people are each spending two hours on them, that's 35,000 eight-hour shifts. Anyway, there might be some actual policing objectives – say, 'Will achieve x detections a month', or 'Will plan and execute at least y operations or warrants per month' – but it's really not about measuring how many people you sent to prison this year versus last year, the really important stuff is all about diversity and the need for me to show 'awareness of cultural and racial differences'. So I'm supposed to actively 'promote equality and diversity' and 'evidence' how I've done so. I usually put that I have engaged with members of the local Bangladeshi community, which basically means that I eat a lot of curries at the Simla in town where my mate is the owner. I don't believe anyone reads the damned things anyway, but it's insulting and unnecessary. When I joined the police I took an oath that I would act at all times with fairness and impartiality and would accord equal respect to all people. The fact that I haven't been fired presumably means I'm doing OK.

PC, 34, Midlands force

Cameron was on the telly saying that state multiculturalism had failed and you think, well, he *is* the Prime Minister so what is this going to mean for the police? Will all the diversity trainers and community liaison officers be sent back to street duties? Will Hate Crime units be abolished, and the same standards of crime investigation applied to everyone? Will diversity requirements be removed from the National Competency Framework? Does it mean that we will no longer have taxpayer-funded interpreters to assist long-established British citizens who are well-acquainted with the police and are quite able to carry on their trade in stolen goods with the local English-speaking community, but have somehow forgotten how to speak the language when it comes to being arrested?

And you watch the news the next day, and the usual suspects are already implying Cameron's a racist and you realise quite quickly that, no, it won't mean any of those things. There might be a bit of window-dressing, like the Hate Crime Unit will be rebranded as the Community Cohesion Team, or something, but nothing will change. Cameron and May and all the rest of them are basically impotent. They make speeches, and everyone inside the force HQs pays lip service to it but carries on as before. You don't get to the top in the police now, almost literally, without having a sociology or criminology degree. This has been going on for 20 or 30 years. There is an institutional culture in the police, but it's not one of racism, it's of soft left-liberalism.

Inspector, 49, Northern force

I don't know if people realise that white victims of crime can often receive a lesser service than victims from ethnic minorities, or that straight victims receive a lesser service than gays. A white victim – white British, that is, as opposed to, say, Eastern European, which would be different – of a standard assault can expect a standard investigation, while a minority ethnic victim of the same assault will receive a far better service, audited and supervised to a level not far off that for a serious crime. A white guy gets punched outside the chippy and gets a fat lip – you'll have a bobby working on it, and it will be one of 15 cases he's dealing with. A black guy gets punched by a white guy and a fat lip – CID are instantly involved, CCTV will be trawled, witnesses will be sought. If I call you a stupid bastard in the street outside the pub, I might get a section 5. If I call you a stupid gay bastard, that is a hate crime and everything grinds into gear. I'm not sure why. We don't put extra resources into other classes of people, like the elderly, or shopkeepers. What's so special about race or sexuality? The whole concept of 'hate crime' is ridiculous. It encourages all the 'isms' it's trying to prevent.

PC, 34, Midlands force

We are the masters of Newspeak. For instance, to the public, 'Hate Crime Unit' sounds like – there's been a hate crime, you ring the police and they transfer you to this unit somewhere where there are loads of top people champing at the bit to deal with the crime and arrest the offenders. In fact, they don't actually investigate crime at all. Almost *all* crime is investigated by ordinary police officers, though a hate crime assault will be dealt with as a higher priority than a *non-*hate crime assault.

All the Hate Crime Units do is 'monitor' the 'performance' of these ordinary cops, send them lots of emails demanding that they detect the hate crime, while they themselves drink coffee and chat in the daily management meetings, produce their Community Impact Assessments and try to ensure that the whole thing doesn't go bent in the media. They work 9 to 5, Monday to Friday, they have car park spaces in the nick, whereas the rest of us have to park half a mile away across enemy territory, and they never, *ever* arrest or interview a suspect. Never get their hands dirty. Never roll around on the ground arresting someone for an assault – just send me lots of emails to ask me why my bods didn't arrest them quicker.

Now, you might say, 'Well, that's OK, we *should* monitor the police's performance.' I would agree, except that our performance is *already* massively monitored.

As a sergeant, I'm monitoring PCs. Our force policy is that the bobbies, if they take crime reports, then have to send these reports up for 'appraisal' to make sure they've done the right thing. If it's a trigger offence such as a burglary or DV, they have to inform a sergeant. If it's a top line trigger offence, like a hate crime or even a hate incident [*i.e. an incident which does not meet the criteria for being a criminal offence*] they tell me and I have to copy the guv'nor and CID in on it. In all cases, the custody sergeants monitor the bobbies' arrests, the shift sergeants appraise the evidence, the crime processing unit then re-appraises the same evidence, even if the shifty is a sergeant with 20 years in. The case is then green-lighted for the next layer of monitoring, the CPS, who then re-re-appraise it. Not forgetting that, for domestics, the PC has to ask a series of demeaning and intrusive questions of people and fill in a DASH [*Domestic Abuse, Stalking, Harassment and Honour-based violence*] risk assessment… Absolutely nothing wrong with this if we've arrested a bloke for stamping on his wife's face, but where it's a pair of pissheads, each of whom literally rings us once a week? This DASH assessment is then appraised by the officer's sergeant and a PPIU [*Public Protection Investigation Unit*] officer. Same with any job involving vulnerable persons: a risk assessment, followed by a thorough check. Again, nothing wrong with this where the person is genuinely vulnerable, but the definition of 'vulnerable' is so wide that this is a mountain of extra work, often for no benefit, at the expense of those jobs where it would help but where the officers are perhaps going through the motions or just incredibly rushed. Not to mention, if it's *not* a crime, the bobbies have to produce a file report explaining why it isn't, which is then checked against the log and signed off by the control room supervisor, then the sergeant, then the divisional boss or his gimp. Just to say something *isn't* a crime!

Then I have an inspector above me, she has a chief inspector above her, and so on; there is a truly massive paper trail to everything we do; my radio tells my bosses where I am at all times and people can listen in through it and monitor what I say without my knowledge; we are encouraged, and in fact instructed in quite an East German way, to inform on each other, and people do this to each other so that they can get good PDRs, and can be promoted. We have internal professional standards departments dedicated to catching us out, we are accountable to various outside agencies – the courts, the IPCC, the media… I could go on. The unaccountable police officer is a myth.

Meanwhile, all these pen-pushers, who no longer do any actual police work, are still called 'police officers', still count in the mythical 140,000 police officer numbers. Still draw salaries and will draw pensions, the same as mine, though that may be about to change, and have no impact whatsoever on whether I do or do not manage to find out who punched you in the face, be you black or white, and bring you before the court. They should disband the Hate Crime Unit and the Public Protection people and put all those shiny-arsed wastes of oxygen back to work, properly. Half of them would immediately go off sick with stress and the other half would leave the Job.

Sergeant, 43, Midlands force

We were recently told that our BCU PACE 1s [*stop-and-searches*] had fallen to an unacceptable level on our internal force league table and that we needed to stop-search more people. A lot of people are asking exactly how you can actually *have* a target for stopping and searching more people? Bearing in mind we can only stop people on reasonable suspicion that they are committing or have committed criminal acts, surely the only way you can stop *more* people on reasonable suspicion that they are committing criminal acts is if you *see* more people of whom you have reasonable suspicion that they are committing criminal acts? An order to carry out more PACE 1s to me sails close to the wind of being an instruction to conduct more unnecessary and illegal searches… Either that, or it's an admission that the crime rate is a lot higher than we say it is, or an admission that there are lots of lazy police who don't *already* stop people when they're four-up in an old car, driving slowly through a known target area with the lights off.

The real reason why we have these stop-and-search targets which are so closely monitored is diversity. If we stop lots of young black youths, because we have reasonable suspicion that the youths in question are involved in street crime – the vast majority of which, I'm sorry, *is* committed by black youths in my area, it will be different in other areas of course – that makes the figures look terrible. Oh look! They're stopping *x* percent black kids and only *y* percent white youths! The racists! So because bobbies won't *not* stop black youths who they suspect, reasonably, might be involved in that street crime, you have a situation where they feel under pressure to stop lots of white youths as well, even if it's on completely spurious grounds, so as to get the proportion of ethnic minorities searched down and make the figures look better.

The numbers game is mad, and also probably illegal, and I consistently refuse to get involved in it. When they raise the fact that my figures might be lower than some other people's I point out that's because I make sure I have grounds. They say, 'Grounds are easy enough, you can always find them,' but they never give you that on a memo or email, and anyway that isn't the point. I accept that we ought to have a lower threshold but we are where we are, I don't make the law and I only *ever* search someone when I know 110 percent that I can justify it in a room in six months' time with a very high-powered lawyer questioning me, because one day someone is going to sue us and when it does it will be the PCs on the ground who are held accountable, not the senior management team who organise the racket.

PC, 34, Midlands force

I think we should do away with all our ethnicity classifications such as IC1, IC3, whatever. [*Identity Code 1 is white, IC3 is, effectively, black.*] We should use a Dulux paint wallchart instead. 'I'm outside HMV, two suspects seen making off along High Street. Suspect one is male, Frosted Dawn with a hint of Garnet Symphony, suspect two is male, Velvet Truffle shading to Totally Cocoa.'

We only have the 16+1 at the moment [*as well as the 'IC' codes, police use 16 Home Office 'self-defined ethnicity' codes to help classify ethnicity, and an additional code, NS, for 'Not Stated'.*] How many colours do Dulux have? Rather than laboriously asking people to self-define their ethnicity, we could hold a Dulux card against their foreheads. Job done.

PC, 34, Northern force

They've taken the word 'prejudice' and changed it to mean something else. *Everyone* is prejudiced. You wouldn't leave your kids with a crackhead, even if he hadn't actually been convicted for it. You wouldn't let a 17-year-old in a Fila tracksuit from inner city Liverpool house-sit for you with three of his mates while you went away for two weeks, even if they told you they were good lads and their mums backed them up. I don't care who you are or what you say, you would not do this. That's because you're prejudiced. And I'm prejudiced, against criminals. I couldn't care two tits what ethnicity they are, I will arrest them if I think they have committed a crime. In nearly 20 years in the police I have yet to hear any officer seriously say anything different.

PC, 33, Eastern force

I was pulled up, or 'challenged' as we say, in an operational planning meeting by a detective inspector for saying that 'Chinese whispers' suggested that a particular person of interest was returning to a given address at a certain time. He advised me that this might be construed as a racist phrase, especially by the Chinese community. As far as I know, the only Chinese people in our entire town run the Chinese restaurant and the two or three takeaways, but even if we had thousands of them, a) they won't know I've said it and b) even if they do, how is it racist? It's just a phrase. You expect it from trainers, or if someone uses the 'N word'. But this is a DI we're talking about, involved in a serious investigation, and he trots out this rubbish.

DC, 40, Southern force

There was a picture in the local paper of my chief constable [*Suffolk Constabulary's Simon Ash*] personally running up the rainbow flag at Martlesham [*Force HQ*] to celebrate lesbian, gay, bisexual and transgender history month. Once I'd recovered from the aneurism that this sight engendered, it raised several important questions in my mind. The first was, *Who the hell designed that? It looks like a beach towel.* The second was, *That Simon Ash is a fat bastard, isn't he?* Try being an officer in the Marines or the Paras, and not being able to do the basic job, i.e. soldiering. I wonder how long it's been since he did a foot chase after a kid legging it from a stolen car? If he tried it now, it would probably kill him. The third was, *What does Ash mean when he says, 'The flag signifies pride and inclusivity'? Pride in what?* If being gay is a natural thing, which we're told it is, how can you be 'proud' of it? I'm not saying you should be ashamed of it, but it's like being proud of having ears. I suppose you could be proud of being transgender, if you'd paid for the op yourself, and maybe had a hand in designing the new you, but really.

He says, 'We have a commitment to tackle hate crimes and we want the message to be clear to victims and offenders that offences involving disability, race, religion and belief, sexual orientation or transgender will not be tolerated.' So what is he saying? That we *will* tolerate offences *not* involving disability, race, religion and belief, sexual orientation or transgender? Silly me. Of *course* we tolerate them. Two blokes get beaten up in the street. One rings and says, 'I've been beaten up by two guys.' The other rings and says, 'I've been beaten up by two guys who called me gay.' No contest.

It doesn't stop with us, either. Assuming in both cases the offenders are brought before the courts, the 'non-gay' assault will result in a fine, irrespective of that fact that they didn't pay their last five fines, or a community sentence, irrespective of whether the offenders have breached their last five community sentences. In the 'gay' assault, you could well be looking at prison. You think I'm exaggerating, but this is enshrined in law. Section 146 of the Criminal Justice Act 2003 imposes a duty on the courts to increase the sentence for any offence aggravated by hostility based on the victim's sexual orientation. Disability and race are the same. What is it about a gay bloke's nose that makes it worse to break it than mine? Can we not just agree that it is wrong to hit people and steal things from them, whatever they do in their bedroom of an evening?

If the police stand for anything, we should stand for equality before the law. It's ridiculous, and 99 percent of the officers are highly embarrassed by the whole thing, though you could be sacked for saying that. Gay colleagues, I mean police officers rather than greasy pole-climbers, are no keener on this enforced diversity than the rest of us. I know a lad who walked out of a training session. He said he didn't need any advice on how to treat gay people, being one himself, and that he tended to treat them the same as straight people. There was a minor panic over that, as they realised that by calling for different treatment he might feel he was discriminated against.

Sergeant, age withheld, Eastern force

There was a lay-by on our area which became a popular haunt of doggers. If you don't know what doggers are, these are people who like to go to public places and have sex, or watch other people having sex. So, you have people wandering around with their cocks out wanking over other people having it away in the back of a Ford Sierra.

First thing to say, this is illegal. Indecent exposure *is* illegal, until the government decides to change the law. We got lots of complaints about it. Children could potentially see what was going on from a primary school, and it wasn't just kids, there could be lone females pulling into the lay-by, old people, whatever. Lorry drivers… You laugh, but are we saying that, if you're a lorry driver, you should be prepared to put up with this? Local people were very angry about it. There was a petition with 300-odd signatures. So what do we do? Do we set up an operation to catch some of these people at it? Thus sending a message that open contempt for the law, and for the feelings of others, will not be tolerated? No, we sent a mobile unit down there to hand round tea and biscuits to the doggers, along with leaflets telling them to wear condoms because of the risk of AIDS and other STDs. It's a 'lifestyle', apparently. We have to 'tolerate' their 'difference'. This isn't just my force. ACPO in Scotland sent round a manual encouraging officers to think about ways of protecting doggers from 'hate crime'. Not, 'Here are some good ways of arresting these people who are breaking the law.'

PC, 40, Midlands force

The town I work in has a large Asian community concentrated in two districts – one, roughly speaking, where the Indian community live and the other where the Pakistani community live.

On the edge of the Pakistani area there is a pub and a public toilet which are both used by members of the gay community. There are lots of 'communities' in our town. The pub is a well-known hook-up point and the toilets are used for sex. As an aside, this used to be called 'cottaging' but we now call it 'activity in a Public Sex Environment', or PSE. We do love our TLAs [*three-letter acronyms*] in the police.

So anyway, we got some complaints about the behaviour of men using these toilets for sex – I mean, full-on shagging and sucking off in broad daylight, and, if people walked in on them, tough shit – but we were told from on high to go easy on the situation as it would be taken to be homophobic if we went round there and started making arrests.

Someone must have mentioned this reasoning to the locals, because the next thing you know there is a small delegation of community leaders in the nick to see the chief inspector complaining that they are offended by this blatant homosexual activity carrying on in the heart of their neighbourhood, that they are unhappy that the police seem to be tolerating this when it's clearly unlawful and, furthermore, warning that if something isn't done about it they cannot guarantee that the elders will be able to restrain the young 'hotheads', that was their word, who would sort the problem out theirselves, doubtless with the aid of Mr Cricket and his friend Mr Bat.

While not condoning people taking the law into their own hands, I had some sympathy with them: the days of arresting and hounding people just for being gay have long gone, but cottaging is still against the law, for very good reasons. So why don't we enforce it? It all left the boss with an exquisite dilemma – does he prioritise the needs of the gays or the Muslims? It's a career-defining thing in the modern police, in the way that arresting a really serious team of blaggers might once have been.

In the end, he had a meeting with the landlord of the pub and a couple of people from a gay rights group and said, basically, 'We'll patrol around there for the next month to guarantee your safety while using the PSE but in the meantime you'll have to be looking for somewhere else to meet up because these locals won't stand for it.'

The upshot was the activity moved to another toilet about a mile further in to town, where there isn't a big Pakistani community and no-one cares that the locals there don't like it, because they aren't a victim group, they're just working class, largely white British and students. So everyone's happy, bar the landlord of the gay pub whose business died overnight.

Sergeant, 43, Midlands force

In my well-known north-western seaside resort town, there's a sizeable gay community. There's also a long-standing issue around acts of indecency in public places. There's a place called Middle Walk which is a half-mile stretch on the seaward-side of the main drag on the North Shore. Basically, it's a big Greco-Roman colonnade, with big pillars and these long, recessed bays, and it would have been nice in its heyday between the wars... The idea being that families and couples take the sea air and stroll along the promenade and take a seat in the recessed bays to relax and watch the waves.

Nowadays it is essentially a meeting place for gay men, who will have sex quite openly there. Everyone knows this, apart from the occasional unwary tourist, so local straight people don't really go there after dark much. But of course, gays are great targets for robbery – they don't always run away from young men, and they're not always keen to make complaints which might in a roundabout way identify them as homosexual – so our local scrotes, of which we have an over-supply, like to go down there, show out a bit to bring them on, and then beat them up and rob them. It's a nightmare for our Robbery Team.

To me the solution is obvious: you don't leave a steak out on the side, where flies can crawl all over it, you put it in the fridge. If we moved the gays on, said, 'Look, there's no shortage of b&bs in this town, why not try one of those?', and stopped *that* particular offence from happening, there'd be no-one to rob, so it would be a win-win.

But what we actually did was institute patrols to protect the gays, to make sure no-one disturbs them whilst they commit criminal acts of gross indecency in a public place. Now, robbery is a more serious crime, sure, but two wrongs don't make a right.

PC, 30, Northern force

We spend our lives pandering on politically-correct issues, instead of telling the truth. Rape is a classic case. We're constantly harangued over the conviction rate… You'll see figures like, 'Only six percent of rapes result in a conviction.' The implication of this is that the police are doing a terrible job, specifically in this area, because the clear-up rates for other offences are much higher. I'm convinced this puts a lot of women off reporting: 'Oh look, the figures prove the police don't care and won't believe me.'

What the lobbyists don't say, or perhaps don't understand, is that, uniquely for rape, that Home Office-approved, six percent clear-up figure is actually what's called the 'attrition rate', which is the rate of conviction against the number of allegations made. In *all* other crime, the indicator used is the *conviction* rate, which is the number of convictions against the number of *prosecutions*, i.e. they weed out all the false allegations, or people who refuse to co-operate *et cetera*. If you deal with rape convictions in the same way as robbery, say, you find a clear-up rate of 50 percent-ish; that is, in 50 percent of the cases we and the CPS take forward to court, the defendant is found guilty.

A long way from the six percent headline figure. Unfortunately, the newspapers like a more dramatic story, so they report 'police solve six percent of rapes' and that's it, unless you look deeper.

I resent this, because I know from personal experience that we take rape extremely seriously, where it is rape. We may not have been that shit hot 20 years ago, and we still make mistakes nowadays because we're human, but where we have a genuine rape… We're almost all either women, or married to women, all of our mothers were women, we have daughters, female friends and colleagues, we don't like rapists – what would *possibly* be our motivation for not wanting to lock them up?

The trouble is that word 'genuine'. There are people who appear to believe that it is inconceivable that a woman would lie about being raped. Probably because they are nice people who are only ever likely to be raped by a stranger, who are unlikely to meet a bloke in a pub, go back to his flat to shag him, and then sober up and wonder how to explain the love bites, ripped knickers and staying out all night to their boyfriend or husband. We get a fair few reports like that. We also get women alleging rape to get at the other side in custody battles, we get prostitutes alleging rape because they haven't been paid by their punter, we get women alleging rape who haven't had sex with anyone in six months. It can be quite bizarre. Often, you do feel sorry for these women, there's problems, they're troubled, vulnerable people – they're just not rape victims.

DC, 33, Northern force

Every rape should be treated as genuine and fully investigated until proven otherwise, that's the start point. But some women, for reasons best known to themselves, *do* falsely report rape. It can be because they have mental health issues, it can be because they've done something stupid with a man at a club and they don't want their boyfriend to find out. I've known cases where women have made allegations out of sheer spite, because the object of their affections doesn't reciprocate.

In my career of 10 years or so, I have dealt with five real rapes and a much greater number of allegations which turned out to be untrue. This is not just my prejudice, this is allegations of rape which were taken seriously, properly and professionally investigated, and which turned out to be untrue.

Off the top of my head, a young woman claimed she had been raped in an alley outside a nightclub. This leads to the man being arrested at home, his home searched and clothing seized, he's brought to the police station, swabbed, fingerprinted, photographed, put in a cell for 12 hours.

Meanwhile, we look at the CCTV footage from the nightclub. The 'victim' is clearly seen dancing happily with the man, then she goes over to her friend, talks to her and the friend hands something over. Then she leaves with the man. We talk to the friend, it turns out that the 'something' she handed over was a condom, which the 'victim' asked her for. At that point, you have to say, is this going anywhere?

The woman retracts, the man is released and the whole thing is NFAd. This particular woman, by the way, had made allegations of rape three times before; this was her fourth. Was she charged with wasting police time? No. A note is made against her name that she alleges, but that's it.

DC, 40, Northern force

I have absolutely no doubt that some rape victims do not report their rapes. Particularly in violent marriages and relationships, I'm sure this happens a lot. Which is a tragedy. I wish we could do more to help those women, but somehow they have to find the courage to leave, and then we have to find a way of keeping them safe. Those are not easy things to do. The best strategy is actually for young women to be more discriminating in the first place. You see some of these women and you look at the blokes they're with, and you wonder how they ever thought that a violent thug with a tattooed neck, no job, a hair trigger of a temper and a criminal record was ever going to be the right man for them. My own daughters, I'm always saying to them, 'Be careful who you fall in love with.' But as we know, women can sometimes fall for the wrong type of man. It's been going on since forever.

There's also the ordeal – do you really want to talk to the police about having had sex with someone, or be examined physically, or go through it all again in public in court? Probably I wouldn't want to myself. But I can't see a way around this – we try to make the process as comfortable as it can be, but we need to ask questions, we need forensic and medical evidence and the case needs to be heard in public, to be fair to the defendant.

I also have no doubt that we, the police, handle some rapes badly. We handle *everything* badly at times, but then even the Space Shuttle crashed, didn't it? Cock-ups are part of life. In our force, we're very hot indeed on rape. We throw a lot of time and resources at it, which is as it should be. However, the other side of this is that we do get false allegations made and it's his word against hers. I don't mean a stranger in the bushes, he's not going to get far claiming the woman consented, but where the people know each other, or met on a night out and ended up in bed together... None of that means it's *not* a rape, it just makes it much harder to prove it *was*. He says she consented, she says she didn't. Juries don't like to send men to jail, particularly if they appear reasonable in the witness box. They'll be well aware of how men and women behave at times. They might well believe the victim, but without something more than she says he raped her they're loath to put a possibly innocent man in jail.

I wonder if we ought to change it so as any previous proven sexual allegations against the defendant are disclosed to the jury? And, to balance that, previous allegations made by the victim? But that's all a long way off my pay grade.

DC, 33, Northern force

Toms [*prostitutes*] do get raped and it should be, and is, taken seriously. But there is no doubt that other toms report rape because they're angling to get compensation. In a way, it's not surprising. If you're prepared to suck fat old Geordies off in the back seats of cars for £20 a throw, you might be the type to tell porky pies to get £10,000 from the Criminal Injuries Compensation Authority. You might not, but you might be.

There's some very interesting research from New Zealand to the effect that, when they stopped paying compensation to rape victims for a period of time, the number of reported rapes fell, and when they started again it rose again. It seems at least plausible that, from this, there was at least *some* correlation for *some* minority of women between making an allegation and getting wedged up. [*It may be, of course, that the prospect of financial compensation helped some victims face the unpleasant ordeal of the investigation and court process.*]

Please note, I am absolutely *not* saying actual rape is ever trivial. It's not. It's disgusting, hateful, and very distressing. It ruins lives. I dealt with a young woman who was raped by a fellow student one Christmas Eve, in some pub toilets. She could hear Slade and *Last Christmas* in the background. Every Christmas Eve forevermore she will remember that. When everyone else is celebrating, she'll be crying. When she hears those songs, they take her back. I think rapists should be sent away for a minimum of ten years.

I'm just saying that it's a challenge for us to sort out the actual rapes from the frauds. Because it is *also* distressing for an innocent man to be hauled out of bed at 6am, handcuffed, walked out with all the neighbours' curtains twitching, then being stripped and swabbed at the nick, interviewed *et cetera*. Speaking as someone who has done the hauling and cuffing, I know. Men have committed suicide, spent years in jail, lost their homes and families as a result of false allegations. That's not to mention the enormous amount of time and manpower involved in ultimately bogus investigations.

I honestly cannot understand why more of the false reporters don't get charged. In my view, they should get the same sentence as the offender would have, had it been real. They should be treated as seriously as corrupt police officers: there's no practical difference between that, and a bobby fitting someone up. The argument is that charging them will somehow put off 'genuine victims' from coming forward, because 'the police won't believe them', but this is wrong and silly. There are rape victims we can prove, rape victims we unfortunately can't prove, and people who make false allegations. It is *never* a case of, 'We don't believe you, therefore you're nicked.'

The question of whether or not a police officer 'believes' you when you report a rape is entirely irrelevant as to whether you end up being charged with wasting police time. You will only be charged with *any* offence if there is *evidence* of that offence, sufficient, in the eyes of the CPS, as to offer a reasonable prospect of a conviction on the traditional beyond all reasonable doubt basis. This is not the same as us being *un*able to prove the opposite, that the offence occurred.

There's a big difference between, 'I'm really sorry, we just can't prove this to the satisfaction of the CPS and a jury,' and 'We know you have made this up.'

Sometimes, undoubtedly and regrettably, rapes slip through because the evidence isn't there: this doesn't mean we don't think it happened, just that a jury won't be prepared to send someone to prison on the basis of the known facts. Genuine victims have absolutely nothing to fear from the police, in fact the reverse.

Sergeant, 40, Northern force

Many officers complain about the constant 'reinvention of the wheel' in British policing. Two key examples are the centralisation of custody and police stations and single-crewing. The move to hubs has seen police stations and cell blocks closing all over the country and moving to fewer, bigger facilities. This can mean officers have to travel as many as 20 or 30 miles to book-in prisoners – whereas previously they might have had a five- or ten-minute trip to a local suite. Single-crewing is also almost universally detested among the officers spoken to.

For some reason, the geniuses at the top of my force think that we can provide a better and more effective service if we close down and sell off all our outlying police stations to property developers and move everything to a hub system. Whereby the control is now done by people 30 miles away with no local knowledge of the area I police – guess what that means for *their* 'effectiveness'? Whereby if I arrest a prisoner I have to transport him 30 miles to the cells – guess what that means for *my* 'effectiveness'?

Not to mention that the old response teams – now renamed 'Targeted Patrol Teams', by the way, as if that makes any difference – have been smashed to bits so that they can take officers out and develop them into SNT teams... I have nothing against neighbourhood policing as such, or neighbourhood bobbies, but those are not magic new bobbies, they are just former response bobbies who are now *not* coming out to you when you ring 999. The chances of seeing an SNT officer any time other than 9-5 Monday to Friday are slim. About the same as seeing anyone across the force establishment over the rank of inspector.

Literally, we are chasing our tails from the start of the shift to the end, and the service we provide is terrible. We end up sending SNT people round to answer jobs three days later on a diary basis, rather than coming out when there's a chance of catching someone in the vicinity. How anyone can say with a straight face that this helps us police better I have no idea.

PC, 29, Southern force

A few years back, everything was devolved to local level – individual nicks had their own control rooms, their own dog teams, their own traffic, their own prisoner handling, their own SOCO, own CID... We were like little town police forces, which funnily enough had already been tried before. It actually worked quite well, you did have slacker periods when the dog – say – wasn't being used, but then policing requires slack to be there because it's unpredictable.

Then someone in the mood cloud at HQ decided that we ought to centralise everything to 'provide a better service', for which read 'cut costs'. One of the ways they did this was by claiming that no-one was visiting the local nicks to report crime, but they forgot to mention that this might be because they virtually closed the front desk except between 1000hrs and 1015hrs, put up a big sign saying, 'Go away, we're not interested', and made members of the public solve a Rubik's Cube before they were allowed in.

The whole previous system was sacked, nicks were shut, teams were disbanded, everyone came into the centre. Now after that proved to be an unmitigated disaster, with the dogs an hour away and being directed to your location by someone with absolutely no local knowledge, some new police-impersonator decided, you know what, we should have all our cops back out in the community... Slight issue, our old nick is now a Wetherspoon's. Meanwhile, HQ is crawling with ACC-this and DCC-that – there's more crappy scrambled egg up there than at a Travelodge breakfast, and more expensive German engineering than Hitler had at his disposal.

PC, 34, Southern force

Single-crewing is stupid. It only makes sense if you think the point of the police is this thing about 'reassurance', which is, the public see lots of police about so they feel better. The logic is, if you have two cops walking or driving down a given street, it's only the public in that specific street that is seeing you at work. If you split those resources into two, you can literally be in two streets at the same time with the same number of officers, and thus you can 'reassure' twice as many members of the public. If they feel better about things, we get better public satisfaction returns in our calls. [*Police officers and civilians are detailed to make thousands of telephone calls each month to members of the public to ask their views on crime in their area. These results are tabulated and help to form public satisfaction scores which are one of many ways in which police forces are ranked against each other. This work obviously takes police officers off the street full-time.*] Plus if you have twice as many cars on the road, the chances are greater that you will hit the target for response time in arriving at a job, even if the first car is as much use as a chocolate teapot. The fact is, it's a tacit admission that we have decided that a certain level of *actual* crime happening to some people is a price worth paying for this spurious reassurance of the rest. It's an admission, actually, that we can't do much about real crime, we can only massage your 'feelings' about it.

I don't personally buy the reassurance argument, anyway. Two years ago, if we went to a proper call needing four cops, we'd go in two cars. Now you'll have four cops in four cars and everyone sees four pandas rock up and immediately assumes world war three is kicking off on their doorstep.

PC, 30, Midlands force

It has been introduced by people who will never have to live the policy they force on the rest of us, and it doesn't work for very obvious reasons, reasons you only wouldn't see if you were a senior policeman or woman who doesn't understand that things have changed on the streets in the 15 years since you last walked them, if you ever did, when single patrolling on a beat was maybe the norm and the word of a police officer was generally believed by the magistrates and complaints from well-known local dregs were ignored. Or if you were more interested in appearances than reality.

Let me give you a very simple example. Last year, a colleague and I went to a report of a fight in a travel agents. Trev had gone in to book his holiday, even though he's on the dole he likes to get away to the sun a couple of times a year, and Kev had seen him going in. Trev owes Kev some money for a little job they did together some time earlier, when – it transpires – they pulled up a sizeable amount of cable from the industrial estate and flogged it off to a mate of Trev's. Trev was less than fair with the proceeds and Kev's not happy.

Anyway, by the time we got there, Trev was lying on the floor outside with a broken nose and Kev was trying to strangle him. There being two of us, we were able to separate them quite quickly, and cuff them both. Trev went in the car, I held on to Kev and my colleague went into the travel agents to have a word with the fairly traumatised ladies inside. It became clear that, for once, Trev was the innocent party, and that he'd been attacked from behind by Kev and hadn't so much as thrown a punch in self-defence. So he was removed from the car, de-arrested and uncuffed, and Kev went into the car instead. Job done. Lots of witness statements and so on to do, but the initial task of arresting the offender is done.

Now, if I had arrived on my own, could I have arrested both men? No, and not many people could. So either two cars would have been sent, or more likely I'd have gone on my own and had to call for back-up. Meanwhile, I'd have to choose one of them to detain and in all likelihood the other runs off. If I nick Trev, then we de-arrest him, that's now two cars on a wild goose chase through the town looking for Kev.

Even if Kev's the right guy, he's a violent thug. His hands are cuffed behind his back but that doesn't stop him leaning forward to spit at the driver and bite or head-butt him, or leaning back and kicking him. So obviously he needs to have another officer sitting with him in the back of the car while he gets transported to custody. We don't have any vans available 90 percent of the time, but that's another story. Last year, this would not be a problem. This year, I have to call a colleague out to help me transport, which means leaving a police car unattended outside the travel agent. There are three or four pubs and slot machine arcades on the row, and the place is heaving with people who hate the police. There's a fair chance that car is going to have its tyres slashed or something. We also have to remove the radio and MDT [*Mobile Data Terminal*] and police signs and stuff from the boot.

Central custody – because all our local cells have been closed as a cost-cutting, sorry, performance-enhancing, measure – is 45 minutes away, so even if the other officer could somehow hitch a lift back to the travel agent as soon as we get to the nick that's him off the road for ninety minutes. In fact, I've known it take two or three hours before someone is free to come back in and transport a bobby back to his car. People have taken taxis back out to get to their vehicles, which is embarrassing, and costly. Not to mention the extra diesel involved in having two or three cars drive around all over the place to deal with the same job that one used to.

Also not to mention the fact that, in many situations where it's an officer's word against a prisoner's, it's very useful to have a corroborating witness, i.e. a colleague. This is important evidence for court, because it is extremely hard – read 'impossible' – to get the CPS to run with anything uncorroborated. It's also important for batting off spurious complaints, of which we get quite a few – PSD, by the way, don't go about single-crewed – and which are very rarely, if ever, prosecuted for wasting police time, even when they are proved to be malicious. I believe double-crewing is a legal requirement in Scotland for exactly this reason.

But if you try to raise any of this, the implication is you're either some sort of dinosaur or you're scared to patrol alone. Leaving aside that, yes, some parts of our force area are very dangerous for lone officers, to have that implication come from people who haven't walked on anything except shagpile carpets for a decade is pretty insulting.

PC, 27, South-western force

In my force, assaults on police increased dramatically after single patrolling was introduced. Scrotes who would have come relatively quietly when there were two of us now will chance their arm, on the basis that they might get away and if they don't the courts will not add anything on to the ticket for assaulting a police officer as it's supposed to be 'part of our job'. Yet, if you raise this, it's ignored or you're threatened with an 'action plan' to improve your 'resilience'.

This from the same people who spend a fortune on health and safety modules for how to position your chair and use a kettle. *Actual* health and safety issues... Not so interested, thanks.

Funny also how the only people in the force who don't travel everywhere on their own are the senior management. The Chief Constable gets driven to his media appearances and committees and meetings, and yet a female officer like me is supposed to drive on her own to reports of five males fighting.

PC, 30, Southern force

Policing only really works as a team, and you don't feel part of a team if you're driving round on your own all day. It helps, mentally and physically, to be able to have a laugh and a joke with colleagues. Not to mention that more inexperienced officers can learn from the more experienced, just chatting as you drive round, just watching them at work, learning the streetcraft, because we don't get taught that at training school, sadly.

Finally, certainly in my training the self-defence techniques we were taught involved having an oppo with you. How does that work, then? And think about the biggest and ugliest doorman you see standing outside the nightclubs in town. Now imagine him off his face with anger and spitting with roid rage because he's just found out his missus is shagging behind his back. Fancy getting between him and the wife, and bringing him in on your own? Especially when the wife will be nailing you with her stiletto as you're trying to get him under control and screaming, 'Leave him along you fucking pig, he ain't done nothing!' It's nice to have someone to back you up at times like that.

The other thing is, the law of unintended and yet somehow obvious consequences which pervades British policing also dictates that single-crewing will inevitably result in more injuries to members of the public, more use of TASER, more use of spray, because it is much easier to subdue and arrest an unwilling person in a way which does not cause serious injury to him or her with two or more officers than it is with one. Then there will be lots of complaints and media stories and the wheel will turn and single patrolling will be banned, like it used to be in the not-too-distant past.

PC, 26, Southern force

The way we take nonsense complaints seriously is frightening. A mate of mine was binned for allegedly sexually assaulting a lone female at an address, when the officer in question had a blemishless 10-year career, commendations, and the female in question was a drug addict with markers for mental health, convictions for offences including dishonesty and who changed her story multiple times. I would bet my life that the guy never touched her, but he was still binned. We get done on the balance of probabilities, not beyond reasonable doubt, and there's no jury, it's all internal. As a result of this, I will not attend any call to any lone female on my own, not ever. I don't care if my boss gives me a direct order, I will find a reason not to go in until I have back-up. I am not losing my house and pension over some lying scummer fitting me up, I'm sorry. If that means genuine vics don't get the service they need, lobby your MP and write to the press about it. I'm sorry, I really am, but no way.

PC, 30, Southern force

A group of kids were winding people up in one of our nightclubs, and one of them picked on the wrong bloke and got glassed. To be brutally honest, he probably got what he deserved. Anyway, the ambo arrived to treat the kid, and his mates attacked the ambo. I was like, 'What the hell do you think you're doing? The ambo are trying to help your mate and you're attacking them? This is mad!'

One of his mates started having a go at me, then. I was like, 'Give it a rest, mate.' Then, 'Listen, shut up.' And finally, 'Get back, now! Get back, now!'

In the end he started throwing haymaker punches at me. So he got nicked. He complained, and the complaint was taken seriously and investigated, that I had said to him, 'if you don't behave, I am going to rip off your arm and beat you with the soggy end.'

It was laughable... As though you're going to say something like that, and that if you did you'd mean it. It got written off and the lad got potted, but the idea that time was taken up investigating it is mad.

PC, 40, Northern force

I do think there are some officers who lack the robustness necessary to patrol alone. We have allowed too many people into the police who are scared of their own shadows and I could name half a dozen or more officers over the past five years or so who have gone off sick with stress or made allegations of bullying simply because they were ordered to do their job and they didn't have the required mettle. But it's an institutional thing – officers have to complete courses to be approved to ride a bike, we get warning emails round advising us that the steps at the front of the nick are being remodelled and until then are a slip/trip hazard, and that we should ensure we keep warm in the winter or cool in the summer. That said, none of this is an argument for double-crewed patrols, it is an argument for those officers not being in the Job. You're going to be on your own sometimes, whatever the policy, and if you go to pieces then you're no good to me.

I also think there's a time and a place for single-crewing. In the far rural parts of the county, daytime shifts, on relatively routine calls – always accepting that there is no such thing as 'routine' – then I don't have a massive problem with it. I would prefer all my officers to be with a crewmate, because of that thing about 'routine' jobs, but I have to accept that life isn't perfect. At night, and during the day in the county's biggest city and surrounding towns, single-crewing in busy high crime areas in 2011 is mental, it's a recipe for disaster. I don't believe it is safe and I have said so in writing to my superiors. On many occasions I have refused to single-crew my team. Sometimes we do this by finding fault with the vehicles, like a light out or a warning light on, and there are always faults to find, but I also do it more openly on officer safety grounds and I have not been challenged about that.

You have to remember that these people [*senior officers*] are generally highly risk-averse and motivated by personal gain and their own careers; the last thing they want is a paper trail that says inspector so-and-so warned that it was not safe to single-crew on the [*name*] estate, we forced his hand and an officer was stabbed to death. I personally patrol alone as I feel that's my role, and I *have* been challenged about patrolling, as apparently I lose 'oversight' of what's going on in the division if I'm out and about. On occasion, when I can, I accompany officers on patrol, because there are not enough PCs.

I accept that my attitude will do my career no good, but I'm not looking for promotion. I have reached the highest rank possible in the police where you are still a policeman, and that will do for me.

Inspector, 44, Southern force

I would really, really love my job if it weren't for all the unnecessary, wheel-reinventing nonsense like this. I don't mind taking on violent thugs, but I do expect not to have one arm tied behind my back. I wonder when my boss last attended a report of burglars-on, and ended up rolling around in the roses with a maniac trying to stab him with a chisel? Or stopped a yoot in Tottenham when a dozen of his mates were only round the corner and he was carrying a knife, as plenty of people do these days? I suspect the honest answer would be either, 'Ten years ago,' or 'Never.'

I'd probably be OK with single-crewing if I didn't keep coming across these kinds of people, or if I had a gun and a car with a cage in it like the Americans do. I'm not a particularly hard bloke, I'm just a normal person, I have some very poor officer safety training which does not turn me into a ninja, and four hours of refresher each year, and it's nice to feel that there's another guy there with me facing the lunatic, or the stroppy kid with a teenth of cannabis and a blade and a bad attitude, a low threshold for violence and no thought of any consequences.

I think the divide between me and my colleagues at the bottom and the uniform carriers at the top is becoming a chasm. They're walking around in their corridor congratulating each other on the latest scheme, pushing non-existent battalions of cops around the map and then knocking off at teatime, just as we're clocking on, to drive home in their expensive unmarked Job car. Vorsprung durch technik, as they say on *Fantasy Island*.

PC, 29, Southern force

When people complained about single-crewing, we were told to make what they call 'a dynamic risk assessment' on arrival at a job. That covers their arses. 'Did you risk-assess before entering the property?' If you say 'No,' whose fault is it when it all goes bent? If you say, 'Yes' – Ah! Obviously your risk assessment was suspect. It's not that black and white, obviously, but the system is gamed in favour of the bosses. Realistically, I don't, and you couldn't, 'risk-assess' every time you go to a job. The whole thing would grind to a halt. Every house our officers go to they could ask whether there are firearms registered to the premises, what intel markers for the premises are on the system, what previous calls have come from there, whether there are any mental health or violence or drugs or other markers against the caller or anyone else believed to be living at the premises... By the time the control room have found all that information, the woman's been stabbed to death. So what we do is we go in, but we go in with a little stick, gritted teeth and bitterness in our hearts.

It's the same mentality which insists that I have to confirm on the radio *en route* to any griefy kind of job that I am wearing my stabbie [*vest*]. They couldn't care less if I'm actually stabbed and hurt as long as they can point to the log and say, 'See, we checked he was wearing his PPE [*personal protective equipment*].'

Digressing slightly, but when I was transferred to SNT I was called in and told there was a health and safety issue, which was that I needed to be trained in the use of a bicycle, which I was going to be using on my beat. I thought it was a joke at first. I'm 40 years of age, I've been riding a bike since I was five.

'Oh, we can never stop learning.'

'I've got my *Blue Peter* cycling proficiency badge at home, if that helps?'

'Now you're being difficult.'

So I had to spend half a day cycling through cones and being told to be aware of the risks from insects, sun exposure, not falling off, risk assessing before I got on the bike *et cetera*. They gave me a leaflet which had a seven point plan for getting off the bike. It tells you to use your brakes to stop, rather than putting your feet down. I haven't done that since I retired the old Raleigh Chopper in about 1977. I know it's funny in a way, but when you start to think of the cost of writing, designing and printing these damn things, and what that money could actually be spent on it's not. I suppose it's down to the lawyers. If you have an accident on your bike and you haven't been properly 'trained', maybe you can sue. Officers *have* sued the Job. So maybe it's our own fault really? I don't know.

Sergeant, 43, Midlands force

The latest figures came out and inevitably showed we were stopping fewer people and vehicles. Our boss was delighted, the implication being we were all being good boys and girls and using discretion rather than doing random stops. Which only goes to prove what a fool you are, Ma'am. Obviously, the real reason was because single-crewed officers are less keen to stop people who also aren't on their own. I hate to admit it, but put yourself in my place, it's 3am and a moody car with four blokes smoking what looks suspiciously like ganja stops at the lights next to you. Would *you* pull them over and spin the vehicle? You ought to, but if you know the nearest back-up is 10 miles away, that the Airwave doesn't work in half the county, that the motor is probably nicked and that you'll spend the next fortnight eating through a straw and they'll probably not get nicked [*because the driver is untraceable via the car registration*], what would you do? Believe me, rolling around in the road trying to press the alarm button on your radio while you're getting a proper shoeing, 30 seconds feels like a very long time, let alone 30 minutes. If there are two of you, you can usually handle a car of lads. On your own it only takes one of them to put two-and-two together and have a go.

That's the hidden truth behind single-crewing – fewer police interventions, fewer searches, means fewer recoveries of drugs, fewer going-equippeds, fewer offensive weapons discovered. All of which means less crime – in the statistical sense. If you were cynical, you might even think that was part of the plan.

PC, 26, Midlands force

The combination of single-crewing and hubs is a nightmare. When I joined 20 years ago, the town I worked at had its own police station, with its own cells and interview rooms and three shifts of eight bobbies and a CID office with, I think, a DS and two DCs. That's for a town of, then, about 30,000 people. We also had a couple of bobbies attached to the nick but effectively permanently out on patrol in the several dozen surrounding villages. Now that town has grown to 50,000 people and the nick has closed. It's policed from the next town on, with at most four officers. They have to transport prisoners to a town another 10 miles over, and if that custody is full, as it very often is, then they have to go south another 20 miles. I mean, this is crazy. The wheel is going to come off big-time one day.

PC, 40, Midlands force

A lot of these changes have been brought about by managerialists and consultants. KPMG are one of the biggest cancers on the police with their QUEST bollocks. [*Highly popular with police officers at the operational levels, Operation QUEST is a refreshingly jargon-free KPMG programme which allegedly (says its website) helps law enforcement agencies 'generate annualised operational efficiency savings whilst simultaneously delivering substantial performance improvements to frontline service provision... To capitalise on the latent passion and ability of frontline staff, it is critical that they drive the change rather then being alienated by it. This "bottom-up" ethos of the QUEST approach ensures staff involvement throughout, helps to foster goodwill, gives discretion back to the frontline and acts as a catalyst for cultural change... (F)rontline staff work "shoulder to shoulder" with KPMG advisors... Opportunities to improve operational performance by designing out wasteful activity are identified...'*]

In our nick, we started a verb, to *QUEST*. 'I wonder if the missus will be up for a good QUESTing tonight?' – that sort of thing. Because we have been thoroughly QUESTed to ensure we conform to the New Policing Model, which appears to be mainly aimed at fucking around our shifts and work-life balance and turning everyone into neighbourhood policemen in a city with a very serious gun crime problem.

I haven't seen any sign of KPMG on the frontline when I'm chasing an addict down a back alley at 2am, yet they are supposedly giving frontline police officers the skills they need to 'work more effectively.' Are these fitness or close control 'skills' to assist them in dealing with cage fighters who don't want to be arrested, or interviewing 'skills', or little wrinkles on how to set up an obbo [*observation*] or whatever? Er, no.

PC, 40, Northern force

I'd like to mention QUEST, so I brought this today [*produces Home Office / QUEST brochure*] which I found lying around in the nick. Honestly, it's a bullshit bingo dream. They write in this way which you'd almost think was designed to obfuscate. I mean, what is a 'workstream'? What are 'stakeholder issues'? What is the 'QUEST sustainability pyramid'? Here's a weird couple of diagrams produced by something called 'Human Synergistics' which seems to be playing off a police force's 'People Orientation', 'Task Orientation', 'Security Needs' and 'Satisfaction Needs' against each other, and comes to the conclusion that the particular force is not 'Self-Actualizing' or 'Humanistic-Encouraging' enough on the 'Satisfaction Needs' side of things, and has too much 'Power' on 'Task Orientation' and too much 'Conventional', if that makes any kind of sense, sort of half-way between 'People Orientation' and 'Security Needs'.

That just means nothing to me, and I suspect if you knocked on the doors of 1,000 actual taxpayers – the people who are paying for this stuff – not one of them would have heard of QUEST. And if you showed them this and said to them, 'Would you like our force to have everyone sitting in a rolling series of meetings designed to draw up, through the medium of QUEST, our Organisational Cultural Inventory so as to help diagnose and tackle any underlying cultural issues which may impact upon delivery, or would you rather we just knuckled down and tried to catch your burglar?', they would opt for the latter in 999 cases out of 1,000, and the only way it wouldn't be 1,000 out of 1,000 is if you happened to knock on the door of someone who worked for fucking KPMG. But they don't tend to live round where I police, so it would be 1,000.

The other thing I notice from this little brochure is, there's a section called 'What the papers say.' And you think, OK, journalists get just about everything wrong but maybe they've knocked on a few doors and asked a few questions and have some feedback from the public about QUEST. But the 'papers' are all government papers – Ronnie Flanagan's Review of Policing, a Green Paper about neighbourhood policing and something called 'Excellence and Fairness –Achieving World Class Public Services', which elicits a hollow laugh from me.

It would be funny if it wasn't so expensive and if my daughter and my mum didn't both live in high crime areas where we are virtually absent. Ask them how they feel about the QUEST sustainability pyramid. And you know what the strangest thing is? In other forces, they've been through QUEST and are now dismantling it.

Inspector, 42, Northern force

I don't want to come across as a moaner. I have a lot of respect for the trade I'm in. I like the fact that by and large we do an important job of work, helping people. I like the variety... No two days are the same. I mean, with experience you learn that Friday night is fight night, Monday is when people crash their cars and come in to work to find their offices have been broken into. But there are always different challenges.

But like my dad was an electrical and mechanical engineer who liked that trade, he might not have liked the actual company he worked for, and I don't like what we have become as a force. We just seem to concentrate on the wrong things. We waste time and money on nonsense... Constant force reorganisations, so you go from a division-based system, to sub-divisions, to OCUs, and back again, roughly every two years. You go from a centralised control room to divisional control rooms, and then back again. Each time, it costs money. We produce glossy brochures telling people how wonderful we are and you think, *Why don't we just do our job?*

Sergeant, 43, Midlands force

I think the long-term goal is the privatisation of the police. Call me paranoid, but ACPO is a private company. The government don't like the fact that we are not answerable, at least in theory, to them and they are determined to make us accountable under the cloak of 'value for money'.

The way to achieve this is first to knock down the police. There was a time when the British bobby was regarded very warmly by the public, generally. Now, if you look at the way that bullshit complaints are taken seriously, the way our own chiefs are always bibbling on about 'learning lessons' about everything, at the way the media constantly knock us, at the way we have been directed to the criminalising of the honest middle and working classes, our traditional supporters, at the expense of targeting actual criminals, that has long gone.

You sell off nicks and training establishments so your fixed costs are lower, and finally you introduce a parallel force in the shape of the PCSOs. They cost pretty much the same as a new PC, yet they have none of the powers. They can't work in the dark, they can't nick people, they can't interview people, they can't crime jobs, they can't drive on blues and twos, they can't search people, they can't issue tickets or producers [*requirements to produce a driving licence or other document at the police station at a later date*]... What on earth is the point of them? Except, unlike bobbies, they can be made redundant. Private employers don't want to take on people who work for the Queen and can't be made redundant, do they? So you build up a force of PCSOs, you get the public used to the concept, and then – bang! You invite tenders.

Inspector, 42, Northern force

A common theme among interviewees was staffing levels, with most response officers complaining of frighteningly low numbers on the streets. Typical was one sergeant who spoke of only six regular police officers being available to police a busy town of 100,000 people, with inexperienced special constables being used to make up the numbers.

I don't care what senior management or politicians say about more police on the streets, it is a lie. I can tell you from my own experience. There may be more police than there were 25 years ago, but there are not more on the streets.

I joined the police in the mid-1980s. Initially, I joined a smaller force which covers the area I grew up in, and then I transferred later to the neighbouring force, which is much bigger. The nearest town to where I lived used to parade a shift of six officers in 1985. I met a sergeant from my old force a week or two back and he said that now they parade two officers to cover that town and all the surrounding villages, up to 15 miles in any direction. In the next town over, which is a bit bigger but still under-policed, they had had a serious incident – one bloke had stabbed another in the street in a row over a girl. It was a serious stabbing, attempt murder. The sergeant had two officers to deal with that. That shocked even me. I said, 'Two officers? For arresting and booking-in, dealing with witnesses, dealing with the CCTV, guarding the scene?'

He shrugged and said, 'I have two officers. That's it.'

In my own force, our OCU [*Operational Command Unit – effectively, a division*] is split into two sub-divisions and we are supposed to parade six cars of two officers in each, so that's 24 officers in total. We regularly put out three cars in each. We drop jobs all the time, but there's nothing you can do about it. Meanwhile, there are reams of people in the back offices doing God knows what. We have an ongoing programme called Continuous Improvement, which is supposed to look constantly at the way we do 'business' with our 'customers'… The joke in the nick is, it's 'continuous' because if you don't reach an end point, you can never be said to have failed. Obviously, getting everyone out of the nick arresting criminals would be simply ludicrous.

PC, 30, Midlands force

If the public at large knew how thinly spread we are they'd be horrified. On the occasions I get chatting to someone who is complaining about a poor police response to a call they've made, I'll ask them how many cops they think we put out on a late shift. They'll say 50 or 60… The actual answer is between six and eight. They tend to think you're making it up. This is the message I try to ram home whenever I can: however many bobbies you think are covering this patch right now, halve it, halve it again and subtract half a dozen, and you're probably not far off.

Sergeant, 40, Midlands force

I attended a PACT meeting where I sat at the front and took all sorts of flak for the poor performance of the police in the area. We hadn't attended various shed breaks particularly quickly, we hadn't responded to calls about kids playing football in the park, we hadn't responded to calls about neighbours parking their cars in front of other people's driveways – as though there's no way people could sort this out without resorting to the police. It went on for quite a while.

Then I said, 'Can I just ask, how many people do you think are on duty at the moment to cover this division, which includes [town] and [town] and two dozen other villages like this one? Which means a population of about 125,000 people, five industrial estates, a hundred or so farms, and 300 miles of roads?'

A guy said, 'Probably a hundred?'

I said, 'Six, including me. It would have been seven, but the other officer is on a course.'

Their jaws hit the floor. One guy said, 'There's more staff in the Queen's Head!'

I said, 'Further, if we arrest anyone, that's two officers off the road for the next three hours, at least.'

They were horrified. I said, 'Please don't tell anyone you heard this from me.'

If they then go back and report to my bosses that I've told them this, I'll be in deep shit for damaging public confidence. It makes me very angry, the lies and the bullshit.

Sergeant, 38, Southern force

In late 2009, we had a meeting with our divisional commander where she told us that they had reviewed our staffing levels on response and it had been proved by the experts that a new minimum level of 10 officers was ideal for our BCU, down from the previous minimum of 14. This in an area where we used to parade two dozen officers not that long ago. The new level was being introduced, and it would no longer be called 'minimum' but 'optimum'. Shades of George Orwell. There were a few murmurs of discontent and she said the change would improve our efficiency by 'ensuring we focus our resources to optimum effect.' More Orwell.

Never mind that we *never* put out 10, thanks to illness, injury, annual leave, courses, abstractions, court appearances and the rest. Spin forward to the beginning of 2011, and she has moved on to head up some other unit at the Centre, and the new superintendent arranged a new meeting and said the experts had reviewed our optimum staffing levels and had decided that eight was the new 10. Most days we're lucky if we put out four or five on shift, to cover a town of more than 80,000 people.

Mind you, the police station car park is absolutely rammed 9-5, Monday to Friday, with all those vitally important people doing public reassurance work, collating statistics and sending emails out to us to ask why we're not hitting our response times and arrest targets.

I genuinely don't understand how there isn't a national outcry. I can only assume it's because the opinion formers and important people either live in London, where the Met actually does have serious numbers, or in the leafy shires where there actually isn't much crime. Who cares if there are no cops in the provincial cities or towns? No-one who counts lives there, do they?

PC, 32, Midlands force

I moved from the Met to a rural force for the quality of life. Basically, I was fed up spending two hours commuting to and from a job where I was increasingly being assaulted, hassled by management and let down by the CPS and the courts.

Out of the frying pan and all that. Management are no better, if not worse, and the CPS and courts are just as bad. I don't get threatened or assaulted as much and I don't have to commute but I do spend all day every day being run ragged, haring from job to job with no back-up or support. All of our vehicles are seriously shagged out – I'm talking hundreds of thousands of miles. There's lots of police in the UK, even in our force, but the actual numbers of frontline officers who will respond to 999 calls are very low in the rural forces. There are plenty in the various offices and units – for instance, we've got a team called some fancy name dedicated to improving 'performance' which has 25 warranted police officers attached to it. They never make any arrests, naturally. Same with the Public Confidence Unit, the Domestic Violence Unit, the Hate Crime Unit... Loads of cops, in offices, not arresting people.

On response, you can *easily* be the only officer out there – all it takes is a couple of arrests and an RTC and that's everyone else either at a scene, on a hospital guard, or back at the nick booking-in and writing up files. I'm TASER-trained, so, OK, I'm on my own, but at least I have TASER. Wrong! Our force policy is that TASER-equipped officers have to be double-crewed. How do you get round that? And who wrote the policy that says the very time you most need TASER you're not allowed to have it?

PC, 29, Northern force

When I was first made inspector, I supervised seven sergeants and nearly 60 PCs on response. Over the next five to 10 years, this has been eroded to the point where I now supervise two Sergeants and 18 PCs. Mind you, that's still more responsibility than some. I know inspectors who are supervising absolutely no-one. Over the years they created all sorts of new squads aimed at tackling the latest pet problems – they took PCs off response and expanded things like the Domestic Violence Team. With the result that we now have police constables who have never policed in the true sense of the word. I can show you people who have spent their entire service of several years in Case Management Teams, Best Value Teams, the Service Definition Unit, whatever the hell that is.

These people basically sit around all day churning out emails. We get dozens of these things, actually reading and digesting them would be a full-time job if you could be bothered, and it's truly frightening when you look at the long list of people who are cc-d in, and you go, '*He's* never policed, *she's* never policed, *he* doesn't know where his cuffs are, it's 10 years since *he* made an arrest…'

I'm not saying nothing else has any value, but in my view everyone who joins the police should have to spend a minimum of five years working shifts before they're even considered for any specialist role or promotion. Anyone who gets promoted above sergeant should be promoted up through uniform response, too. I might make an exception for career detectives, but if you're a skipper in some office buried deep in force HQ cranking the magic email machine, and you want to get your two pips, you should go out and do a couple of years dealing with Friday night drunks before you get to scurry back to your desk. It's the only way we will develop a cadre of senior officers who actually know what we do, because believe me, most of them currently are clueless.

Inspector, 39, Northern force

We just don't have the time to do a proper job any more. In my force, in my opinion, as response officers we deliver an absolutely terrible service to members of the public. We spend our lives blatting about the place as fast as we're allowed and we never have the time to do anything creative. I'd like to be able to sit with some of the people who call us – often they're old people, or vulnerable people, and they would really value that. But it's knock the door, hello, goodbye, and off we go to the next job. We never get the time to go back to see our victims and update them. It's just constantly reacting to the jobs as they come in.

There's an industrial estate on us in a town on the edge of [city] which is always getting screwed. When I first joined, we did a lot of dressing up in plain clothes and hanging around there of an evening, and we nicked loads of these scrotes. Now that's all gone.

PC, 40, South-Western force

I had a very bog standard call the other day. Youths hanging around, throwing bottles in the street and a fence had been damaged. Now, the person who made that call wanted us there quickly so as we could apprehend the offenders and deal with them, instead of what actually happened, which was me and my mate turning up two hours later, by which time the youths had long gone.

Now, actually, I have a lot of sympathy with the decent, law-abiding public who get annoyed when they call us and we take forever to get there. I can understand their frustration, in fact I feel it myself. The trouble is, people don't seem to understand why it is that we aren't there immediately. I said to this guy with the bottle-throwing youths, who was pretty angry, there are only two possibilities. The first is that we're basically too busy eating doughnuts or watching telly to come out to you. I'm lucky if I get five minutes to eat a sandwich most days, so that's not it. The second is that we're really busy dealing with other offences that either happened before this or are more important. And I'm sorry, but I got here as quick as I could.

I'd *like* to have added, 'Actually, there's a third possibility. There are plenty of people called "police officers" in this town, with warrant cards and handcuffs hidden away in their desk drawers, but they never, ever, come out to calls from members of the public. Police officers who actually respond to calls from members of the public in this town, at this moment... There are six of us. And if we arrest a pair of shoplifters, a couple of drunks and a husband and wife who are shouting at each other in the street, then the paperwork and the assorted rigmarole can easily keep us off the street for the next three or four hours. So that's the whole town's police cover gone, just like that. Now, someone might come over from the other side of the county, and if world war three erupts they'll find some bodies from somewhere, but youths throwing bottles? Not a chance.'

And the crazy, crazy thing about this... Well, there are two crazy things. The first is that the officers sitting in the nick 'working' on the various squads or auditing response's performance and monitoring us 24/7 are mostly there to improve public confidence by massaging the figures, and the second is that what people *really* want, and what I think would be better, is more of us responding to calls from the public about crimes. People don't care about the crime figures, they don't even see them; all they want is us to come round and deal with youths vandalising their streets, and I think that's fair enough.

Sergeant, 40, Southern force

There are roughly 140,000 police officers covering the whole of the UK, 70 million people and however many square miles and miles of road, but the majority of them never respond to 999 calls – traffic officers, CID, domestic violence teams, burglary squads, car crime squads, custody officers, front desk, Neighbourhood teams, licensing officers, armed officers, schools liaison, community liaison, diplomatic protection, PSD, British Transport Police, and all the office-bounds and senior ranks. Of those who do, there's annual leave, rest days, appearing in court, courses, maternity leave, sickness and injury, and, increasingly, stress. We police 24/7, 365 days a year, in shifts. If you look at it like that, you begin to see how thinly spread we are.

As someone once said to me, if a man breaks his arm, he doesn't mind waiting in casualty, but if they call us because a neighbour swore at them they expect us there inside five minutes. Yet casualty has three times the staff that we have on division, and we have a thousand calls to deal with every day, whereas A&E has a couple of dozen.

The main problem with the generally honest, law-abiding public is one of expectations. On the telly, you call 999 and the cops are there in five minutes. Somehow, we have let it become part of the national folklore that we're all sitting there champing at the bit waiting for the phone to go. Maybe it stems from a previous era, when a town like mine used to parade 30 PCs per shift, instead of now where it will be five or six.

Inspector, 44, Southern force

As well as low numbers, frontline officers feel passionately that the equipment they are given is of poor quality.

Our equipment is almost uniformly terrible. Maybe other forces are different, but ours all seems to have been ordered with short-term cost in mind.

Our radios don't work if you're indoors, or outdoors, or it's cloudy, or too sunny, or you're near a big tree, or you're in one of the black-spots all over the force area where we can't get any service, no matter what the conditions, which is not very good at all when you're being assaulted or need to get some other urgent message across. Many's the time I've had to ring in with my personal mobile.

The MDTs in the cars don't work. The cars themselves are fecked. Our shirts cost something like 35p a piece, and you can wear them about twice before they look terrible, and another twice before they start to fall apart. Particularly when you wear them under body armour. They bobble up, they go out of shape with all the sweat, they look really scruffy.

The body armour itself is rubbish, though admittedly it's better than it used to be. Until recently, we had pool armour, and you sweat a lot in it, particularly in the summer, so you end up wearing some gorilla's soaking-wet armour which doesn't really fit you properly, which is a safety compromise, and is all scuffed up and in some cases even damaged. Who bothers to look after pooled equipment? Now we have individual issue, which is a bit better but only because you're not absorbing someone else's BO. They trialled various types and ended up choosing the cheapest, shoddiest available, which made me wonder why they bothered with the trials. A year down the line, we all look like scarecrows.

PC, 39, Northern force

In our force, it used to be that you had to wear your PPE at all times. This annoyed some people – in our nick, the heating only goes off when it gets to about 100°F outside, so the summer months are almost literally unbearable. Then a PCSO sued because he sustained a spinal injury from being ordered to wear unsuitable armour, and it all changed. Now it's down to you to make your own 'dynamic risk assessment', which is a bizarre phrase to me. I get told to carry out these things by people who only leave the nick for a fag or to go shopping. The idea is, I get about a third of a second to make my mind up on a matter of life and death, at night, in the pissing rain by a broken streetlamp, and then the SMT, PSD, IPCC, the papers and half a dozen lawyers get to sit down in and air-conditioned room six months later and spend several weeks gaming my actions. Given that you never really know *what* you're going to find at any job, if I actually risk-assessed jobs I wouldn't go anywhere without a dog van, firearms, a PSU and a helicopter filming from above. But I imagine the body armour policy will stay that way until someone unfortunately makes the wrong risk assessment, dynamically-speaking, and his or her family sue the Job because there wasn't a policy in place to ensure he or she was wearing the body armour, at which point the policy will reverse through 180 degrees.

Personally speaking, I've always worn it and I always will. The very nature of the Job is that it's unpredictable, so the whole concept of deciding when you need to get the armour out of the boot and when you can leave it there is nonsense. I would certainly never enter the police station without it. I've seen too many good men stabbed in the back in there to make that mistake.

PC, 40, Eastern force

We can choose whether to wear it, and I do have colleagues who, certainly in the warmer months, don't bother. Fair enough, it's their funeral, I hope not literally. But my experience is that the times you decide you won't bother is when you'll very suddenly wish you had. Like, I stopped two youths for a chat round the back of our local shopping centre, all very friendly, and the next minute a third, entirely unrelated guy has come out of nowhere from behind some big wheelie bins and tried to do me in the back with a screwdriver. It skidded up where the armour protected my ribs and went nearly an inch into the right tricep. I'm not saying I'd have been killed, but I think it's highly likely that I'd have been in shit state. The guy was mad and should have been in hospital, but he'd walked out a day or two before and no-one had bothered trying to stop him.

PC, 29, Midlands force

Our control now asks that you confirm you're wearing your vest when you are *en route* to a job. I'd *like* to think that this is because they give a monkey's about me, but in reality it's obviously an arse-covering exercise so that if I get stabbed, they can say they told me to wear a vest. We do a lot of this sort of thing, drown the radio in pointless bollocks. It's almost more important than what you do when you get there. They want the right boxes ticked on the transcript of the radio for later on, so they can load it all on you if it goes pear-shaped. There is absolutely no culture of supporting the troops on the ground.

PC, 34, Midlands force

One of our bosses is obsessed with making sure we're wearing the stabbie, to the point where it gets a bit irritating. But he has been stabbed himself and a few years back he almost lost one of his officers to a knife. So it's understandable. Another of them *doesn't* like us wearing vests... He's always moaning that they look scruffy and give off the wrong impression to the public. He's obsessed about hats, too. 'Why is that officer not wearing his hat? It gives a bad impression.' You despair.

PC, 28, Eastern force

I suppose as a community officer I should expect that the kit we get issued is not brilliant, but my brother's an ARV [*Armed Response Vehicle officer*] in [*a northern force*] and his is even worse. His PPE doesn't fit – it ends about level with his navel, just where you want to get stabbed – and the chest plate doesn't fit. Even worse, he struggles to actually use his pistol in a firing position because the damn thing's so bulky it constrains his arms. I'd love to know how much they cost.

PC, 30, Eastern force

They don't last forever, Kevlar degrades over time. I think they're guaranteed for five years but there are all sorts of conditions like, you have to store it properly, not throw it in the back of your car or stuff it in a locker every night, you can't expose it to prolonged moisture, or direct sunlight… I mean, how can you avoid that if you spend any time outdoors? A lot of our vests expired a long while ago, but we were told not to worry, the use-by date was only for guidance and they'd been tested and found to be OK. I was told that this testing involved some random bloke attacking one of the vests and trying to get through it with different knives. A Samurai sword apparently managed to get through, but that's fine because we never come across those in real life.

The thing that confuses me about this is, I can't square it in my mind with the general culture of risk aversion in the police. I assume that someone somewhere has put his name to this, that the vests are OK, even though the paperwork presumably says they should have been swapped for new ones. So if someone is badly hurt, surely that's an open-and-shut case, compo-wise? I understand the cost issue at the present moment, but when *is* a good time to spend millions on replacing the entire force stock of body armour?

PC, 30, Eastern force

In 2000 we were told to change all our cars [*in the officer's covert surveillance team*] due to age and mileage. The DS in charge was asked to submit a list of the vehicles we needed, so he put down six different makes, models and colours. Then we waited and waited, can't rush these things, to finally receive a telephone call from the civilian buyer that the vehicles were at the traffic garage ready for collection. We all went down full of anticipation to be confronted by six dark blue Ford Mondeos with sequential number plates. Absolutely brilliant for following a suspect. The civilian responsible for buying the said cars said he thought we were only joking when we gave him the list of vehicles we wanted.

It's not just the civvies, mind you. Our detective superintendent retired and was replaced with a transferee who was an ex-graduate and had no experience of surveillance whatsoever. He decided that the team was claiming too much in expenses and therefore introduced the following policy. Surveillance officers could no longer claim for meals and would have to eat in police buildings during a tour of duty. Also, officers would no longer purchase Tube tickets but show their warrant cards. [*Officers in London are allowed – currently – to travel free on the London Underground, on the basis that this helps to protect other travellers from crime.*]

Madness. How you can follow someone if you have to break away to go back to the nick for your tea is beyond me. Plus on the Tube thing, guess what, the guy we were following eventually saw one of the officers show his warrant card... End of that job. This bozo also introduced similar policies with the area intelligence unit and crime squad. The end result was he lasted three months in post. I'm sure it had nothing to do with him finding his car up on bricks one afternoon.

DC, Southern force

A common self-description among response police officers is 'uniformed social worker'. Much of their work involves liaising with social services, mental health teams and other agencies. It's not always a happy experience.

We got a call to a mental health unit, where one of the patients had gone berserk with a knife. So we all coded up in the black ninja gear [*put on protective clothing and equipment*] and started going through the building. It was a long building with lots of rooms, and we basically had to go through and systematically clear each one, because the guy had free rein around the building.

Eventually, we found him and subdued him. Now, when we do this it is not a gentle experience: there's a mental patient with a knife, that's our lives at risk, so we are very aggressive and forceful. And when we got this kid on the floor, I found he was armed with a plastic butter knife.

I said to the unit manager, 'What the hell did you call us over this for?'

He said, 'He could hurt someone with that.'

I said, 'It's a plastic butter knife, for God's sake,' and I snapped it in half and handed it to him. 'He can't hurt anyone with it. This is ridiculous.'

Bear in mind that this guy has mental health problems, the last thing he needs is a gang of us jumping on him yelling and wearing helmets and carrying shields. It was disgusting.

Sergeant, 43, Midlands force

There's a 17-year-old burglar in our town, Lee. After being convicted of his third wave of dwelling burglaries, he was sent to prison for 12 months, much to the relief of the folk on the local housing estate. Lee lives among them, he knows when they're in or out, what property they have and when to take it. He sold what he stole and spent the money on cannabis and, no doubt, cocaine. You'd think we'd be happy with the sentence – we can now go after other crooks for at least a few months. Except that we can't, because Lee appealed the sentence and was out after six weeks. He is apparently classed as 'vulnerable' as he is 17, with a whole entourage of social workers and youth offending team officers responsible for him back in the 'community'. In the system's eyes, Lee is as much a victim as those he stole from.

His mother didn't want him back – he bullies the other members of her extensive brood and kicks the dog. The local authority's accommodation for 'vulnerable youths' won't have him, either, because last time he was there he was caught smoking cannabis and trashed his room. He also owes them a few hundred quid in rent – I suppose it's tough to remember to spend your benefit handouts on accommodation when there's drugs to buy. So the local authority has housed him in a hotel. This is not a 4 star with pool – it's more a set of knocked-through terraced houses in an old mining town – but it's a hotel, all the same. I am not sure if the hotelier was told of Lee's previous behaviour, but he appears not too troubled. This may be due to two facts. One, police offender management officers call there often to check on Lee, and two, he is rarely there.

He bobs in for a shower when he's passing, but he prefers to crash at his mates' houses, where he can sit up all night smoking weed, playing computer games and drinking. He also keeps a distance from the cops in this way, which allows him to continue stealing, drug taking and indulging in his favourite pastime of riding motorbikes at breakneck speeds around the place. It goes without saying Lee does not have a driving licence or insurance and the origin of the bikes is very questionable.

Lee is 'managed' by a multi-agency panel which I have the pleasure of being part of. At the last meeting, 13 professionals attended and spoke about Lee for two hours. Prison staff even attended to report on how great Lee had been doing during his recent very short spell inside, and how he had only five warnings about his behaviour – the last for giving abuse to a prison officer. Someone from I can't remember which department of the Social/Health service reported that on their last meeting with Lee they noticed he appeared a little gaunt and unwell. I think we can make an educated guess as to where his benefit monies are being spent, instead of food. The meeting spun into action and all sorts of ideas were discussed. The result was his empty hotel room was visited, and £80-worth of groceries were left for him at taxpayers' expense. I have no doubt the bulk of this was sold on for a few tenner bags of bush.

There is another meeting shortly about Lee. I am trying to find a reason not to attend. I doubt whether I'll be able to be restrained enough not to pass comment about the colossal amount of money spent on this lost cause. I really want to tell the truth and shout out that it is cheaper for Lee to be in prison. I am told he needs 'structure' and 'stability' in his life – prison would no doubt provide this. Or I might send my apologies, saying 'Whilst you are sat there discussing Lee, I'm out protecting his old neighbours from him.'

PC, 34, Northern force

I was moved to my current role as a MAPPA* liaison officer – I won't give the exact title – after suffering serious injury at work. To be honest, I'd rather be stabbed again than carry on with it. I spend half of my life sitting in meetings, and the other half reading, writing and responding to emails. This is not why I became a policeman.

To give you one for-instance, on Monday I presented myself at the local authority at 9am sharp with 'professionals' from the council, the NHS, the social services, probation, housing and the DSS. If you looked around that room, there must have been a quarter of a million pounds in salaries sitting there. We were there to discuss a woman I'll call Kerry. She is a chaotic, drug-using alcoholic single parent in her early 40s. She has never worked, not even for one day. She is very well-known to us. She has had several moves from various flats because of problems with the neighbours, caused by her. The meeting was to discuss her in general and then specifically what to do with her daughter. I won't give any details of the child, obviously. She has two other adult children, both in prison. The father of the little girl is also in prison, and has never even seen his child. I put forward, as I have on previous occasions, my view that the little girl should be taken into care. It is as plain as the nose on your face that growing up in this madwoman's company is going to end in tears of one sort or another. In my opinion, the best she can hope for is to make it to adulthood and a life of unemployment, pregnancy and crime. At the other end of the scale, would I be surprised if something really terrible happened to her? Frankly, no. One thing I can say with some certainty, she will not go to school on a regular basis, with a full tummy, washed hair, clean clothes and make something of her life.

So we sit there for hours and hours talking about this little girl. The social worker tells me I need to be careful not to judge 'mum' for her lifestyle choices, and how 'mum' is 'trying really hard', how she has her rights, how the child's interests will be best-served by 'staying with mum'. At 1pm we break for lunch, we resume at 2pm and we carry on until 4pm, when the decision is made that we'll carry on monitoring the situation. Out there in the real world, blokes are grafting in all weathers digging ditches or laying bricks. In here, all nice and warm, all talk. It makes me want to scream.

Sergeant, 40, Northern force

MAPPA – Multi-Agency Public Protection Arrangements, where police officers, staff from the probation and prison services and others sit around eating biscuits and discussing how to 'manage' violent and sex offenders who should actually be in prison.

Partner agencies can be brilliant, or terrible. My experiences are mixed. When I PBO-d [*worked as a permanent beat officer, i.e. not on response*], I said to the local council housing officer, 'You work here, I work here, we've got problems with the same people – let's patrol together.'

And we did, and it worked brilliantly. Years later, it's become a standard thing, but at the time no-one else did it. I wish I'd put it forward as part of my portfolio – then I'd have got my two pips by now. But then, another time, we were called to the DSS to deal with someone. I needed to get an address for this bloke and the DSS manager refused to give it to me.

I said, 'Hang on. *You* called me, and I need this information to help *you*.'

She said, 'Well I can't give you the information. It's data protection.'

I said, 'Well, without it, I can't help you.'

She said, 'You've got to.'

I said, 'I can't unless you give me the information.'

She said, 'I'm not giving you the information.'

Crazy.

Another time, a social worker called us to locate a missing girl from a care home. This girl was known to be sexually active and there was concern for her welfare. Her social worker knew the address where the girl had gone, but she wouldn't tell me. She said it was a matter of client confidentiality.

I said, 'You know where she is, but you won't tell me?'

She said. 'Yep.'

I said, 'So you want us to go out just looking for her, when you know all along where she is?'

She said, 'Yep.'

Then she started talking to me in patois. 'Ya just dun't gettit, innnit, officer? She ain't gwan trust me if a tell ya.'

I said, 'Hang about, stop talking like that. You're supposed to be a professional social worker. I'm a professional police officer. You weren't talking like that a moment ago. Now, just give me the address.'

She wouldn't, but I happened to know her boss. I called the boss, she told the social worker to give me the address and that was job done. But it was very irritating.

Sergeant, 43, Midlands force

Above all, most officers still love the job – although some, like the author, have moved overseas to police.

I was inspired by PC Copperfield to seek my fame and fortune in Canada. I don't work in the same town as him, though I do work in the same province. Back in England, I was a response bobby for a shade over 10 years, and I can vouch for all the things most cops at that level talk about. We had declining numbers of operational officers and ever-increasing numbers of desk jockeys. We had terrible kit – cars that were held together by sticky tape, 10-yaer-old computers that kept crashing, the usual. We had spineless, cowardly senior officers who could give you chapter and verse on health and safety and diversity but hadn't got a Scooby [*Doo – clue*] about how to deal with angry drunks. We would put the same faces before the courts time and again and see them walk away. I loved the basic tenets of policing, I wanted to help the victims, but I was completely hog-tied by the crapness of it all.

I moved to Canada just before they stopped recruiting, and I've been out here for a shade over three years now. Some things are the same. There is a lowlife element to the population, the same kind of people who take a lot of drugs, drink too much, don't work, and spend their leisure time beating each other up and generally molesting each other. Even relatively law-abiding Canadians do get drunk and they do fight the police, though not so much in the winter. Like PC Rain back home, the weather doesn't half help – not too many folks want to go burgling or rioting when it's 30 below. The big difference is, there is still a good deal of respect for the uniform, and whereas if you wanted to take us on back home we were treading on eggshells and we were often outnumbered, over here, we'll get the back-up and our colleagues are not afraid to use force. There's far less bureaucracy, far less tolerance for lazy and workshy officers, and for lazy and criminal members of the public. So we get to offer a far better service to the decent, law-abiding majority.

My standard of living out here is better – with overtime, I currently earn more than my old chief inspector did back in the UK. My house is twice the size, I eat better, I live better. I have next to no job-related stress. I miss the cricket and proper beer, and my old mates, but that's about it.

Police officer, 36, Alberta

I remember, it was one of the proudest days of my life when I found myself at the Scottish Police College wearing my crisp, new police uniform for the first time, fresh-faced and as keen as mustard. I then spent the next six months with my head in the books reciting legislation and hitting a pad with my baton to represent an imaginary offender during officer safety training, before graduating in front of my family and a number of overseas dignitaries on the parade square in front of Tulliallan Castle. Unfortunately for us, the marching didn't go quite to plan, as the band was out of sync with the parade sergeant calling 'time', which resulted in all the squads tripping over each other. When we attempted to perform the 'about turn on the march' just before we reached the edge of the parade square, which co-incidentally was aligned with a hedge, the dysfunction with the marching resulted in half of the squad being pushed into the hedge. It provided a bit of entertainment for all the spectators.

I was then unleashed onto the mean streets of a major city in Scotland for my first foot patrol with my tutor Constable. I was distinctly apprehensive, and I remember feeling very self-conscious in my shiny new uniform.

Things I quickly learned: where to buy the best kebabs and deep-fried haggis, that the locals favoured term for their police brethren was 'black bastards', that some gypsies had a penchant for copper and not to park the patrol car underneath the tower blocks lest some of the less friendly natives throw bricks onto it.

The next five years or so were a blur. I worked in the housing schemes, which were something of a shock to a young lad who'd been to boarding school, and who, like most people, had never previously had much reason to venture into these intimidating areas. My memories are of grey concrete as far as the eye could see – depressing tower blocks blending into the grey sky, with small areas of grass covered in dog turds. Whatever improvements the council attempted to make to beautify the area were quickly trashed by the locals.

I soon realised that many members of our local 'community' did not seem to appreciate my efforts. I always found it somewhat perplexing when they told me they hoped I died of cancer. Given the amount of deep fried food I was eating, I took some consolation in the fact I was more likely to die of a heart attack first.

Another interesting experience was attending my first football match. Being more of a rugby man, I was used to attending matches where opposing fans are integrated, and where you could chat to anyone about the Scotland rugby team's latest thrashing; attending football matches as a police officer was an educational experience. It was a Celtic game – a fact I vividly remember because, along with about five other colleagues, I ended up confronted by a couple of hundred Neanderthals wearing their green-hooped club strip at one of the stadium's exits, all of whom were screaming at us for some reason about wanting a 'piece of me'. This was what I would politely describe as a 'brown pants' situation as I stood there, terrified, holding my aluminium stick to defend myself.

During this baptism of fire, the senior police management also thought it would be entertaining to send a small group of us up into the stands to seize an Irish flag, no doubt having placed bets as to how long we would last. Not to worry, we were told, the CCTV cameras would be following us continually to record our demise and identify any offenders who might stamp on our heads.

My policing experiences continued in this vein for some years. One of the schemes I worked in was not too far away from the city's airport, and I often found myself standing in the middle of the estate looking up at the planes passing overhead, and dreaming of the sunnier climes they were flying to. I would invariably be brought back to reality by one of the kindly locals shouting 'black cunt' from a neighbouring tower block, or by realising that I had managed to step in another dog turd.

I somehow heard that the Australian police were recruiting experienced officers from overseas. Given that I'd spent a lot of time watching *Home & Away* and *Neighbours*, I felt I knew something of contemporary Australian issues. I was also partial to a Foster's beer every now and then. There were issues to consider – crocodiles, snakes and feral pigs, for example – but I decided to apply. Ironically,

I needn't have worried; the feral pigs turned out to be far more well-mannered than most of the criminal underclass I had to deal with in Scotland.

I spent a couple of months on a policing course at the Aussie police academy. The main difference from Scotland, apart from the sun, was the officer safety training. This was mainly because we were trained to use firearms and TASER, which we would carry with us at all times whilst patrolling. This was refreshing; clearly the senior police management appreciated that the days of *Dixon of Dock Green* had gone, and we needed modern tools to do our job. To start with, carrying a firearm took a little getting used to. I was aware that my hand eye co-ordination was somewhat lacking, having previously driven a police van at slow speed in broad daylight into a skip situated at the side of a road back home. I was slightly worried that I'd inadvertently shoot myself in my leg, or, even worse, my crotch. In the end, after a while I forgot I was carrying a firearm, it was just another tool in our box of tricks. Currently, both my legs and crotch are intact.

The officer safety training also consisted of a serious assault course, including a six foot wall which even the more physically adept amongst us found challenging. Ironically, those of us who had made the biggest effort to integrate into Australian society by consuming vast quantities of Foster's and BBQ were most disadvantaged. Also on offer was 'grappling', which was always interesting after a heavy lunch of steak and shrimp, and mandatory circuit training at 6am for those who were not physically making the grade.

In the end, while I had visions of strutting out of the academy like Mick Dundee, there was no training in the art of wrestling crocodiles, avoiding feral pigs or sucking the venom out of snake bites. In fact, I've only seen one snake, which was a python having a siesta at the side of the road. One of my colleagues did have to rescue a baby crocodile that crawled out of a drain onto a main road, and another inadvertently ran over an adult croc which was crossing the road at night

My first day of work in Australia was not that different from my first day in Scotland, except that the sun shone for the full eight hours of the shift rather than eight or so minutes. I also identified some important cultural differences, such as the fact that 'Burger King' is called 'Hungry Jacks' in Australia, and like all good police officers I quickly established which food establishments in the area offered police discount.

As a police officer in my area of Australia, you have quite a bit of freedom. When you turn up at incidents, you have a large amount of discretion as to whether you want to record the incident by creating a crime report. As the investigating officer, you decide whether or not you want to proffer a charge, and if there is sufficient evidence to proceed. If you decide to proffer a charge, depending on the circumstances you can give the offender a form out on the streets which gives them a court date, effectively 'charging' them, or you can take them into custody and charge them in the watch-house. It takes between five to 10 minutes to process a prisoner in the watch-house, and for your average street offence, 40 minutes is ample time to complete all the paperwork, have a coffee and that all important kebab with extra chilli sauce to sustain you for the remainder of your shift. Back home, this would all take much longer.

Another consideration is the scale of the area in which you work. Back in Scotland, I could drive from one end of my police district to the other in about 20 minutes, and if I had the blues and twos on – say to get back for my meal break in time – I could probably do it in about 10. The distance from one side of my current police district to the other is in the region of 1,200km, much of which is bush and mangrove swamps full of hungry reptiles. The distance from one end of the force area to the other is in the region of 3200km. If you want to get back to the station before your kebab gets cold or eaten by a crocodile, over here a panda car is not much use, so we have a police air wing, which has a number of aircraft to transport us to more remote parts of the district.

The obligatory diversity training so prevalent in most police forces in the mother country is almost nonexistent here, and what a happy situation this is. Perusing the local force directory one day, whilst munching on a Hungry Jacks burger with beetroot – weirdly, Australians put beetroot in their burgers – I was unable to find a diversity department. It's not that Australians are racist – I've found them to be very fair and equitable. It's just that they have not had diversity awareness training rammed down their throats for the last decade. They say it as they see it, and have not been programmed to be as politically correct as many people are in the United Kingdom.

Friends who I served with in Scotland often ask me if things are better in Australia. When I was a fresh-faced probationer back in Scotland, one of my tutor's many pearls of wisdom was, 'Same shit, different bucket.' (His other favourite phrase for me was, 'Everything you touch turns to shite.') And, by and large, the work is the same wherever you are in the world. In Scotland, some of the locals would affectionately refer to me as an 'English cunt.' Here, our indigenous friends prefer 'Captain Cook cunt.'

Some things are better, some things are worse; in the end it really comes down to the lifestyle. I still miss curry and scotch eggs − for some strange reason, you just can't get a decent curry here, and scotch eggs are non-existent. However, though I face these challenges on a daily basis, the outdoor lifestyle and relaxed Australian approach to life more than makes up for it. Plus I've found an Aussie chocolate biscuit called a Tim Tam which, to make more Scottish, I cover in batter and deep fry.

Senior Constable, 35, Australian force (ex-Scotland)

Yes, there's lots of mither and nif naf in the Job, but at the end of the day you have moments which make all of that worthwhile. I arrested a lad who was on the edge of going bad, he was hanging around with all the bad yoot, he was causing a nuisance, and one day he was part of a group who boshed a bus shelter in. He wasn't the prime mover, so I gave him words of advice in a very severe way, in front of his mum, who was a good sort. I said to him, 'You're a good lad, basically, you're not daft. You're at a fork in the road, here. You can go one way and you and I'll be seeing a lot more of each other, and that will end up with you in prison and your mum crying. Or you can go the other way and make something of yourself and make your mum proud of you.' He was suitably shame-faced. Anyway, after that he was off my radar for a long time until I got a letter in the nick inviting me to his passing-out parade. He'd been accepted into the Army, and he was thanking us for helping to keep him on the straight and narrow.

PC, 40, Welsh force

I'd hate people to think I don't like my job. I hate the bullshit that goes with it, but the job itself is great. Dealing with the appreciative public, working with your mates, it's all good. You have some great laughs. Like, we were called to reports of prowlers outside a house at about 2am on a pitch black night. It was a big old house, almost a mini-stately home, with what we later found out was a stone verandah and lawns stretching off into the distance. My partner and I were sent to investigate, and as we arrived at the property the radio operator said, 'The caller states that the prowlers are still outside the rear of the property, advises that officers come quietly to the front door to be admitted.'

So we parked in the road outside and tiptoed up the gravel to the front door. As we got there, it opened and this little old lady peered out, shaking a bit. 'Oh, officers,' she whispered, she had a very plummy voice. 'I can't tell you how pleased I am to see you. Come in, come in. They're still there.'

We followed her through the darkened hall and into the living room, which was like something out of a Harry Potter film, and she motioned to us to stop. 'There they are,' she says. 'They've been standing there for an hour at least.'

Which sounded a bit odd. But I looked, and there were two figures standing there, looking in at the big French windows. Well over six feet tall, both wearing hoodies, neither of them moving. My colleague's only about 5ft 6in tall and I'm not the biggest bloke myself, so we radioed for back-up. And we crouched there, watching them all the time. They never moved a muscle. After about five minutes, this began to strike me as *really* odd. There were no lights on inside, so why weren't they either trying to get in or at least walking around looking for an entry point?

I said, 'This is weird isn't it?' My colleague nodded. The old lady nodded. All three of us just kept staring.

Then my colleague said, 'Er, do you have any patio furniture outside?'

'Patio furniture?' says the old biddy. 'Actually, my son bought me some at the weekend.'

She had some sort of open gardens or village fête planned, and she'd needed some chairs buying.

'Is there an outside light?' says my colleague.

'Yes,' says the old lady.

'Can you turn it on please?' says my colleague.

The old biddy tootles off somewhere out back and then the lights come on to reveal… Two big parasols sticking out of the middle of a couple of wooden patio tables.

Embarrassing, that's all I can say. We got a cup of tea out of it, though, and we did manage to reassure a frightened old lady that she wasn't going to be burgled by a B&Q umbrella, so all was not lost.

PC, 29, Midlands force

It was 3am and had been a quiet night. I'd been crawling around the street in my panda looking for anything moving, but there was nothing much doing. Not even a stray dog or curious fox was out.

Then a call came in – thieves-on at a bungalow on the far side of town and out into the countryside. I put my foot down and sped through the deserted, neon-lit streets.

As I approached the area, I turned off my headlights and continued in *Knight Rider* mode. A few hundred yards from the property, I turned off the engine and glided up to the bungalow amongst a small copse of trees.

Off the road, I climbed the steps to the front of the bungalow and crept around the side of the property. I peered at the conservatory, and saw there was a broken window, and just then I heard a noise in the field to the side of me. I span round and just made out in the dark a figure in a white jacket sprinting away from me across the field to my left.

'Bastards!' I thought – I couldn't believe I'd been heard despite my stealthy approach. I leapt off the patio and into the field in hot pursuit of the figure.

Now, I'm no gazelle – but this guy was moving at an extraordinary speed. I shouted up on the radio. 'Collar number XXX, chasing on foot over the fields to the rear of the property.' Over the sound of my own panting, I could hear others on the radio making their way.

The field dropped down before rising towards the orange-lit skyline of the next town. I continued running, or at least stumbling at speed, across the field but no matter how hard I tried the guy was getting further and further away. I'd obviously caught Haile Gebrselassie or Steve Cram at it.

As he got to the horizon, I could make out the jacket, the legs, and, er, the very long neck.

It was a horse – with a winter rug on. A pissed off horse that had now reached the end of its paddock and had just turned and was now running back at me, snorting.

I did the smartest about-turn since training college and set off back across the field. I could hear the bloody thing behind me, and had visions of it trampling me. A small whimper may have escaped my lips. I realised I'd never outrun it back to the house, but out of my peripheral vision I spied a gate onto a country lane and made for that. I got there with seconds to spare and vaulted over it head first onto the side road.

I stood there panting and thanking my lucky stars, until I remembered the officers making their way to assist me in the apprehension of a fugitive. What the hell could I say over the radio? How can I get out of this one? How can I cough to chasing a horse?

I put my hands on my knees, gulping in the air, and then I noticed it. To my right, parked under a tree, was a clapped-out old Peugeot with what looked like, and turned out to be, plumes of cannabis smoke coming from the interior. A knock on the window, and two detained.

They were interviewed about the broken window at the bungalow which they denied smashing – but coughed to the bags of weed in the car.

Everyone assumed I had been chasing one of the youths and I walked into the custody office that night's hero. One of the youths later asked me how we had found them, and I told him a heavily edited version of events.

He said, 'You know, I wouldn't be surprised if the horse put the window through.'

'Yeah, right,' I said.

'Well,' he said, 'it was certainly kicking fuck out of that gate next to our car before you lot arrived!'

PC, 38, Northern force

When I was in uniform, which was until only a few months ago, we went to a drunken domestic argument at around 4am one weekend morning. Bloke ended up being arrested to prevent a breach of the peace. Handcuffed, popped into the back of our patrol car, and, after a couple of minutes of taking details, off to the station we went.

Bloke booked into custody, no problem.

I then went back outside to our marked car to see, sat on the parcel shelf, the bloke's cat, which must have jumped in unnoticed while we were outside the house and which had then remained silent in the footwell during our journey. Unable to let even this get in the way of the ubiquitous paperwork, I let the cat out, assuming it would find its own way back home. Two hours later, shift finished, I left the locker room to see the cat skulking around near the entrance to custody. I felt bad as it looked to have no homing instincts, and I knew I wouldn't be able to sleep when I got in if I hadn't helped it out. So I gave the cat a taxi ride home in my own car, doing a subtle-as-possible drop-and-run at the end of the street. Never got any recognition for my humanitarian action that day.

DC, 27, Northern force

I love this job, after 18 years I still get a massive buzz out of arresting criminals and helping people. Last year I was involved in an operation targeting burglars, and we were quite successful, both in detections and in recovering property. The feeling you get when you knock on the door of an old lady's house and tell her you've recovered her stolen property, you can't buy that. It's the same as that *bingo!* feeling you get when you catch a burglar in a house, or stop a car full of known local nominals and find the proceeds of burglaries in the boot.

My colleagues say I'm Job-pissed, but I don't care. There are things I don't like about it, but broadly, I'd still recommend it as a career to anyone.

Sergeant, 40, Eastern force

If you have enjoyed this book, please do mention it to your friends and family. As a small, independent publisher, Monday Books unfortunately lacks the resources for nationwide publicity campaigns, and so relies greatly on, and is very grateful for, word-of-mouth recommendation and support.

Our books are available in most good bookshops, from various online retailers and from our own website, www.mondaybooks.com (with free p&p through the UK on all titles, and worldwide on all paperbacks). Our titles are also available as eBooks at Amazon and iTunes.

Our blog, at www.mondaybooks.wordpress.com, carries information about forthcoming titles and the company generally.

Perverting The Course Of Justice / **Inspector Gadget**
(ppbk, £7.99)

A SENIOR serving policeman picks up where PC Copperfield left off and reveals how far the insanity extends – children arrested for stealing sweets from each other while serious criminals go about their business unmolested.

'Exposes the reality of life at the sharp end'
– The Daily Telegraph

'No wonder they call us Plods… A frustrated inspector speaks out on the madness of modern policing'
– The Daily Mail

'Staggering… exposes the bloated bureaucracy that is crushing Britain' *– The Daily Express*

'You must buy this book… it is a fascinating insight'
– Kelvin MacKenzie, The Sun

In April 2010, Inspector Gadget was named
one of the country's 'best 40 bloggers' by *The Times*.

From all good bookshops, online from
www.mondaybooks.com or via 01455 221752.
All of our titles are also available as eBooks from amazon.co.uk

Wasting Police Time / **PC David Copperfield** (ppbk, £7.99)

THE FASCINATING, hilarious and best-selling inside story of the madness of modern policing. A serving officer - writing deep under cover - reveals everything the government wants hushed up about life on the beat.

'Very revealing' – *The Daily Telegraph*

'Passionate, important, interesting and genuinely revealing' – *The Sunday Times*

'Graphic, entertaining and sobering' – *The Observer*

'A huge hit… will make you laugh out loud' – *The Daily Mail*

'Hilarious… should be compulsory reading for our political masters' – *The Mail on Sunday*

'More of a fiction than Dickens' – *Tony McNulty MP, former Police Minister*

(On a BBC *Panorama* programme about PC Copperfield, McNulty was later forced to admit that this statement, made in the House of Commons, was itself inaccurate)

From all good bookshops, online from www.mondaybooks.com or via 01455 221752. All of our titles are also available as eBooks from amazon.co.uk

Not With A Bang But A Whimper / **Theodore Dalrymple**

(hbk, £14.99)

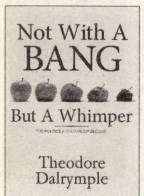

IN A SERIES of penetrating and beautifully-written essays, Theodore Dalrymple explains his belief that a liberal intelligentsia is destroying Britain. Dalrymple writes for *The Spectator*, *The Times*, *The Daily Telegraph*, *New Statesman*, *The Times Literary Supplement* and the *British Medical Journal*.

'Theodore Dalrymple's clarity of thought, precision of expression and constant, terrible disappointment give his dispatches from the frontline a tone and a quality entirely their own... their rarity makes you sit up and take notice'
- Marcus Berkmann, The Spectator

'Dalrymple is a modern master'
- The Guardian

'Dalrymple is the George Orwell of our times... he is a writer of genius'
- Dennis Dutton

From all good bookshops, online from www.mondaybooks.com or via 01455 221752.
All of our titles are also available as eBooks from amazon.co.uk

Second Opinion: A Doctor's Dispatches from the Inner City
Theodore Dalrymple (hdbk, £14.99)

THEODORE DALRYMPLE has spent much of his working life as a doctor in a grim inner city hospital and the nearby prison; his patients are drug addicts and drunks, violent men and battered women, suicidal teenagers and despairing elderly. For many years, Dalrymple - acknowledged as the world's leading doctor-writer - wrote a column in The Spectator in which he recounted his experiences. This collection of those shocking, amusing and elegant columns offers a window into a world many of us never see.

'The harsh truths he tells are all the more shocking because the media, in general, is unwilling to tell them' - *Daily Telegraph*

'He actually cares about the people at the bottom of the social heap while public sector jobsworths and slimy politicians only pretend to' - *Daily Express*

'A rare voice of truth' - *The Spectator*

'He could not be further from the stereotype of the "little Englander" conservative... he is arguably our greatest living essayist' - *Standpoint*

From all good bookshops, online from www.mondaybooks.com or via 01455 221752. All of our titles are also available as eBooks from amazon.co.uk

Sick Notes / **Dr Tony Copperfield**
(ppbk, £8.99)

WELCOME TO the bizarre world of Tony Copperfield, family doctor. He spends his days fending off anxious mums, elderly sex maniacs and hopeless hypochondriacs (with his eyes peeled for the odd serious symptom). The rest of his time is taken up sparring with colleagues, battling bureaucrats and banging his head against the brick walls of the NHS.

If you've ever wondered what your GP is really thinking - and what's actually going on behind the scenes at your surgery - *SICK NOTES* is for you.

'A wonderful book, funny and insightful in equal measure'
– *Dr Phil Hammond (Private Eye's 'MD')*

'Copperfield is simply fantastic, unbelievably funny and improbably wise… everything he writes is truer than fact'
– *British Medical Journal*

'Original, funny and an incredible read' – *The Sun*

Tony Copperfield is a Medical Journalist of the Year, has been shortlisted for UK Columnist of the Year many times and writes regularly for *The Times* and other media.

**From all good bookshops, online from
www.mondaybooks.com or via 01455 221752.
All of our titles are also available as eBooks from amazon.co.uk**

When Science Goes Wrong / **Simon LeVay**

(ppbk, £7.99)

WE LIVE in times of astonishing scientific progress. But for every stunning triumph there are hundreds of cock-ups, damp squibs and disasters. Escaped anthrax spores and nuclear explosions, tiny data errors which send a spacecraft hurtling to oblivion, innocent men jailed on 'infallible' DNA evidence…just some of the fascinating and disturbing tales from the dark side of discovery.

'Spine-tingling, occasionally gruesome accounts of well-meant but disastrous scientific bungling'
– The Los Angeles Times

'Entertaining and thought-provoking'
– Publisher's Weekly

'The dark – but fascinating – side of science… an absorbing read' *– GeoTimes*

From all good bookshops, online from www.mondaybooks.com or via 01455 221752. All of our titles are also available as eBooks from amazon.co.uk

A Paramedic's Diary / **Stuart Gray**
(ppbk, £7.99)

STUART GRAY is a paramedic dealing with the worst life can throw at him. *A Paramedic's Diary* is his gripping, blow-by-blow account of a year on the streets – 12 rollercoaster months of enormous highs and tragic lows. One day he'll save a young mother's life as she gives birth, the next he might watch a young girl die on the tarmac in front of him after a hit-and-run. A gripping, entertaining and often amusing read by a talented new writer.

As heard on BBC Radio 4's Saturday Live and BBC Radio 5 Live's Donal McIntyre Show and Simon Mayo

In April 2010, Stuart Gray was named one of the country's 'best 40 bloggers' by *The Times*

From all good bookshops, online from www.mondaybooks.com or via 01455 221752. All of our titles are also available as eBooks from amazon.co.uk

So That's Why They Call It Great Britain / Steve Pope
(ppbk, £7.99)

FROM THE steam engine to the jet engine to the engine of the world wide web, to vaccination and penicillin, to Viagra, chocolate bars, the flushing loo, the G&T, ibruprofen and the telephone... this is the truly astonishing story of one tiny country and its gifts to the world.

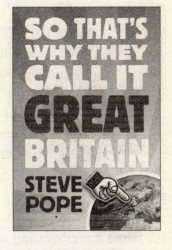

From all good bookshops, online from www.mondaybooks.com or via 01455 221752. All of our titles are also available as eBooks from amazon.co.uk

It's Your Time You're Wasting
– A Teacher's Tales Of Classroom Hell **/ Frank Chalk**
(ppbk £7.99)

THE BLACKLY humorous diary of a year in a teacher's working life. Chalk confiscates porn, booze and trainers, fends off angry parents and worries about the few conscientious pupils he comes across, recording his experiences in a dry and very readable manner.

'Does for education what PC David Copperfield did for the police'

"Addictive and ghastly" – *The Times*

**From all good bookshops, online from
www.mondaybooks.com or via 01455 221752.
All of our titles are also available as eBooks from amazon.co.uk**

Generation F / **Winston Smith**

(ppbk, £8.99)

YOUTH WORKER Winston Smith - winner of the Orwell Prize for his edgy, controversial and passionate writing - opens a door on the murky, tragic world of children's care homes and supported housing schemes. Frightening, revealing and sometimes very funny, *Generation F* is his story.

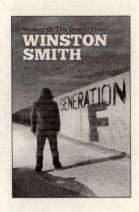

'**Winston Smith paints a terrifying picture**'
- The Daily Mail

'**What carried the day was his passion and conviction that we should know what wrongs had been done in our names**' - *Orwell Prize judges*

From all good bookshops, online from www.mondaybooks.com or via 01455 221752.
All of our titles are also available as eBooks from amazon.co.uk

In Foreign Fields / **Dan Collins**

(ppbk, £7.99)

A STAGGERING collection of 25 true-life stories of astonishing battlefield bravery from Iraq and Afghanistan... medal-winning soldiers, Marines and RAF men, who stared death in the face, in their own words.

'Enthralling and awe-inspiring untold stories'
– *The Daily Mail*

'Astonishing feats of bravery illustrated in laconic, first-person prose' – *Independent on Sunday*

'The book everyone's talking about... a gripping account of life on the frontlines of Iraq and Afghanistan'
– *News of the World*

'An outstanding read' – *Soldier Magazine*

From all good bookshops, online from
www.mondaybooks.com or via 01455 221752.
All of our titles are also available as eBooks from amazon.co.uk

Kidnapped / **Colin Freeman**

(ppbk, £8.99)

WHAT'S IT like to be kidnapped by khat-chewing Somali pirates who are armed to the teeth and would kill you in a heartbeat? Colin Freeman, *Sunday Telegraph* foreign correspondent, found out the hard way. This is the story of his terrifying ordeal in captivity – an astonishing adventure told in a surprisingly funny and fond way.

'More than simply a terrific book on the scourge of Somali piracy, Freeman's wry style and heartfelt candour raises *Kidnapped* to the highest rank'
– Tim Butcher, author of *Blood River*

'A witty and admirable account... Self deprecating humour which makes you laugh out loud'
– *The Daily Telegraph*

'Brings humour to otherwise serious proceedings, from the complexities of toilette in arid mountains to talking football with his abductors, and also gives a frank account of the nuts and bolts of foreign news reporting'
– *The Independent*

From all good bookshops, online from www.mondaybooks.com or via 01455 221752.
All of our titles are also available as eBooks from amazon.co.uk